Financial Management for Hospitality Decision Makers

To Dawne, Logan and Matthew

Financial Management for Hospitality Decision Makers

Chris Guilding

ELSEVIER
BUTTERWORTH
HEINEMANN

AMSTERDAM BOSTON HEIDELBERG LONDON NEW YORK OXFORD
PARIS SAN DIEGO SAN FRANCISCO SINGAPORE SYDNEY TOKYO

Butterworth-Heinemann is an imprint of Elsevier
Linacre House, Jordan Hill, Oxford OX2 8DP, UK
30 Corporate Drive, Suite 400, Burlington, MA 01803, USA

First published 2002
Reprinted 2003, 2005, 2006, 2008

Notice
No responsibility is assumed by the publisher for any injury and/or damage to persons
or property as a matter of products liability, negligence or otherwise, or from any use
or operation of any methods, products, instructions or ideas contained in the material
herein. Because of rapid advances in the medical sciences, in particular, independent
verification of diagnoses and drug dosages should be made

British Library Cataloguing in Publication Data
A catalogue record for this book is available from the British Library

Library of Congress Cataloging-in-Publication Data
A catalog record for this book is available from the Library of Congress

ISBN: 978-0-7506-5659-7

For information on all Butterworth-Heinemann publications
visit our website at books.elsevier.com

Printed and bound in *China*

08 09 10 10 9 8 7 6 5

Working together to grow
libraries in developing countries

www.elsevier.com | www.bookaid.org | www.sabre.org

ELSEVIER   BOOK AID International   Sabre Foundation

Contents

Hospitality, Leisure & Tourism Series

Preface

Welcome to *Financial Management for Hospitality Decision Makers*. The current era of growth and dynamic change in hospitality signifies that it is an exciting time to be involved with the industry. Like many other industries, the hospitality sector is experiencing heightened levels of competition and a growing need to apply appropriate management techniques to ensure commercial success. These factors increasingly signify that a hotel manager needs a working knowledge of pertinent financial management tools, techniques and procedures.

From my experience as an instructor of financial management and accounting generally, and hospitality financial management and accounting in particular, I have found students tend to approach their first class with a degree of trepidation and an expectation that the subject will be dry and difficult to master. Through this book, I endeavour to make the subject material accessible and to demonstrate the relevance of financial management to decision making and control in today's increasingly dynamic business environment. Recognition of financial management's value to the modern manager is a critical factor that can facilitate a student's understanding of the subject. Once relevance is appreciated, the student starts to explore the range of ways in which financial management can serve the hospitality manager.

The book has been designed to encourage confidence in financial management so that current and future managers can demand excellence from their financial management information system. Too frequently, managers are 'turned-off' by accounting language and the presentation of reports produced by the accounts department. It is an unfortunate reality that financial reports frequently appear to be designed by accountants for accountants. This problem is partially attributable to the fact that most qualified accountants have gained their qualification through demonstrating their mastery of the rules of external reporting (i.e. financial accounting, which is the branch of accounting concerned with the preparation of annual accounts for external parties such as shareholders). When providing financial management information to managers within the hotel, however, reports should be designed with the decision-making needs of the managers in mind.

The book has been written with two specific audiences in mind. First, it can serve as a valuable self-help tool for the practising hospitality manager interested in improving their appreciation of financial management techniques and procedures.

Second, it has been designed to serve as a text that can be used in a financial management or accounting course in a hospitality-related course of study. The book is compatible with stage two of the Butterworth-Heinemann hospitality, leisure and tourism series of texts, and is therefore consistent with level two of an undergraduate degree. While the depth of the material covered signifies it would serve well as a stage two text, it could also be used in a first year of study as no prior study of accounting or financial management is presumed.

In my view, not only can a well-designed book meet the needs of both the practitioner and student audiences, a well-balanced book is likely to result from addressing the needs of both audiences. Addressing the practising manager audience ensures that the book imparts information that is relevant to today's hospitality manager in a direct and readily accessible style. The reader will be able to quickly see the wood from the trees and gain an early appreciation of how concepts introduced can be applied in practice. Addressing a student audience ensures that the material covered provides a broad foundation. A set of problems addressing the main issues raised appears at the end of each chapter. Inclusion of these problems was motivated primarily by a desire to provide students with an opportunity to practise applying issues raised in the chapters and also to gain exposure to the type of problems that can be encountered in examination situations. A review of these problems will also prove extremely beneficial to the practising manager, however, as deeper understanding of the material introduced in the text will result from exposure to a range of real-world decision-making scenarios. Solutions to the first three problems in each chapter appear at the back of the text. This is a self-help feature designed to further facilitate learning and enable students to appraise their understanding of concepts covered by the book. Additional solutions to problems are available to lecturers on a password protected site which can be accessed at: http://www.bh.com/manuals/075065659X.

A distinctive aspect of the book is its international orientation. The hospitality industry is becoming increasingly international with large multinational chains dominating the 5- and 4-star market segments. This factor, together with the drawing together of countries to form economic alliances such as the European Economic Union, signifies that the career path of hotel managers increasingly involves some international work experience. Further, the clientele base of hotels is becoming more international as a result of increased international business and tourist travel. In combination, these factors highlight the need for a book that views hospitality financial management in a globalized context. International differences in key accounting terms used in different countries as well as the format of key financial statements such as the profit and loss statement ('income statement' in the USA and Canada) will be noted. In addition, scenarios introduced and problems posed will draw on a range of international settings. This will develop the reader's familiarity with addressing financial problems in the context of a range of countries and currencies.

A second distinctive aspect of the book is its hospitality decision makers' orientation. This theme will be apparent from the problem-solving approach used throughout the text. In each chapter this approach is supplemented by the inclusion of a case that takes a particular hospitality manager's perspective on an issue raised. Each of these cases is headed 'Financial Decision Making in Action'.

The book is structured according to three main parts: an introduction (Chapter 1), hospitality financial accounting (Chapters 2–4), and financial information and hospitality management (Chapters 5–12). Each part can be approached independently of the other parts, i.e. if the reader is exclusively interested in financial management, they can commence their reading at Chapter 5.

In Chapter 1, in the course of providing an overview of the nature of financial management, the contents of the book are introduced. Chapters 2, 3 and 4 build on one another to provide a basic understanding of financial accounting. While financial accounting does not represent the primary orientation of the book, a basic understanding of the workings of the financial accounting system can be highly beneficial to the hospitality manager, due to the importance of financial statements such as the balance sheet and profit and loss statement. It is difficult to overstate the importance of these statements as they represent a key resource used by outsiders to gauge an organization's performance. The need for management to understand the mechanisms by which they are judged externally is clearly important.

The theme of Chapter 5, analysing financial performance, moves us more towards financial management. In this chapter a detailed review of how management can monitor financial dimensions of a hotel's performance is undertaken. Chapters 6–12 consider hospitality management decision making from the following perspectives:

- Classifying costs in order to facilitate decision making
- Cost–volume–profit analysis
- Budgeting and responsibility accounting
- Flexible budgeting and variance analysis
- Cost information and pricing
- Working capital management
- Investment decision making.

Again, an accessible and problem-orientated approach has been taken in presenting this subject matter.

The book has been designed to facilitate a flexible teaching and learning approach. While the sequencing of the chapters results from my view of the most appropriate order in which to present the material covered, many of the chapters can be read out of sequence. The only chapters that build on one another to such a degree that they should be read consecutively are Chapters 2, 3 and 4 and Chapters 8 and 9.

I hope you find this book to be a stimulating read and that your career benefits from your enhanced ability to recognize how financial management techniques and procedures can be applied in hospitality management.

Chris Guilding

PART 1

Introduction

Hospitality decision makers' use of financial management

Learning objectives

After studying this chapter, you should have developed an appreciation of:

1 The financial management implications of key hospitality industry characteristics

2 The nature of financial management

3 Some of the ways hospitality managers become involved in financial management

4 What is meant by the *Uniform System of Accounts for the Lodging Industry*

5 The focus of this book.

Introduction

This book describes financial management procedures and analytical techniques in the context of hospitality decision making. The purpose of this introductory chapter is to set the scene for the remainder of the book.

The next section of this chapter describes key characteristics relating to the hospitality industry and outlines financial management implications associated with these characteristics. Next, an overview of the nature of financial management and its relationship to accounting is provided. We will see how financial management is closely related to accounting, as accounting information represents a key resource extensively drawn upon in financial management decision making. In the course of describing the nature of financial management, the overall structure of the book will be introduced. We will see that Chapters 2–4 provide a grounding in hospitality financial accounting and Chapters 5–12 introduce a range of topics that show how financial management techniques and procedures are critically important to a host of hospitality decision-making situations. The chapter's subsequent section highlights some of the many ways that different hospitality managers can apply financial management techniques and procedures to inform their decision making.

The chapter's final section introduces an important accounting report: the profit and loss statement. This statement is introduced in the context of a description of the *Uniform System of Accounts for the Lodging Industry*. This system was developed in the USA and is being increasingly used in large hotels internationally. This signifies increased standardization of the classification scheme used by hotels to record their financial transactions, and also greater standardization of the financial performance reports produced by hotels.

Key characteristics of the hospitality industry

The hospitality industry encompasses a broad range of activities and types of organization. Some of the industry's primary players include restaurants and bars that provide dining and beverage service and also lodging operations that offer accommodation facilities. Restaurant organizations range from multinational companies to small street-corner cafés. Similarly, lodging operations range from multinational hotels offering thousands of rooms worldwide to bed and breakfast operations offering a single guest room. At the bed and breakfast extreme we have small family-run concerns with a limited service range, while at the other extreme we have multinational companies offering a range of services that transcend accommodation, dining and a breadth of sports and leisure activities. The hospitality industry's heterogeneity becomes apparent when we recognize that its diversity encompasses the following:

- Hotels
- Motels
- Restaurants
- Fast-food outlets
- Pubs and bars
- Country and sport clubs
- Cruise liners.

This book's primary focus is on hotel management. This focus has been taken because the majority of large hotels provide most of the service elements offered by the hospitality organizations listed above. In addition, as many large hotels have to coordinate provision of a range of hospitality services, they confront a degree of management complexity not encountered in many other hospitality organizations that offer a narrower range of services. For example, a large hotel's organizational structure and financial management system must be designed with due regard given to coordinating a range of disparate functions that, in most cases, will at least include the provision of accommodation, restaurant and bar facilities. The disparity of these functions is apparent when we recognize that the sale of rooms can be likened to the sale of seats in the airline or entertainment industries, a parallel exists between food preparation in restaurant kitchens and production activities in the manufacturing industry, and bar operations can be likened to retailing. In addition to managing this disparate range of services, a hotel needs to coordinate a set of distinct support operations such as laundry, building and grounds maintenance, information systems, training, marketing, transportation, etc.

This disparate range of hospitality activities are housed within a single site (i.e. building and surrounds), that we refer to as a hotel. This creates a degree of site complexity which is exacerbated when we recognize that the location of the service provider is also the place where the customer purchases and consumes the services offered. While this is patently obvious to anyone who has been to a hotel, we should not forget that it is not the case in many other service industries (e.g. banking, transportation, telecommunications, law, accounting), or the manufacturing industry. This factor highlights a further dynamic of the hotel industry. Not only is a hotel site the place where a broad range of activities is undertaken, it is the focal point of extensive and continual vigilance with respect to cleaning, maintenance and security. We can thus see that a hotel represents a complex site where distinct activities are conducted in close proximity to one another. Where the performance of one functional activity (e.g. cleaning) can be affected by the way another is conducted (e.g. maintenance), high interdependency is said to exist. Such high interdependency can create problems when attempting to hold one functional area (e.g. cleaning) accountable for its performance.

Not only is functional interdependency an issue when trying to hold a manager accountable for costs, it can be a problem when attempting to hold a manager responsible for a particular department's level of sales. For example, through no fault of her own, a food and beverage (F&B) manager may see her profits plummet as a result of a relatively low number of rooms sold by the rooms division. Such cross-functional interdependency needs to be recognized when identifying which aspect of a hotel's performance a particular manager should be held accountable for.

Sales volatility

The hotel industry experiences significant sales volatility. The extent of this volatility becomes particularly apparent when we recognize it comprises at least four key dimensions:

- Economic cycle-induced sales volatility
- Seasonal sales volatility

- Weekly sales volatility
- Intra-day sales volatility.

These dimensions of sales volatility and the implications they carry for hotel financial management are elaborated upon in Box 1.1.

High product perishability

Relative to many other industries, in foodservice operations there can be limited opportunities to produce for inventory. A significant proportion of food inventory is purchased less than 24 hours prior to sale, and much food preparation is conducted within minutes of a sale. There is thus a very short time span between purchase, production and sale. Many menu items cannot be produced in advance of sales due to their high perishability.

Box 1.1
Dimensions of sales volatility in the hospitality industry

(1) *Economic cycle-induced sales volatility.* Hotels are extremely susceptible to the highs and lows of the economic cycle. Those with a high proportion of business clients suffer during economic downturns due to significantly reduced corporate expenditure on business travel. Hotels offering tourist accommodation also suffer during economic downturns due to families reducing discretionary expenditure on activities such as holidays and travel. This high susceptibility to the general economic climate highlights the importance of hotels developing operational plans following careful consideration of predicted economic conditions.

(2) *Seasonal sales volatility.* Many hotels experience seasonal sales volatility over the course of the year. This volatility can be so severe to cause off-season closure for some resort properties. The decision whether to close can be informed by an appropriately conducted financial analysis such as that described in Chapter 6. Seasonal sales volatility can also pose particular cash management issues. During the middle and tail-end of busy seasons, surplus cash balances are likely to result, while in the off-season and the build-up to the busy season, deficit cash balances are likely to result. The need for careful cash planning and management is discussed in Chapter 11.

(3) *Weekly sales volatility.* Hotels with a high proportion of business clients will experience high occupancy (i.e. a high proportion of rooms sold) from Monday to Thursday, and a relatively low occupancy from Friday to Sunday. By contrast, many resort hotels have relatively busy weekends. Accurate forecasting of demand will inform management's decision making with respect to the amount and timing of room rate discounting. Forecasting is discussed in the context of budgeting in Chapter 8.

(4) *Intra-day sales volatility.* Restaurants experience busy periods during meal times, while bars tend to be busiest at night times. This intra-day demand volatility has led to widely used pricing strategies such as 'early bird specials' in restaurants and 'happy hours' in bars. Hotel pricing issues are discussed in Chapter 10. In addition to these dimensions of intra-day activity volatility, staffing needs have to be considered in light of issues such as the front desk experiencing a frenetic early-morning period processing check-outs and a second, more protracted, busy period in the late afternoon processing check-ins.

Perishability is even more apparent with respect to room and banquet sales. If a room is not occupied on a particular night, the opportunity to sell is lost forever. No discounting of a room's rate the following day can reverse this loss. This situation also applies to conference and banqueting activities. The high perishability associated with rooms, conferencing, banqueting and food underlines the importance of accurate demand forecasting. With respect to food, an accurate forecast of the mix and level of demand can result in the maintenance of all options on a menu during high-demand periods, and minimal cost of food scrapped during low-demand periods. With respect to rooms, an accurate forecast of room demand can enable appropriate pricing decisions to be made as part of an attempt to maximize revenue. Appropriate room demand management is particularly important, as room sales can be the prime determinant of sales of many of the hotel's other activities (e.g. restaurant, bar, etc.).

High fixed component in cost structure

A high proportion of a hotel's costs do not vary in line with sales levels. These costs are referred to as 'fixed'. The high fixed cost structure of hotels results from rent (a significant investment is required to buy land and build a hotel), as well as fixed salary costs associated with administrative and operational staff needed to manage, operate and maintain a hotel. The high proportion of fixed costs signifies that an important issue in hotels concerns the determination of the level of sales necessary to achieve breakeven (i.e. cover all fixed costs).

A considerable proportion of fixed costs result from periodic refurbishment of rooms and also investment in the hotel's physical infrastructure such as kitchen and laundry equipment. In financial management we refer to such long-held assets of the organization as 'fixed assets'. In Chapter 4 we will see how the purchase of a fixed asset results in depreciation (the allocation of a fixed asset's cost over its useful life), and in Chapter 12 techniques that can be used to appraise fixed asset investment proposals will be described.

Labour-intensive activities

If you visit the typical modern factory, you are likely to be struck by the highly automated and capital-intensive nature of the production process. Procedures are scheduled by computers and robotic engineering is used extensively in physical processing. This capital intensity in the conduct of work lies in stark contrast to what you see when entering a hotel. Major hotel activities include room housekeeping, restaurant food preparation and service as well as bar service. Despite the advent of the machine and computer age, the physical conduct of all these activities has changed little over the last fifty years. They continue to have a high labour component. Relative to many other industries, we can conclude that activities conducted in the hotel industry are still highly labour intensive.

The high labour intensity of the hospitality industry signifies the importance of performance measures that monitor labour productivity. Indices such as restaurant sales per employee-hour worked are described in Chapter 5. In addition, the need to analyse the difference between the actual cost of labour and the budgeted cost of labour can represent a significant dimension of labour cost management. In

Box 1.2
The financial management implications of distinctive hospitality industry characteristics

Hospitality industry characteristic	Financial management implication
1 Disparity and interdependency of functions	Care must be taken when determining a functional area's scope of accountability. Due to their influence on sales and expenses, some managers can be held profit accountable (e.g. a restaurant manager). Due to no direct influence on sales, others can only be held cost accountable (e.g. a training manager). Factors affecting departmental performance can be complex in hotels, however. If room occupancy affects F&B sales, care must be taken if attempting to hold an F&B manager profit-accountable.
2 High sales volatility	Hotel activity can be highly volatile over the course of an economic cycle, a year, a week, and a day. As noted in Box 1.1, this issue highlights the importance of accurate budgeting and forecasting systems to aid discounting decisions with respect to room rates and restaurant menu prices.
3 High product perishability	The absolute perishability of rooms, conference and banquet facilities and the relative perishability of food underlines the importance of accurate hotel demand forecasting as part of the budgeting process. Generally, the most important aspect of forecasting is room occupancy, as room sales drive sales levels of other hotel activities. Accurate restaurant forecasting provides the basis for maintaining a full menu of options and minimizing the cost of food wastage. With respect to rooms, forecasting accuracy can enable appropriate room rate discounting decisions.
4 High fixed costs	Hotels involve considerable investment in fixed assets such as buildings on prime land as well as extensive furnishings, fittings and equipment. This investment generates high rent and depreciation cost (discussed in Chapter 4), which, together with significant salary costs, result in hotels having a high fixed cost structure. High investment highlights the importance of using appropriate financial analysis when appraising the relative merits of proposed investments.
5 Labour-intensive activities	The high labour intensity apparent in many hotel activities highlights the importance of monitoring differences between actual labour cost and budgeted labour cost and also using performance measures that focus on labour productivity.

Chapter 9 we will see how differences between budgeted and actual labour cost can be segregated into labour rate and labour efficiency variances.

The distinctiveness of these hotel characteristics that have just been described underlines the degree to which hotel financial management systems must be tailored to the particular needs of hotel management. In combination, these characteristics signify that a hotel represents a fascinating arena in which to consider the application of financial management. Box 1.2 provides a summary of financial management implications associated with each of the hospitality industry characteristics just described.

Financial management: its nature and relationship to accounting

Finance is generally viewed as a body of principles and theories concerned with the generation and allocation of scarce resources (generally money). The most relevant aspect of finance to most managers within a company concerns the effective and efficient use of resources that fall within their particular sphere of activity. Accordingly, in this book we are concerned with describing the financial tools and techniques that can aid hospitality managers in their efforts to ensure efficient and effective management of resources.

Financial management draws extensively on accounting information. The distinction between financial management and financial accounting can be difficult to discern in many small hotels as the financial controller is often responsible for overseeing the hotel's financial management function as well as its accounting function. Although the distinction can be blurred, we tend to view financial management as a decision-making role that uses accounting information, while the financial accounting function is concerned with 'recording, classifying and reporting' (Cooper and Ijiri, 1983) the financial transactions of an organization. The closely related nature of financial management and accounting signifies that gaining a basic understanding of accounting procedures is a prerequisite to becoming a financially astute manager.

For most organizations, the accounting system represents the most extensive and all-encompassing information system. This is because accounting information is based primarily on the most fundamental common denominator in business, i.e. money. A front-office manager might talk of the number of check-ins processed, a restaurant manager may talk of the number of covers served, a laundry manager may talk of the weight of linen laundered and a housekeeping manager may talk of the number of rooms cleaned. While each manager uses different operational units when talking of their respective activities, they are all familiar with terms such as 'cost' and 'profit'. Cost and profit are denominated in monetary terms and this underlines the degree to which the accounting system is the organization's most pervasive and all-encompassing information system. It is also the only information system that measures the economic performance of all departments within an organization. When we recognize the pervasive nature of the accounting information system and the fact that we are living in a time that is frequently described as 'the information age', we begin to appreciate the critically significant role of accounting in business management generally and financial management in particular.

Individuals from different functional areas should play an active financial management role by demanding excellence in the design of accounting systems. We sometimes need to remind ourselves that accounting system design is too important to be left solely to accountants. Specific financial management information needs that fall outside the scope of a conventional accounting system design will have to be flagged by managers with decision-making and control responsibilities. There is boundless scope for tailoring an accounting information system, but the onus is on managers to inform the accounting service providers how the information provided should be tailored to meet their decision-making needs.

In the last few years there appears to have been a strong movement away from accounting's traditional 'command and control' philosophy to more of an 'inform and improve' philosophy. Despite this, some question the appropriateness of using financial measures to direct and control businesses. Criticisms include:

- Financial measures focus on symptoms rather than causes. Profit may decline because of declining customer service. It might therefore be more helpful for management to focus on monitoring factors such as customer service rather than profit.
- Financial measures tend to be oriented to the short-term performance of the past. This can hinder forward-looking, longer-term initiatives such as the development of a strong hotel chain image among customers.

Some of these criticisms have led to greater importance attached to a breadth of financial and non-financial performance indicators, e.g. Kaplan and Norton (1992, 1996) talk of the 'Balanced Scorecard'. Despite such developments, given the importance attached to published financial statements by the investing community, continued management emphasis on financial controls is to be expected.

Chapters 2, 3 and 4 provide a progressive introduction to the workings of financial accounting systems. In Chapter 2 we will see how, like a coin, a financial transaction has two sides. These two sides signify that all financial transactions have a double impact on the business. In Chapters 3 and 4 we will see how the two sides of the 'financial transaction coin' are referred to as debits and credits. It is important that you gain an understanding of the double entry bookkeeping system as it is a fairly fundamental aspect of accounting. An analogy can be drawn between the manner in which knowing the alphabet serves reading and writing and the way in which an appreciation of the double entry bookkeeping system will aid your capacity to exercise appropriate financial management. Once you have mastered the basics of double entry accounting, you will have a grounding that will allow you to begin considering how accounting information can be tailored to the specific financial decision-making needs that arise in a hotel. It is from the information stored in the double entry record-keeping system that a profit and loss statement and balance sheet are periodically prepared. These statements, which represent key indicators of an organization's financial health and performance, are also described in Chapters 2 and 3.

The book's subsequent chapters have more of a financial management orientation. The financial management issues addressed concern: analysis of performance (Chapter 5), decision-making and control implications associated with cost manage-ment (Chapters 6 and 7), responsibility accounting and budgetary control (Chapters 8 and 9), using cost information to inform pricing decisions (Chapter 10), managing elements of working capital such as cash, accounts receivable, inventory and accounts payable (Chapter 11), and conducting financial analyses of investment proposals (Chapter 12).

Financial management and hospitality decision makers

A theme of this book concerns viewing financial management from the perspective of a range of different hospitality management functions. This theme will be evident from the book's many worked examples that show how particular financial management applications are pertinent to a range of hospitality management decision-making situations that can arise. To underline the theme still further, however, each chapter contains a particular case that shows how a financial management issue raised in the chapter can be considered from a particular hotel manager's perspective. Each case is headed 'Financial Decision Making in Action' and has a sub-heading relating to the particular hospitality decision maker and also the aspect of financial management in question.

To provide you with an early sense of the importance of financial management to a range of hospitality decision makers, an overview of these cases is provided in Box 1.3. The hospitality functions identified are based on Burgess's (2001) listing of the typical executive committee in a large leisure hotel.

Uniform system of accounts

There is a uniform accounting system for the hotel industry that has been developed in the USA. It was initiated in 1925 by the Hotel Association of New York City. Application of this uniform system has grown in the USA and it is now increasingly recognized across the world. The current version of the uniform system, entitled the *Uniform System of Accounts for the Lodging Industry (USALI)*, was produced collaboratively by the Hotel Association of New York City and the American Hotel & Motel Association. The following significant benefits derive from this uniform system:

- It represents an 'off the shelf' accounting system that can be adopted by any business in the hotel industry
- The system can be viewed as 'state of the art' as it benefits from the accumulated experience of the parties that have contributed to the system's development over many years
- By promoting consistent account classification schemes as well as consistent presentation of performance reports, it facilitates comparison across hotels
- It represents a common point of reference for hotels within the same hotel group.

A profit report for Canberra's KangarooLodge Hotel is presented in Exhibit 1.1. This statement is presented in a format consistent with *USALI*. In the UK, Australia and New Zealand this statement is called a 'profit and loss statement', while in the USA and Canada it is referred to as an 'income statement'. Profit can be viewed as synonymous with income. To minimize any potential misunderstanding, the terms 'profit' and 'profit and loss statement' will be used throughout this book.

Box 1.3
Some perspectives of hospitality decision makers on aspects of financial management

Hospitality function	Financial management aspect or tool	Significance of the financial aspect or tool
General Manager	A general manager needs to understand the nature and workings of the main financial statements. Many managers incorrectly believe that asset values recorded in the balance sheet represent the assets' worth (see Chapter 2).	Senior managers are increasingly benchmarking the performance of hotels within chains. Real estate inflation rates need to be considered if conducting an analysis using asset values of hotels bought in different time periods. This is because balance sheets report historical cost and not current value of assets.
	Senior managers with no accounting training also sometimes incorrectly believe that the retained earnings account in the balance sheet represents cash that can be accessed (see Chapter 3).	Retained earnings is frequently a large account appearing in a balance sheet. It represents the accumulation of all profits reinvested in the hotel since its inception. Poor cash planning will occur if senior management believe it represents cash.
Rooms Division Manager	The Rooms Division Manager can use cost–volume–profit analysis to determine occupancy levels necessary to achieve breakeven (see Chapter 7).	Appreciating the dynamics of breakeven will help the Rooms Division Managers take steps to ensure that sales do not fall below the breakeven level.
	Variance analysis is a tool that can help a range of managers, including the Rooms Division Manager, when investigating differences between budget and actual performance (see Chapter 9).	Appraising the efficiency of activities such as room cleaning represents an important and on-going aspect of management. Variance analysis is a technique that helps a manager determine the factors causing room cleaning costs to be above or below budget.
F&B Manager	What type of inventory recording system should be used? (see Chapter 4).	If stock loss represents a problem in F&B, a perpetual rather than a periodic system may be warranted.
	Appropriately using cost information to support decision making such as whether to outsource (Chapter 6).	Hotels are increasingly outsourcing, and managers need to know how to correctly draw on cost data when making such decisions.
Human Resource Manager	Determining staffing needs from budgeted sales levels (see Chapter 8).	In the light of the hospitality sector's volatility, matching labour supply with hotel activity is an important aspect of human resource management.
Financial Controller	Use of debt financing to lever up returns to shareholders (see Chapter 5).	Appropriate use of debt finance can have a significant impact on returns earned by shareholders.
	Applying an appropriate financial analysis when deciding whether to take a supplier's offer of a discount for early payment (see Chapter 11).	Many suppliers offer a discount for early settlement of an account. In the light of this, it is important that the accounts payable department is appropriately informed on when to make an early payment.
Sales & Marketing Manager	The use of yield management in pricing (see Chapter 10).	Demand volatility highlights the importance of sales staff varying room rates charged through the year as part of a strategy to maximize profit.
Chief Engineer	Financial analysis of investment proposals (see Chapter 12).	Chief engineers are key players in building equipment investment decisions. Appropriate investment analysis is vital, as these decisions often involve large amounts of money.

Exhibit 1.1
Profit and loss statement prepared in *USALI* format

KangarooLodge Hotel
Profit and loss statement
for the year ended 30 June 20X1

	Net revenue $	Cost of sales $	Payroll and related expenses $	Other expenses	Profit (loss) $
Operating departments					
Rooms	1,232,000	0	193,000	101,000	938,000
Food	404,000	171,000	159,000	48,000	26,000
Beverage	221,000	54,000	58,000	27,000	82,000
Telecommunications	64,000	59,000	4,000	2,000	(1,000)
Total operating departments	1,921,000	284,000	414,000	178,000	1,045,000
Undistributed operating expenses					
Administrative and General			51,000	28,000	79,000
Human Resources			25,000	6,000	31,000
Marketing			29,000	36,000	65,000
Energy			0	79,000	79,000
			105,000	149,000	254,000
Profit after undistributed operating expenses					791,000
Rent, rates and insurance					182,000
Loan interest					102,000
Depreciation					123,000
Profit before tax					384,000
Tax					110,000
Net profit					274,000

The *USALI* profit and loss statement comprises three sections. In the top section, net revenue (i.e. net sales) for each functional area is identified in the first data column. This is followed by three columns that identify expenses that can be directly related to the functional areas listed, i.e. cost of sales, payroll & related expenses, and other expenses. Cost of sales refers to the cost of items that are sold, e.g. the cost of wine sold through a restaurant. Each department's profit is determined by deducting the sum of the three expense items from net revenue. The statement's middle section is headed 'undistributed operating expenses'. In this section the expenses relating to a hotel's service departments (e.g. administrative and general, human resources, marketing, etc.) are identified. The distinction between the hotel's service departments and the functional areas listed in the top section of the statement is that no revenue can be traced directly to the service departments. The statement's lower section includes expenses that are generally not traceable to a hotel's operating management. Expenses such as rent, insurance and interest on debt are generally traceable to a tier of management that lies above a hotel's operational staff. The last line of the statement presents the net profit, i.e. all hotel revenue minus all hotel expenses.

It is apparent from Exhibit 1.1 that a profit and loss statement presented in accordance with the *USALI* provides much profitability information at the hotel department level (e.g. rooms, food, beverage department, etc.). This format supports financial management as it allows a hotel's management to consider the relative profitability levels of its different functional areas, e.g. from Exhibit 1.1, it can be determined that following the deduction of expenses directly related to rooms, 76.14% of room revenue remains as a contribution to general hotel expenses and profit ($938,000 ÷ $1,232,000 × 100).

The *USALI* is introduced in this first chapter in order to give you an early appreciation of a typical hotel's profit and loss statement. It is also useful to note differing terms used around the globe to describe the surplus of revenue over expenses ('income' in the USA and 'profit' in the UK). This provides you with an early warning to tread a little warily when consulting accounting and financial management texts written in different countries. Your understanding of the nature of the profit and loss statement will be reinforced in the next chapter which, among other things, focuses on the relationship between the profit and loss statement and the balance sheet.

Summary

This chapter has set the scene for the remainder of the book. We have reviewed the particular characteristics of the hospitality industry and considered their implications for financial management. We have also considered the nature of financial management in general and also its relevance to a range of hospitality decision makers. Finally, the chapter provided a short introduction to financial accounting by outlining the nature and presentation of a profit and loss statement produced using the standard that is generally referred to as the *Uniform System of Accounts for the Lodging Industry*.

Having read the chapter you should now know:

- Some of the hospitality industry's particular characteristics and their financial management implications
- What is meant by financial management and how it relates to accounting
- Some of the ways that different hospitality decision makers draw on financial information and analyses in their decision making
- The nature of information provided in a profit and loss statement.

References

Atkinson, H., Berry, A. and Jarvis, R. (1995) *Business Accounting for Hospitality and Tourism & Leisure*, International Thomson Publishing, London, Chapter 1.

Burgess, C. (2001) *Guide to Money Matters for Hospitality Managers*, Butterworth-Heinemann, Oxford, Chapter 1.

Cooper, W.W. and Ijiri, Y. (eds) (1983) *Kohler's Dictionary for Accountants*, 6th edition, Prentice Hall, Englewood Cliffs, NJ.

Harris, P. (1999) *Profit Planning*, Butterworth-Heinemann, Oxford, Chapters 1 and 2.

Kaplan, R.S. and Norton, D.P. (1992) The Balanced Scorecard – measures that Drive Performance, *Harvard Business Review*, **70**, 1, 71–79.

Kaplan, R. S. and Norton, D.P. (1996) *The Balanced Scorecard – Translating Strategy into Action*, Harvard Business School Press, Boston, MA.

Kotas, R. (1999) *Management Accounting for Hospitality and Tourism*, 3rd edition, International Thomson Business Press, London, Chapter 1.

Schmidgall, R. F. (1997) *Hospitality Industry Managerial Accounting*, 4th edition, Educational Institute – American Hotel & Motel Association, East Lansing, MI, Chapter 3.

Uniform System of Accounts for the Lodging Industry (1996) 9th edition, Educational Institute of the American Hotel & Motel Association, East Lansing, MI.

Problems

✓ indicates that a solution appears at the back of the text

✓ 1.1 (a) Describe what is meant by functional interdependency.
(b) Describe why functional interdependency is an issue that needs to be considered when designing a hotel's system of accountability.

✓ 1.2 (a) What are the four main dimensions of sales volatility in the hotel industry?
(b) What are the accounting implications arising from these four dimensions of sales volatility?

✓ 1.3 (a) Describe what is meant by high perishability of the hotel product.
(b) Describe the accounting implications arising from high product perishability.

1.4 Describe the factors causing hotels to have a high proportion of fixed costs.

1.5 (a) Describe the manner in which hotel activities tend to be labour intensive.
(b) Describe the accounting implications arising from the high labour intensity of hotel activities.

1.6 Give one example of how a particular financial management tool or technique might be drawn upon in the context of a particular hospitality management function.

1.7 Identify three advantages that derive from using the *Uniform System of Accounts for the Lodging Industry* (*USALI*).

PART 2

Hospitality Financial Accounting

Analysing transactions and preparing year-end financial statements

After studying this chapter, you should have developed an appreciation of:

1 How there is a double financial implication arising from every financial transaction undertaken by an organization

2 The nature and format of the balance sheet

3 The nature and format of the profit and loss statement

4 How profit computed in the profit and loss statement flows into the owner's equity section of the balance sheet via the statement of owner's equity.

Introduction

This is the first of the three chapters concerned with **financial accounting**. Financial accounting concerns the preparation of **financial reports** that are made available to external users such as shareholders. This chapter provides an overview of the main financial accounting statements that appear in annual reports prepared by publicly listed companies (i.e. companies with shares listed on a stock exchange). Although this is not a long chapter, the material presented is fairly concentrated. A considered review of this material will provide you with a good basic appreciation of the nature of the year-end financial statements. To achieve this appreciation you will need to carefully follow through the chapter's worked example that illustrates how a set of financial transactions impact on the year-end accounts. Once you have gained an appreciation of the nature of the year-end financial statements, the next chapter will introduce the 'debit/credit' double entry record-keeping process that underlies the financial accounting system. Finally, Chapter 4 introduces some more advanced aspects of double entry record-keeping by reviewing year-end adjustments that need to be made to the financial records in order to recognize time-related issues such as asset depreciation.

It may appear a little strange that a book concerned with hospitality decision making has devoted three chapters to financial accounting. There are, however, several reasons why a hotel manager should have a basic familiarity with financial accounting. Of particular significance is the fact that most professional accounting courses of study have a bias towards financial accounting, rather than management accounting, which is the branch of accounting concerned with the provision of accounting information for management decision making and control. Once qualified, many accountants secure jobs working in industries such as the hospitality sector, with the result that a financial accounting mentality frequently prevails in organizations' internal accounting departments. It is important that all managers appreciate the potential for this tendency and have an ability and willingness to 'think outside the square' by asking for accounting information and analyses to be presented in a way that **supports management decision making rather than the needs of external reporting**.

An example of 'thinking outside the square' might be a marketing manager who feels that a customer profitability analysis would help management deliberations concerned with allocating a promotion budget. The manager might feel reluctant to ask for such information, however, as the accounting system has never provided it in the past. If you review the material presented in Chapter 4, it will become apparent that a key concern of financial accountants is the accurate allocation of profit earned to particular periods of time. The financial accounting system does not require, however, that profit be allocated across customer segments. As the impetus for allocating profit across customer segments is unlikely to come from an accounting department, it will have to be initiated by the manager needing the information. (For a further discussion of the customer accounting issue in hotels see Guilding *et al.*, 2001.) A second reason why a hotel manager should understand the basics of financial accounting is that two outputs of the financial accounting system, the **balance sheet** and the **profit and loss statement**, represent important sources of information that can further management control of the company. The manner in which these statements can be used to facilitate management control will be extensively explored in Chapter 5.

The balance sheet and profit and loss statement

In most Western countries, four financial statements are presented in the published annual reports of publicly listed companies. These reports are the balance sheet, the profit and loss statement, the statement of owners' equity and the statement of cash flows. As noted in Chapter 1, in the USA and Canada the profit and loss statement is called the 'income statement'.

The elements comprising the balance sheet, profit and loss statement and statement of owner's equity are described in this section. Following this, the worked example in the next section will show the extent to which these statements can be seen as direct outputs of the financial accounting record-keeping process. No detailed review will be undertaken of the statement of cash flows which classifies cash inflows and outflows and identifies the net change in cash held by the firm over the reporting period. Relative to the balance sheet and profit and loss statement, this statement is not used as much for decision making and control purposes. Although it will not be considered further in this book, if you see a cash flow statement you will have an immediate rudimentary understanding of it, due to its resemblance to an aggregated version of your monthly bank statement.

The balance sheet is a schedule summarizing what is owned and what is owed by a company at a particular point in time. Its three main sections which comprise assets, liabilities and owners' equity, are described in Box 2.1.

From Box 2.1 it is apparent that profit earned increases owner's equity. It is also evident that the profit computed through the profit and loss statement can be seen to feed into the owners' equity section of the balance sheet via the statement of owner's equity. For this reason, at the year-end we need to prepare the profit and loss statement and statement of owner's equity in advance of preparing the balance sheet.

One key difference between the profit and loss statement and the balance sheet pertains to time. The profit and loss statement (like the statement of owners' equity) always relates to a period of time, i.e. the time taken to make the profit reported in the profit and loss statement. The balance sheet, however, relates to a particular moment in time.

Let's draw on the analogy of your own financial situation to highlight this important time distinction. If you were asked 'How much do you earn?' you can only respond in the context of a time period, i.e. you could talk of your earnings last month or your earnings last year. Your earnings are analogous to the profit of a firm, in fact, a firm's profit represents what the business has earned for the owners of the firm (note how a time period is referred to in the heading of the profit and loss statement presented in Exhibit 2.2 below). Similarly, if you were asked 'What is your wealth?' your answer would have to be in the context of a particular moment in time, as the value of your assets are constantly changing, i.e. you might receive weekly payments for work rendered, you buy and consume things such as food on a daily basis, etc. To determine your wealth you would have to identify everything you own (your assets) and deduct everything that you owe (your liabilities) at a particular point in time. The issue of determining personal wealth is analogous to the preparation of a company's balance sheet which can be seen as a representation of the wealth of the firm, i.e. it summarizes assets and liabilities. Like the wealth of an individual, the wealth of a firm can only be conceived in the context of a particular moment in time (note how a point in time is referred to in the wording of the balance sheet heading presented in Exhibit 2.2 below).

> ## Box 2.1
> ## The main sections of a balance sheet
>
> - **Assets** are 'things' that are owned (most usually purchased) by the organization. They are assets if the organization can derive some future value from ownership. Typical hotel assets include: cash, accounts receivable, prepayments, inventory (sometimes referred to as 'stock'), cars, china, silver, glass, linen, uniforms, equipment, land and buildings. Assets are generally recorded in the accounting system at their cost, although in some countries such as Australia, New Zealand and the UK, asset revaluations can be made (asset revaluation is not permitted under the generally accepted accounting principles of Canada and the USA).
>
> - **Liabilities** may be seen as the opposite of assets. They reflect financial obligations of the organization. Typical liabilities include: wages & salaries payable, accounts payable and bank loans.
>
> - **Owners' equity** reflects the financial investment of the owners in the organization. It includes the owners' original investment plus all profits not paid out to the owners (i.e. profits retained in the business). For financial accounting purposes, profit is typically determined on an annual basis. This computation is achieved through the **profit & loss statement** (termed the 'income statement' in Canada and the USA). In the profit and loss statement, expenses for the year (which represent resources consumed such as housekeeping wages and cost of beer sold through a bar) are deducted from revenue earned during the year to give profit for the year. If expenses are greater than revenue, a loss results. Some profit may be withdrawn from the business by the owners. That portion of profit that the owners choose not to withdraw is effectively a further contribution to the business by the owners. It is therefore treated as an addition to owners' equity (at the end of the accounting year), and is generally termed 'retained earnings' or 'retained profit'. Computation of the year-end owners' equity balance is achieved through the **statement of owners' equity**. The first line of this statement identifies the owners' equity balance at the beginning of the accounting year. To this we add net profit for the year as well as any new equity capital raised. Finally, any profits distributed to the owners during the year (termed 'drawings' or 'dividends') are deducted to give the closing owners' equity balance.

A balance sheet can be presented in one of the following two basic formats:

Assets – Liabilities = Owners' Equity

or

Assets = Liabilities + Owners' Equity

As both formats represent an equation, some people talk of 'the balance sheet equation'. Underlying the first equation is the notion that the value of the owners' equity (the owners' stake) in the company equals the surplus assets that would remain after the acquittal of all liabilities. Underlying the second equation is the notion that money raised by a business is invested in various assets. The 'money raised' notion is on the right-hand side of the equation as liabilities include sources of finance such as bank loans, while owners' equity refers to money invested in the business by the owners. With respect to the left-hand side of the second equation, the money raised finances the purchase of assets and any money raised but not used to purchase assets must be held as cash, which is itself an asset.

Classifying transactions according to assets, liabilities and owners' equity

Like a coin, a financial transaction has two sides. These two sides signify that all financial transactions have a double impact on a business. We will now consider a set of transactions and see how, as a result of their double impact, the balance sheet equation is always left intact. In this worked example the balance sheet equation is stated as 'assets = liabilities + owners' equity'. The same exercise could be performed using a format based on the alternative balance sheet equation, however.

In Exhibit 2.1, transactions undertaken in the first ten days of trading for Joe Blow, a small hotel offering seminar facilities close to Montreal's Ile Notre-Dame Formula One Grand Prix circuit, are summarized. Following this, the way in which each of the transactions affect the balance sheet are noted in the 'account' columns appearing under the main balance sheet headings: assets, liabilities and owners' equity. In the interests of capturing all the transactions in one matrix, transactions that affect profit (i.e. a sale or the incurrence of an expense) appear in the final column headed 'profit and loss'. As profit affects owners' equity, this column appears under the owners' equity heading. Investments in the business by the owners are recorded in the 'capital' column which also appears under the owners' equity heading.

Following the steps undertaken in Exhibit 2.1 represents a learning activity designed to develop your appreciation of the fact that every transaction has a double impact on the balance sheet equation. As will be seen later in Exhibit 2.2, in reality, transactions affecting profit flow first into the profit and loss statement and then flow into the balance sheet via the statement of owners' equity.

Following through the steps involved in Exhibit 2.1 is an important exercise. Not only do they clearly demonstrate how every transaction has a double impact on the balance sheet, the exercise also lays the basis for your appreciation of the workings of the balance sheet. You should approach Exhibit 2.1 by considering each transaction in turn and noting its double impact on the balance sheet in a manner that leaves assets equal to the sum of liabilities and owners' equity. A description of how each transaction results in a double impact is provided in Schedule 2.1.

We can present the results of the ten transactions described in Exhibit 2.1 in a more conventional accounting format by compiling Joe Blow's profit and loss statement and statement of owner's equity for the first ten days of May and also Joe Blow's balance sheet as at 10 May. These statements are presented as Exhibit 2.2. Note how the column totals in the balance sheet equation matrix appearing at the bottom of Exhibit 2.1 feed into the statements compiled in Exhibit 2.2. Also note how the profit determined in the profit and loss statement feeds into the balance sheet via the statement of owners' equity.

The balance sheet presented in Exhibit 2.2 has been compiled according to a horizontal format whereby assets appear on one side and liabilities and owners' equity appear on the other. You may also encounter balance sheets presented using a vertical format in which the totals of assets, liabilities and owners' equity appear one above another (see, for example, the balance sheet presented later in the book as Exhibit 5.2).

Exhibit 2.1
Illustration of how transactions affect the balance sheet equation

May

1 Owner contributes $30,000 cash to commence business.
2 Purchased a van for $12,000, paying $3,000 in cash and obtaining a loan for the balance.
3 Purchased non-perishable food stock including a large maple syrup shipment on credit for $800.
4 Billed clients $19,000 for use of conference facilities.
5 Received $6,000 from customers billed in (4) above.
6 Paid $500 to trade creditors to reduce amount owing for inventory stock purchased.
7 Owners withdrew $1,500 from the business.
8 The accountant has determined that $600 of inventory stock has been used.
9 Paid $250 for miscellaneous expenses (telephone, electricity, etc.).
10 Repaid $5,000 of the loan taken out for the van.

Balance sheet equation

| May | Assets | | | | = | Liabilities | | + | Owners' equity | |
	Cash at bank $	Accounts receivable $	Inventory $	Vehicles $		Accounts payable $	Loan payable $		Capital $	Profit & loss $
1	+30,000								+30,000	
2	−3,000			+12,000			+9,000			
3			+800			+800				
4		+19,000								+19,000
5	+6,000	−6,000								
6	−500					−500				
7	−1,500								−1,500	
8			−600							−600
9	−250									−250
10	−5,000						−5,000			
Total	25,750	13,000	200	12,000		300	4,000		28,500	18,150
	$50,950				=	$4,300		+	$46,650	

While both the horizontal and vertical balance sheet formats are widely used within the same countries, some different balance sheet formatting conventions do exist internationally. Relative to other English-speaking countries, some distinct conventions are particularly evident in the UK. In Australia, Canada, New Zealand and the USA, the convention is to present assets in order of liquidity, i.e. the assets that are closest to cash are presented first. If a business has cash, marketable securities, accounts receivable and inventory, then cash is presented first, marketable securities are second (marketable securities are readily convertible into cash), accounts receivable are third (accounts receivable are converted into cash in the short term in the normal course of business), and inventory appears fourth (with the

Schedule 2.1
The impact of Exhibit 2.1's ten transactions on the balance sheet

Transaction date	Description of balance sheet impact
1 May	The business now has $30,000 in cash (increase cash account). The capital account records all financial investments in the business made by the owners (increase capital account).
2 May	This transaction is slightly awkward as it affects three accounts. The business now has a motor vehicle which is an asset that cost $12,000 (increase vehicles account). It paid for the van by using $3,000 cash (reduce the cash account) and by borrowing $9,000 (increase loan payable account).
3 May	The business now has $800 in inventory (increase inventory account). It owes money for this purchase (increase accounts payable account).
4 May	The business is now owed $19,000 for services rendered (increase accounts receivable account). The business has now made a sale (increase the revenue account – treated in this exercise as positively affecting owners' equity by increasing profit).
5 May	The business now has a further $6,000 in cash (increase cash account). The money it was owed with respect to the sale made on 4 May is now $6,000 less (reduce accounts receivable account).
6 May	Cash has now declined by $500 (reduce cash account). The amount owing with respect to the purchase made on 3 May is now $500 less (reduce accounts payable account).
7 May	The business cash balance has now declined by a further $1,500 (reduce cash account). The net investment in the business made by the owners has declined by $1,500 (reduce capital account).
8 May	The cost of stock held in the business has declined by $600 (reduce inventory account). This decline in stock signifies that resources have been consumed (increase cost of sales account – treated in this exercise as negatively affecting owners' equity by reducing profit).
9 May	Cash has declined by $250 (reduce cash account). The use of telephone and electricity signifies resources have been consumed (increase miscellaneous expense account – treated in this exercise as negatively affecting owners' equity by reducing profit).
10 May	Cash has declined by $5,000 (reduce cash account). The amount owing on the loan taken out for the van is now $5,000 less (reduce loan payable account).

Exhibit 2.2
Illustration of how the profit and loss statement is linked to the balance sheet via the statement of owners' equity

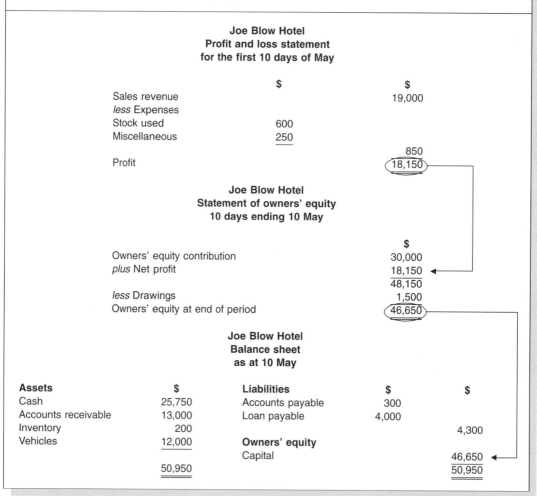

exception of cash sales, a sale from inventory will become an account receivable prior to translation to cash). In these countries, a similar rationale is applied to the sequencing of liabilities, i.e. those liabilities with the shortest term to payment appear first. In the UK, however, this sequencing for assets and liabilities is reversed. A further distinguishing feature of balance sheets in the UK concerns the positioning of the three main balance sheet sections. In a UK horizontal balance sheet, the convention is to place owners' equity and liabilities on the left-hand side (owners' equity above liabilities) and assets on the right-hand side. To illustrate this distinct nature of the balance sheet format used in the UK, the same balance sheet numbers as those appearing in Joe Blow Hotel's balance sheet in Exhibit 2.2 are presented using a UK horizontal format in Exhibit 2.3 (in this exhibit £s replace $s).

Exhibit 2.3
Illustration of a UK balance sheet prepared in a horizontal format

Joe Blow Hotel
Balance sheet as at 10 May

	£	£		£
Owners' equity			**Assets**	
Capital		46,650	Vehicles	12,000
Liabilities			Inventory	200
Loan payable	4,000		Accounts receivable	13,000
Accounts payable	300		Cash	25,750
		4,300		
		50,950		50,950

The importance of understanding financial accounting basics

In your working life you are highly likely to meet senior managers who have a poor understanding of the mechanics of financial accounting. In the financial decision-making case presented below, we see how an unfamiliarity with the basics of financial accounting can be a recipe for poor decision making.

Case 2.1

Financial Decision Making in Action – The General Manager's use of balance sheet information

Senior managers are increasingly using the performance of other hotels as a benchmark for appraising their own performance. A widely quoted performance indicator is return on investment (ROI) which is computed by stating a hotel's annual profit as a percentage of the investment in its assets (ROI will be more extensively discussed in Chapter 5). Considerable care needs to be exercised in this type of analysis, however, as balance sheets record assets (i.e. investment) at their historical cost and not their current value.

Imagine hotels A and B are in the same hotel chain and are highly comparable in terms of markets served, size, quality and profits generated. Hotel A was purchased seven years ago at a price that was 30% less than the price paid for Hotel B five years ago. The difference in the amount invested resulted from rapid inflation around the time the two hotels were acquired. If ROI is calculated based on conventional accounting records, it will appear that Hotel A is the better performer. This will be attributable more to the time it was purchased than good management by the general manager, however. To provide a better basis for benchmarking the relative management performance in the two hotels, current market value rather than historical cost could be used as the basis for valuing the investment in each hotel.

This issue of assets being recorded at their historical cost is also pertinent to insurance decisions taken. Senior managers should ensure that all assets are insured for what it would cost to replace them. Replacement cost can be significantly different from the historical cost recorded in a balance sheet.

Summary

In this chapter we have seen how two financial implications arise from every financial transaction undertaken by a business. We have also reviewed the nature and content of the main financial reports: the balance sheet and the profit and loss statement. We have seen that the balance sheet comprises assets, liabilities and owners' equity accounts. The profit and loss statement comprises revenue and expense accounts.

Having read the chapter you should now know:

- The main account headings in a balance sheet and profit and loss statement
- The layout of a balance sheet and profit and loss statement
- How to classify transactions according to their impact on assets, liabilities and owners' equity accounts
- How profit is determined in the profit and loss statement and flows into the balance sheet via the statement of owners' equity
- The importance of senior managers having a basic understanding of the balance sheet.

References

Atkinson, H., Berry, A. and Jarvis, R. (1995) *Business Accounting for Hospitality and Tourism & Leisure*, International Thomson Publishing, London, Chapters 3 and 4.

Carnegie, G., Jones, S., Norris, G., Wigg, R. and Williams, B. (1999) *Accounting: Financial and Organisational Decision Making*, Irwin/McGraw-Hill, New York, Chapter 3.

Coltman, M. M. and Jagels, M. G. (2001) *Hospitality Management Accounting*, 7th edition, John Wiley, Chichester, Chapter 1.

Guilding, C., Kennedy, D. and McManus, L. (2001) *Journal of Hospitality and Tourism Research*, **25**, 2, 173–194.

Harris, P. (1999) *Profit Planning*, Butterworth-Heinemann, Oxford, Chapter 2.

Kotas, R. and Conlan, M. (1997) *Hospitality Accounting*, 5th edition, International Thomson Publishing, London, Chapter 1.

Owen, G. (1994) *Accounting for Hospitality, Tourism & Leisure*, Pitman Publishing, London, Chapter 4.

Schmidgall, R. F. (1997) *Hospitality Industry Managerial Accounting*, 4th edition, Educational Institute – American Hotel & Motel Association, East Lansing, MI, Chapters 2 and 3.

Problems

✓ indicates that a solution appears at the back of the text

✓ 2.1   Describe what is meant by:

(a) an asset
(b) a liability
(c) owners' equity.

✓ 2.2   Describe what is meant by the term 'balance sheet equation'.

✓ 2.3   Describe the difference between a profit and loss statement and a balance sheet.

2.4   Identified below are a set of transactions for the SerenitySleep Hotel which commenced business in Wellington, New Zealand on 1 June.

June
1   Owner commenced business by depositing $20,000 in a new business bank account.
2   Purchased some basic office furniture for $3,000 cash.
3   Purchased inventory stock for $900 cash.
4   Purchased more inventory stock on credit for $1,400.
5   Purchased an office computer for $6,000, paying $1,500 in cash and obtaining a loan for the balance.
6   Billed clients $1,000 for use of conference facilities.
7   The owner withdrew $800 from the business.
8   Banked the first week's cash revenue $1,300.
9   It was determined that $400 of inventory has been used since the commencement of business.
10   Paid $240 for miscellaneous expenses (telephone, electricity, etc.)

Required • • •
Using a format similar to that appearing in Exhibit 2.1, demonstrate the impact each transaction will have on the balance sheet equation.

2.5   The Johnson Hotel is located in Perth, Western Australia. Identified below are the account balances for the Johnson Hotel following its commercial activities through the month of December 20X1.

	$
Accounts payable	10,000
Accounts receivable	12,000
Cash	5,000
Linen	8,000
Uniforms	7,500
Buildings	250,000
Loan payable	100,000
Owners' equity	148,000
Sales revenue	38,000
Inventory stock used	6,500
Miscellaneous expenses	3,000
Owners' drawings	4,000

Required • • •
(a) Prepare the Johnson Hotel's profit and loss statement for December 20X1.
(b) Prepare Johnson Hotel's statement of owner's equity for December 20X1.
(c) Prepare Johnson Hotel's balance sheet as at 31 December 20X1.

2.6   In April 20X1, Jock MacNoodle opened the MacNoodle Italian Restaurant in Glasgow. Identified below are the restaurant's financial transactions in its first month of business.

Date	Transaction
1 April	Jock MacNoodle deposited £10,000 in a newly opened business bank account.
2 April	Paid £400 cash for non-perishable food items to build up an inventory of food.
4 April	Purchased a photocopier costing £1,000. 10% of the purchase price was paid in cash and a loan was taken to cover the balance.
5 April	Purchased £500 of wine stock on credit.
7 April	Banked the £350 received for cash sales made in first week.
8 April	Paid £450 rent for April.
14 April	Paid a kitchen assistant and waiter wages of £100.
18 April	Paid £300 as part settlement of the wine merchant's account.
27 April	It was noted that half of the stock of wine purchased on 5th of April had been sold.
28 April	Banked £460 received from cash sales.
29 April	Paid a kitchen assistant and waiter wages of £280.
30 April	It was noted that £60 of food inventory had been used.
30 April	It was noted that credit sales made in the first month of business were £340.

Required . . .
Using a format similar to that appearing in Exhibit 2.1, demonstrate the impact each transaction will have on the restaurant's balance sheet equation.

2.7   In connection with the information provided in problem 2.6 above, prepare the following:

(a) The MacNoodle restaurant's profit and loss statement for April 20X1.
(b) The MacNoodle restaurant's statement of owners' equity for April 20X1.
(c) The MacNoodle restaurant's balance sheet as at 30 April 20X1.

Double entry accounting

After studying this chapter, you should have
developed an appreciation of:

1 The mechanics of double entry bookkeeping

2 How the terms 'debit' and 'credit' are used in
   financial accounting

3 The fact that asset and expense accounts
   normally have a debit balance

4 The fact that liability, owners' equity and revenue
   accounts normally have a credit balance

5 The distinction between current assets and fixed
   assets and also current liabilities and long-term
   liabilities.

Introduction

This chapter focuses on the fundamentals of **double entry accounting** and will reinforce the understanding of the **balance sheet** and **profit and loss statement** that you acquired from reading Chapter 2.

Double entry accounting: some background concepts

In Chapter 2 we saw how a double impact arises from any financial transaction. In the light of this, it is not surprising that the financial accounting recording process is based on a system of double entries. In this chapter we will see that the columns in the previous chapter's Exhibit 2.1 represent 'accounts' in a real accounting system. In Exhibit 2.1 there were columns pertaining to cash, accounts receivable, inventory, etc. In double entry accounting we have a cash account, an accounts receivable account, an inventory account, etc. Further, we will see that the '+' and '−' symbols that indicated the directional change for each of the accounts in Exhibit 2.1 represent a 'debit' or 'credit' in double entry accounting. An important word of caution is warranted at this point, however. A '+' does not always represent a debit or credit and a '−' does not always represent a debit or credit. As we will see in Exhibit 3.1 presented below, the relationship between the '+' and '−' used in the previous chapter and the debit and credit terms used in double entry accounting depends on the nature of the account in question.

Before exploring the workings of the double entry bookkeeping system, it is helpful to review the nature of the five basic account categories. In an accounting system these comprise: assets, liabilities, owners' equity, revenues and expenses. Asset, liability and the owners' equity accounts relate to a certain point in time (they are sometimes referred to as 'snapshot' accounts). Their 'snapshot' nature should be apparent from the fact that they all appear in the balance sheet. We noted in Chapter 2 that the balance sheet refers to a particular point in time, and not a period of time. Revenue and expense accounts are 'flow' accounts (they only make sense when referring to a period of time). Again, this should be apparent from the fact that expense and revenue accounts appear in the profit and loss statement which, unlike the balance sheet, refers to a time period and not a particular point in time.

Let us now turn to the fundamentals of double entry accounting. In Box 3.1 there is a summary of key principles that can help when first confronting the debits and credits of double entry accounting.

The first two principles in Box 3.1 provide a framework that can serve as a highly valuable reference point when learning the double entry accounting process. This framework is also depicted as a matrix in Exhibit 3.1. From this matrix we can see that asset accounts usually have a debit balance (column 1). It follows that a debit entry is made to record an increase in an asset account (column 2), and a credit entry is made to record a decrease in an asset account (column 3). Similarly, it is also evident from Exhibit 3.1 that liability accounts usually have a credit balance (column 1), we credit a liability account to increase it (column 2), and debit a liability account to decrease it (column 3).

The fourth principle of double entry accounting referred to in Box 3.1 concerns the workings of the cash account. Gaining a familiarity with the workings of the cash account is a useful first step when attempting to understand the double entry accounting system. This is because many transactions affect cash. Cash is an

---

Box 3.1
Key principles of double entry accounting

- With respect to balance sheet accounts: asset accounts normally have a debit balance, liabilities and owners' equity accounts normally have a credit balance. This is a helpful rule, however be warned that in some situations it can be broken, e.g. while we normally think of a bank account as an asset (i.e. debit balance), if it becomes overdrawn it will represent a liability (i.e. credit balance).

- With respect to profit and loss accounts: revenue accounts have a credit balance, expense accounts have a debit balance.

- For every debit entry, there must be an equal credit entry.

- Where there is a cash inflow we debit the cash account. For a cash outflow, we credit the cash account.

Exhibit 3.1
The double entry accounting framework

Type of account	(1) Usual balance	(2) If increasing the account	(3) If decreasing the account
Asset (balance sheet account)	Debit	Debit	Credit
Liability (balance sheet account)	Credit	Credit	Debit
Owners' equity (balance sheet account)	Credit	Credit	Debit
Revenue (P&L account)	Credit	Credit	Debit
Expense (P&L account)	Debit	Debit	Credit

example of an asset account, and once you have mastered the way this account works, you will have gained an insight into the workings of all asset accounts. As cash is an asset, it is evident from Exhibit 3.1 that a receipt of cash (i.e. an increase in cash) will be recorded by debiting the cash account and a disbursement of cash (i.e. a decrease in cash) will be recorded by crediting the cash account.

The cash account's workings can be illustrated using a 'T account', as depicted in Exhibit 3.2. The left-hand side of all T accounts (regardless of whether they are assets, liabilities, etc.) is the debit side (sometimes abbreviated as 'Dr') and the right-hand side of all T accounts is the credit side (sometimes abbreviated as 'Cr'). Some find it helpful to visualize money flowing through the cash T account from left to right, i.e. money flows into the left-hand side of the account (the arrow on the left in Exhibit 3.2), and flows out of the right-hand side of the account (the arrow on the right in Exhibit 3.2). Consistent with this visualization, a receipt of

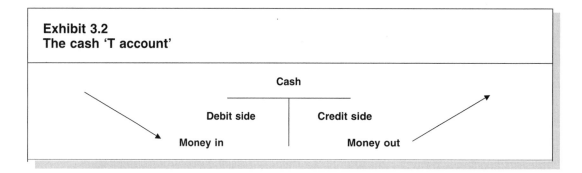

Exhibit 3.2
The cash 'T account'

Cash

Debit side | Credit side

Money in | Money out

money is recorded as a debit to the cash account and an outflow of cash is recorded as a credit to the cash account.

Because of the terminology used by banks, many students of accounting are confused when introduced to the workings of the cash account. They are used to their bank informing them that a deposit of funds in their account represents a credit. This confusion arises because the bank is using terminology from its perspective and not the account holder's perspective. This will be illustrated by the following small example. Imagine that Monica Miser deposits $300 in her savings account held with the Loyalty bank. The double entry that the Loyalty bank will record in its accounting system is as follows:

Cash		M. Miser Savings Account	
300			300

Note that the cash account (which is an asset from the bank's perspective) has been debited. This is consistent with Exhibit 3.2. Note also that the bank's record of Monica Miser's savings account has been credited. This account represents a liability from the perspective of the bank (i.e. it records what the bank owes to M. Miser). As the bank's liability to Monica Miser has increased, the savings account has been credited (check back to column 2 in Exhibit 3.1). When Monica Miser receives a statement from her bank, she will find that the $300 deposit has been recorded as a credit to her savings account. The confusion for the student of accounting stems from the fact that the savings account represents a liability for the bank, but an asset for the account holder.

Double entry accounting: a worked example

We are now in a position to explore the nature of double entry accounting through a worked example comprising several transactions. In the following example we will see the double entry recording of a series of transactions and the subsequent preparation of a profit and loss statement and balance sheet.

Imagine that on 28 June the Winnie Pooh Hotel Ltd commenced business next to a children's theme park in Cardiff, Wales. On 30 June the only balances in W. Pooh Hotel Ltd's accounting system were as follows:

	£
Cash	8,000
Revenue	300
Owners' Equity	7,700

Identified below are nine transactions that occurred in July, together with the double entry necessary to record each transaction in the accounting system. The circled numbers in the 'T-accounts' highlight the entry necessary to record the transaction in question.

Transaction 1

1 July: From the £8,000 balance in the bank account, beverage stock was purchased for £200 cash.

Cash		Inventory	
Opening balance (OB) 8,000			
	(200)	(200)	

Both cash and inventory are asset accounts. From Exhibit 3.1 it can be determined that the decrease in cash necessitates a credit to the cash account, and the increase of stock necessitates a debit to the inventory account.

Note: Exhibit 3.1 indicates that we expect to see a debit balance in an asset account (e.g. cash or inventory).

Transaction 2

4 July: At an American Independence Day banquet function the beverage stock bought on 1 July was sold for £500 cash.

Note: this is a slightly tricky transaction to record as we have to complete two sets of entries. The first set deals with the sales aspect of the transaction, the second set deals with the expense aspect of the transaction.

Cash		Revenue	
8,000			OB 300
	200		
(500)			(500)

Note: Exhibit 3.1 indicates that we expect to see a credit balance in a revenue account.

Cost of sales		Inventory	
(200)		200	
			(200)

Note: Exhibit 3.1 indicates that we expect to see a debit balance in an expense account (e.g. cost of sales). Cost of sales includes the cost of all goods and services consumed in making a sale.

Transaction 3

5 July: Purchased inventory stock on credit from Ripoff Ltd for £1,000.

Inventory		Accounts payable	
200	200		
(1,000)			(1,000)

Note: Exhibit 3.1 indicates that we expect to see a credit balance in a liability account (accounts payable is an example).

Transaction 4

10 July: Sold conferencing services on credit to Ripoff Ltd for £2,000.

Accounts receivable		Revenue	
			300
			500
(2,000)			(2,000)

Transaction 5

11 July: Purchased 10 kitchen ovens on credit for £250,000 from Rusting Ltd.

Kitchen equipment		Accounts payable	
			1,000
(250,000)			(250,000)

Kitchen equipment is an example of a 'fixed asset'. 'Fixed assets' is the term given to all physical assets that will be held by the purchasing company for more than a year. Fixed assets are acquired for use in operations rather than for resale to customers.

Transaction 6

18 July: Paid Rusting £250,000 to settle the outstanding account.

Cash				Accounts payable	
8,000					1,000
	200				
500					250,000
	(250,000)			(250,000)	

Transaction 7

20 July: Paid £300 for electricity bill.

Cash			Electricity expense	
8,000				
	200		(300)	
500				
	250,000			
	(300)			

Transaction 8

24 July: To correct the business bank overdraft, the owner invests a further £500,000 into the company.

Cash			Owners' equity	
8,000				
				OB 7,700
	200			
500				(500,000)
	250,000			
	300			
(500,000)				

Note: Exhibit 3.1 indicates that we expect to see a credit balance in the owners' equity account.

Transaction 9

31 July: The owner realizes that in the previous week he had taken too much out of his personal account and that he now faces a shortfall of cash. As a result, he took £1,500 back out of the business account and put it in his personal account.

Hospitality, Leisure & Tourism Series

Cash		Drawings	
8,000			
		(1,500)	
	200		
500			
	250,000		
	300		
500,000			
	(1,500)		

Note: Drawings is the term used to describe the transaction occurring when an owner takes funds out of the business. In the case of companies with shareholder ownership, drawings are referred to as 'dividends'. Drawings is the one account that does not lend itself to interpretation through the framework outlined in Exhibit 3.1. If attempting to use Exhibit 3.1, it is best to view drawings as a negative owners' equity account. If an owner adds to his investment in the business (increase in owners' equity) we credit the owners' equity account. It follows that a debit to the owners' equity account refers to a decrease in owners' equity. Instead of debiting the owners' equity account directly, however, when an owner removes funds from the business, we debit the drawings account.

Assuming there were no further transactions for the W. Pooh Hotel, the profit and loss statement can be produced as follows:

Winnie Pooh Hotel Ltd
Profit & Loss statement
for the period ended 31 July

	£	£
Revenue	2,800	
Cost of Sales	200	
Gross Profit		2,600
Electricity Expense		300
Net Profit		2,300
less Drawings		1,500
Retained Earnings		800

In Chapter 2 we saw that the owners' equity balance can be computed by way of a 'statement of owners' equity'. It is also common practice to segregate owners' equity into two underlying elements: the capital account and the retained earnings account. The capital account records direct investments made into the business by its owners, the retained earnings account records all business profits made and not distributed to the owners. The retained earnings balance can be computed in the manner noted above, i.e. by deducting drawings from the net profit figure in the profit and loss statement.

In the following balance sheet for the Winnie Pooh Hotel, assets have been segregated between current assets and fixed assets. Current assets include cash and other assets that through the business's operating cycle will be converted into cash, sold or consumed within one year of the balance sheet date. As noted earlier, fixed assets include all physical assets that will not be sold in the next 12 months. Similarly, a distinction can be drawn between current and longer-term liabilities. Current liabilities include those liabilities that are due for payment in the course of the next 12 months, while long-term liabilities include liabilities that are not due for payment in the next 12 months.

Winnie Pooh Hotel Ltd
Balance Sheet as at 31 July

	£	£		£	£
Current Assets			*Current liabilities*		
Cash	256,500		Accounts payable		1,000
Accounts receivable	2,000		*Owners' equity*		
Inventory	1,000		Capital account	507,700	
		259,500	Retained earnings	800	
Fixed Assets					508,500
Kitchen equipment		250,000			
		509,500			509,500

For well-established companies, the retained earnings account can be one of the largest accounts appearing in a balance sheet. As highlighted in the financial decision-making case presented below, it is an account that is frequently misunderstood by managers.

Case 3.1

Financial Decision Making in Action –
The General Manager's interpretation of the retained earnings account

The retained earnings account records the accumulated profits earned by a company and retained in the business. There is a common tendency, however, for managers who have had no accounting training to believe that the retained earnings account represents cash held.

It is imperative that senior management do not fall prey to this misconception of the retained earnings account because:

- As will be seen in Chapter 11, careful cash management is fundamental to maintaining business solvency. The immediate factor that causes a bankruptcy is a shortage of cash.
- The retained earnings account is frequently one of the largest accounts appearing in a balance sheet.

Senior managers should not allow the retained earnings balance to influence their thinking in any decision that carries significant cash management implications. To determine how much cash a business holds, look at the cash (or bank) balance that appears as an asset in the balance sheet.

Summary

This chapter has built on Chapter 2's introduction to financial accounting by describing the 'debit and credit' system of double entry bookkeeping. A framework was introduced showing you that a debit increases asset and expense accounts and that a credit increases liability, owners' equity and revenue accounts. In connection with a worked example, you were shown an accounting transaction affecting each of these main account groupings.

Having read the chapter you should now know:

- How to increase or decrease asset, liability, owners' equity, revenue and expense accounts
- That profits not paid out to the owners of a business as dividends or drawings are generally credited to an owners' equity account called 'retained earnings'
- That current assets include cash and other assets that through the business's operating cycle will be converted into cash, sold or consumed within one year of the balance sheet date
- That current liabilities include those liabilities that are due for payment in the course of the next 12 months.

References

Carnegie, G., Jones, S., Norris, G., Wigg, R. and Williams, B. (1999) *Accounting: Financial and Organisational Decision Making*, Irwin/McGraw-Hill, New York, Chapter 4.

Coltman, M. M. and Jagels, M. G. (2001) *Hospitality Management Accounting*, 7th edition, John Wiley, Chichester, Chapter 1.

Kotas, R. and Conlan, M. (1997) *Hospitality Accounting*, 5th edition, International Thomson Publishing, London, Chapter 2.

Owen, G. (1994) *Accounting for Hospitality, Tourism & Leisure*, 1st edition, Pitman Publishing, London, Chapter 2.

Schmidgall, R. F. (1997) *Hospitality Industry Managerial Accounting*, 4th edition, Educational Institute – American Hotel & Motel Association, East Lansing, MI, Chapter 1.

Problems

✓ indicates that a solution appears at the back of the text

✓ 3.1 Describe whether we can say that a debit to an account signifies that something beneficial has happened for the business concerned.

✓ 3.2 Are we able to say that in double entry accounting a debit represents a plus and a credit represents a minus?

✓ 3.3 What is the difference between fixed assets and current assets?

3.4 Record a hotel's following five transactions in appropriately headed T-accounts.

(a) Hotel receives $500 for room sales.
(b) Hotel pays staff $400 in wages.
(c) Hotel makes $600 of restaurant sales all on credit.

(d) Hotel owner withdraws $1,000 from the business.

(e) Hotel buys $700 of inventory stock on account.

3.5 Dublin's BlarneyStone Pub opened on 1 April and the following six transactions occurred in its first week of business. Record the transactions in appropriately headed T-accounts for the BlarneyStone Pub's manager.

(a) Owner invested €4,000 in a newly opened bank account for the pub.

(b) Purchased €5,000 of 'Old Black Creamy' stout on account.

(c) Paid cash €450 for a delivery of potato crisps and salted peanuts.

(d) Purchased a cash register for €1,000 on credit.

(e) Banked the first week's bar takings of €350.

(f) Determined that the cost of 'Old Black Creamy' sold in the first week was €150.

3.6 (a) Using 'T-accounts', record debit and credit entries for each of the following transactions that all occurred in January 20X1 for a San Francisco restaurant. The T-accounts you will need are: Cash, Food Inventory, Beverage Inventory, Accounts Receivable, Furniture and Equipment, Accounts Payable, Bank Loan, Owners' Equity, Revenue, Food Purchase Expense, Beverage Purchase Expense, Wage Expense, Supplies Expense, Rent Expense, Interest Expense.

a Mr T. Francis commenced business by investing $30,000 cash in the restaurant.

b Purchased on credit food stock for $4,000, and beverage stock for $6,000.

c Purchased furniture and equipment for $20,000, paying $12,000 cash and owing the balance.

d The bank extended a loan of $20,000 to the business.

e Made sales of $40,000 during the month – 75% of this was cash sales, the remainder was on credit.

f Purchased $9,000 of perishable food items (food purchase expense) on credit and paid $2,000 cash for beverages (beverage purchase expense). The business has established that both these purchases should be immediately expensed.

g Paid $12,000 to trade creditors.

h Repaid $2,000 of the bank loan plus interest of $100.

i Paid $10,800 of wages.

j Paid $4,000 for miscellaneous supply items. The business has a policy of expensing these items on purchase.

k On the last day of the month, paid $1,500 rent for January.

(b) Once the T-account entries have been recorded, prepare a profit and loss statement for January 20X1 and a balance sheet as at 31 January 20X1.

3.7 The following transactions occurred during the first month of operations for 'Oz Hinterland', a hotel proprietor's new business located in the Australian Kimberleys:

a Owner invested $80,000 of her own money in Oz Hinterland.

b In order to provide further capital, a bank extended a loan of $40,000 for the business.

c Paid cash for land and buildings $99,500.

d Purchased kitchen equipment for $20,000. $8,000 of this was paid for in cash, with the balance owing.

e Purchased on credit a stock of linen and uniforms for $5,800.

f During month received revenue of $12,000 for room sales and restaurant revenue.

g Paid $1,500 for first month's wages.

h Paid $300 covering one month's interest on the bank loan.

i Paid $1,200 insurance premium covering the first year of operations.

j Paid $6,000 of the balance owing for kitchen equipment.

k Purchased beverage stock of $1,500 for cash. By the end of the first month it was determined that one third of this stock had been sold in the restaurant.

l Determined that during the month the kitchen had purchased $1,800 of perishable food supplies for cash. No balance of food stock remained at the end of the month.

Required • • •

(a) Enter these transactions on T-accounts.

(b) Prepare a profit and loss statement for the first month and a balance sheet as at the month-end.

Adjusting and closing entries

After studying this chapter, you should have developed an appreciation of:

1 What is meant by 'closing entries'

2 What is meant by 'adjusting entries'

3 The distinction between periodic and perpetual inventory accounting systems

4 How the accountant accounts for bad debts

5 How the accountant accounts for depreciation.

Introduction

This chapter focuses on adjusting entries and closing entries. '**Adjusting entries**' is the term used to describe the set of bookkeeping entries that need to be made in order to **update** some accounts prior to the preparation of the accounting year-end profit and loss statement and balance sheet. '**Closing entries**' is the term used to describe the set of year-end accounting entries that are made in order that all accounts relating to a period of time (i.e. revenue, expense, and the drawings or dividends account) **begin the new accounting year with a zero balance**. It is only once all adjusting entries have been completed that closing entries can be made. This is because closing entries result in the transference of account balances to the profit and loss account.

As the mechanics of adjusting entries are more challenging than those of closing entries, the chapter is structured around the different types of adjusting entries that can be encountered. In the course of considering a range of adjusting entries, the mechanics of making closing entries will also be demonstrated.

Why do we need closing entries?

Immediately prior to entering the new accounting year, all accounts that relate to a period of time (i.e. those accounts that do not flow directly to the balance sheet) need to be wound back to zero. If these accounts were not wound back to a zero balance on an annual basis, their balances would not reflect the current year's sales revenue (for a revenue account) or the current year's expenses (for an expense account). In effect, failure to close these accounts would result in the revenue account and also all expense accounts showing balances that reflect sales achieved and expenses incurred since the inception of the business. The term 'closing entry' is used to describe the year-end transference of balances in these accounts to the profit and loss account (the profit and loss statement can be thought of as an account in which revenues are credits and expenses are debits).

In Chapter 2, we saw that the balance on the profit and loss account (i.e. net profit) is transferred to the owner's equity section of the balance sheet by way of the statement of owner's equity. This highlights the fact that all accounts flow eventually into the balance sheet. This flow is direct for those accounts that are sometimes described as 'permanent' (i.e. asset, liability and owner's equity accounts) and indirect via the profit and loss statement for other accounts that are sometimes referred to as 'temporary' (e.g. revenue and expense accounts).

Why do we need adjusting entries?

In many cases the need for adjusting entries arises because the timing of cash flows (either receipts or disbursements) does not coincide with the period in which it is appropriate to recognize the related revenue or expense. This distinction between the timing of a cash flow and the timing of the recognition of a revenue or an expense item stems from the accrual concept of accounting. The nature of this concept, as well as some examples of year-end adjusting entries are presented in Box 4.1.

The examples of year-end adjusting entries referred to in Box 4.1 will be more fully explained in the next section which provides a worked example of year-end adjusting entries.

Box 4.1
Adjusting entries and the nature of the accrual concept

Most year-end adjusting entries arise because of the accrual concept of accounting which holds that:

- Revenue is recognized when it is earned and certain, rather than simply when cash is received

- An expense is recognized in the period when the benefit derived from the associated expenditure arises (e.g. wages for work conducted during the current period are treated as an expense of the current period, regardless of whether or not they have been paid for during the current period).

Examples of year-end adjusting entries include:

- Recording wages accrued (at the year-end there are wages owing for employee work conducted but not yet paid for)

- Allocating the cost of a fixed asset to those accounting periods in which the benefit of owning the fixed asset occurs (this is 'depreciation')

- Allocating a pro-rated portion of prepaid insurance to the most recent accounting period

- Adjusting accounts receivable (debtors) to recognize that some of the balance appearing in the accounts receivable ledger may prove to be uncollectible.

Worked examples highlighting types of adjusting entry

In this section, the following four basic types of adjusting entry will be explained by way of worked examples:

- Costs paid for but not yet incurred (i.e. expenses pre-paid)
- Costs incurred but not yet paid for (e.g. money owing for wages)
- Unearned revenue (i.e. cash received prior to delivery of a good or service)
- Revenue earned but no cash received (e.g. interest on an investment account that is earned but not yet received).

In addition, three further commonly confronted situations that give rise to adjusting entries are explored:

- Supplies used
- Bad debts (uncollectible account receivables)
- Depreciation.

Adjusting entry type 1: Costs paid for but not yet incurred

This situation arises for insurance and rent (in rental and insurance situations the payee typically pays prior to the period in which the rental or insurance benefit is received).

Hospitality, Leisure & Tourism Series

Imagine that on 1 January 20X1 Winnipeg's TrudeauInn took advantage of a special insurance offer and purchased 18 months' insurance coverage for $3,000. On 30 June 20X2 this policy was renewed for a further 12 months at a cost of $2,400. TrudeauInn's accounting year-end is on 31 December.

To compute the insurance expense to be charged to the P&L statement, prorate the amounts paid to the periods of time in which the insurance coverage expired, i.e.:

20X1 Insurance expense = two thirds of $3,000 = $2,000.

20X2 Insurance expense = one third of $3,000 + half of $2,400 = $2,200.

Accounting treatment:

1 January 20X1:

Insurance prepaid		Cash	
(3,000)			(3,000)

Note: The insurance cover is paid for in advance of the period of time that it pertains to. This signifies that immediately following the payment of the insurance premium we have an asset (i.e. insurance coverage) that runs for the life of the insurance contract. This asset is referred to as 'insurance prepaid'.

31 December 20X1 (adjusting entry):

Insurance expense		Insurance prepaid	
(2,000)		3,000	(2,000)

Note: The need to make this year-end entry can be viewed from an asset-depletion perspective or an expense-incurred perspective. With respect to the asset-depletion perspective, two thirds of the insurance coverage paid for at the beginning of the year has now expired due to the passage of time. This signifies that the $3,000 asset (i.e. prepaid insurance) has diminished by $2,000. With respect to the expense perspective, 12 months of insurance cover was 'consumed' in 20X1. From the prorated calculation above, we found that the 20X1 insurance cover effectively cost $2,000.

31 December 20X1 (closing entry):

Insurance expense		P&L account	
2,000	(2,000)	(2,000)	

Note: Prior to entering the new accounting year, all revenue, expense and drawing accounts (i.e. 'period related' or 'temporary' accounts) need to be wound back to zero in order that their balance at any time reflects the revenue, expense or drawings for the current accounting year. This process is generally referred to as making closing entries. These accounts are closed by transferring their balances to the profit and loss account, which results in the compilation of the profit and loss statement for the year.

30 June 20X2:

Insurance prepaid		Cash	
3,000			(2,400)
	2,000		
(2,400)			

This 30 June 20X2 entry is to record the $2,400 insurance premium paid.

31 December 20X2 (adjusting entry):

Insurance expense		Insurance prepaid	
(2,200)		3,000	2,000
		2,400	
			(2,200)

Note: Again, we can take an asset depletion or an expense incurred perspective on this adjusting entry. With respect to the asset depletion perspective, in the first six months of 20X2 $1,000 of the $3,000 prepayment expired. In the second six months of 20X2, $1,200 of the $2,400 prepayment expired. From the expense perspective, this signifies that insurance coverage costing a total of $2,200 is attributable to 20X2. Note also that a rationale can be offered for the $1,200 year-end debit balance remaining on the insurance prepaid account. This represents the cost of acquiring insurance cover for the first six months of 20X3, i.e. the cost of insurance cover that is prepaid as at 31/12/X2.

31 December 20X2 (closing entry):

Insurance expense		P&L account	
2,200		(2,200)	
	(2,200)		

Finally, on 31 December 20X2, all revenue and expense accounts are closed off to the profit and loss account.

In this example, it has been presumed that on payment of the premium, 'insurance prepaid' is debited. In some accounting systems this amount may be charged immediately to 'insurance expense'. This approach is referred to as 'expensing on purchase'. If this alternative approach is taken, the year-end adjusting entry will have to set up the prepaid amount. For example, in the case described above, if the company had immediately expensed the $3,000 insurance cover purchased on 1 January 20X1, the year-end adjusting entry would be as follows:

31 December 20X1 (adjusting entry):

Insurance expense		Insurance prepaid	
3,000		(1,000)	
	(1,000)		

Note: Regardless of the initial method taken to record the insurance cover purchased, once the year-end adjusting entries have been made, the insurance expense account has a debit balance of $2,000 and the insurance prepaid account has a debit balance of $1,000. Some find it helpful to approach adjusting entries by first considering what year-end balance is needed in the prepaid account and the expense account. If you can determine what year-end balance needs to be reflected in these accounts, you can work out what adjusting entry needs to be made.

Adjusting entry type 2: costs incurred but not paid for (accrued expenses)

Costs incurred but not yet paid are frequently referred to as 'accrued expenses'. One of the main examples of accrued expenses arises in connection with wages and salaries. If, at the end of the accounting period, employee work costing $1,000 has been performed but has not yet been paid for, accrued wages are recorded as follows (the wages accrued account is a liability account that reflects wages owing):

Wage expense		Wages accrued	
(1,000)			(1,000)

Like all expense accounts, at the year-end the debit balance of the wage expense account will be closed off to the P&L account. In the new accounting year, if the first wage bill paid amounts to $5,000, the following entry will have to be made:

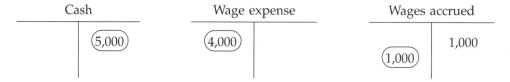

Cash		Wage expense		Wages accrued	
	(5,000)	(4,000)			1,000
				(1,000)	

Note: This first entry in the new accounting year is slightly complicated as it involves three accounts. The cash account credit entry of $5,000 is straightforward as $5,000 has been paid out. The wage expense account starts the new year with a zero balance as a result of the closing entry made at the end of the previous year. Of the $5,000 wage payment, $1,000 relates to the previous year (this is evident from the $1,000 credit balance in the wages accrued account). $4,000 of the $5,000 wage payment must therefore relate to work conducted this year. As the wage expense account reflects the cost of work completed this year, it is appropriate that it be debited with $4,000. Finally, prior to the wage payment, the wages accrued account reflects a liability of $1,000. Immediately following the payment of wages the liability to employees is removed, therefore it is appropriate that a zero balance be reflected, i.e. a $1,000 debit entry is warranted. The intricacies of this particular set of accounting entries only arise around the year-end, as in most accounting systems this is the only time that entries are made to the wages accrued account.

Adjusting entry type 3: unearned revenue

Imagine that on 1 December the Captain Cook Hotel in Whitby, Yorkshire received £50,000 as an advance payment from a conference organizer, covering the cost of a 5-day conference that the hotel will host commencing on 30 December. At the close of business on 31 December (the hotel's accounting year-end), 40% of the conference service can be seen to have been provided (i.e. the hotel has completed the hosting of 2 days of the 5-day conference).

Accounting treatment made in the hotel's records would be as follows:

1st December accounting entry:

Note: Unearned revenue is the name of the account that is credited when cash is received in advance of the provision of goods or services associated with a sale. This is a liability account. In the above example, in the period following the £50,000 receipt but prior to hosting the convention, the £50,000 can be seen to represent a liability. Under a typical conference contract, if a contingency arises preventing the hotel from hosting the convention, it will have to refund the conference organizer.

31 December accounting entry (adjusting entry):

Note: As 40% of the work contracted for (i.e. hosting the conference) has been completed by the year-end, 40% of the original unearned revenue amount can be viewed as earned by 31 December. We therefore make a credit entry of £20,000 (40% of £50,000) to the revenue account and reduce the balance on the unearned revenue account by making a debit entry of £20,000.

Adjusting entry type 4: Revenue earned but no cash received

The issue of accounting for 'unearned' revenue frequently arises when a reporting entity has an investment in an interest bearing account. Imagine Aberdeen's Scrooge Hotel has an investment of £24,000 yielding 10% annual interest with cash interest paid semi-annually. The last time Scrooge updated its records with respect to this investment occurred on 30 September which is when it last received an interest payment of £1,200 earned for the six months commencing 1 April. If Scrooge has a 31 December year-end, the year-end adjusting entry required to record the interest that it is owed as a result of holding the investment through October, November and December is as follows:

31st December accounting entry (adjusting entry):

Interest receivable		Interest revenue	
(600)			(600)

Note: Scrooge's investment is earning interest at the rate of £200 per month. At the year-end it has not recorded the interest earned in the final three months of the year. A £600 credit entry to the interest revenue account updates the company's record of interest earned in the year. The £600 debit entry to the interest receivable account highlights that the company has an asset in the form of interest that it is owed at the year-end.

Adjusting entry type 5: accounting for supplies

Supplies such as office stationery generally represent a relatively small investment for most hotels. As a result, many hotels adopt the relatively simple accounting procedure of periodically determining the supplies balance by conducting a stock-take (this approach is generally referred to as a periodic inventory accounting system). Under a periodic inventory system, the purchases of supplies are simply recorded by debiting a 'supplies purchases' account. Operation of a periodic inventory system and the adjusting entry that it gives rise to are demonstrated through the worked example in Exhibit 4.1.

The year-end adjusting entries that would have to be made in the scenario described in Exhibit 4.1 can be managed in two stages. First, the purchases account balance can be transferred to the supplies inventory account. Consistent with the philosophy of closing entries, this results in the purchases account starting the new accounting year with a balance of zero.

Supplies purchases		Supplies inventory	
14,000	(14,000)	2,800	
		(14,000)	

Hospitality, Leisure & Tourism Series

Exhibit 4.1
Determining stock used in a periodic inventory system

Suzy Defoe is the office manager of Manchester's Old Trafford Hotel. The hotel operates a periodic inventory system with respect to office supplies. At the year-end, the hotel accountant asked Suzy to oversee a year-end stock-take of supplies, in order that the cost of supplies used during the year could be determined. The year-end stock-take revealed that £2,000 of office supplies were held on 31 December 20X1. Suzy then consulted the supplies inventory account which had last been updated 12 months previously (i.e. following the previous year-end's stock-take) and noted a debit balance of £2,800. Throughout the year she debited the 'supplies purchases' account whenever purchasing supplies. She notes that prior to making any adjusting entries, this account had a year-end debit balance of £14,000.

Calculation of the cost of supplies used in the year can be determined by solving for ? in the schedule below.

	£
Opening balance	2,800
add Supplies purchased	14,000
Supplies made available	16,800
less Supplies used	?
Closing balance	2,000

As we have determined that the cost of supplies made available is £16,800, and we know that at the end of the year the stock of supplies available cost £2,000, we can conclude that £14,800 of supplies must have been used during the year.

Second, the supplies expense account can be debited with the £14,800 cost of supplies used that was calculated above. The corresponding credit entry should then be made to the supplies inventory account. These entries result in the recognition of an expense (the supplies expense account will be closed to the profit & loss statement). They also result in a £2,000 debit balance in the supplies inventory account, which reflects the result of the year-end stock-take. This inventory account balance will comprise part of the total assets recorded in the year-end balance sheet.

Supplies expense		Supplies inventory	
(14,800)		2,800	
		14,000	
			(14,800)

Using a periodic inventory control system signifies that a degree of control is lost with respect to inventory. Between stock-takes the manager responsible for ordering supplies will have no administrative record of the supplies held in stock. If this is believed to represent a significant problem, the manager could consider using a perpetual inventory system. The relative merits of perpetual and periodic inventory systems are outlined in the following financial decision-making case.

Hospitality, Leisure & Tourism Series

<table>
<tr><td></td></tr>
</table>

Case 4.1

Financial Decision Making in Action –
The F&B Manager's choice of inventory control procedures

Rather than depending on a periodic stock-take to determine what amount of stock is held, a perpetual inventory system can be operated. A perpetual inventory accounting system involves debiting the inventory account every time inventory is purchased and crediting it every time a sale or issue of stock is made. Deciding between a periodic and perpetual inventory approach can be a significant issue for an F&B manager due to the many low-cost food items that can be held.

Perpetual accounting systems are generally more expensive to operate due to the number of individual inventory records that have to be maintained. Despite this, an F&B manager would consider adopting a perpetual inventory accounting approach for particular food and drink items if one or all of the following issues is believed to be significant:

1. Significant stock shrinkage is occurring due to theft.
2 A significant loss of customer goodwill would result if certain menu items were to become unavailable.
3 Observing whether the stock item in question needs to be reordered is awkward and time consuming.

Adjusting entry type 6: Bad and doubtful debts

An initial word of warning is warranted here. Without wanting to sound alarmist, accounting for bad debts gives rise to what is probably the most complicated set of accounting entries described in this book. Proceed at a gentle pace through this section!

At the end of the accounting period, an adjusting entry needs to be made to reflect the fact that some of the balance in 'accounts receivable' may prove to be uncollectible. If some of the accounts receivable balance does prove to be uncollectible, the revenue account will be overstated as it will include 'bad sale' entries, i.e. sales for which we will obtain no receipt of funds.

The following three steps outline a widely adopted approach to accounting for bad and doubtful debts.

Step 1: The provision

Periodically (say, every month-end during the accounting year) update records to reflect and provide for the problem of potentially non-collectible accounts. If every month we make $100,000 of credit sales and we believe on average 2% will prove to be uncollectible, having already debited 'accounts receivable' $100,000 and credited 'revenue' $100,000, we can make the following month-end 'adjusting entry'.

Bad debts expense	Allowance for doubtful accounts
(2,000)	(2,000)

The 'bad debts expense' account can be described as a 'contra' account, as it flows through to the profit and loss statement where it will off-set the revenue account's credit balance. The 'allowance for doubtful accounts' account can also be described as a contra account as its credit balance will be recorded in the balance sheet in a manner that off-sets the account receivables' debit balance.

Step 2: An account turns bad ● ● ●

Imagine that half-way through the accounting year one of our clients, Untrustworthy Ltd, went bankrupt while owing us $3,500. It is determined that we are unlikely to collect any of the amount outstanding. The 'step 1' month-end entry is designed to **provide** for this type of eventuality. Now the eventuality has been **realized** and we need to update the books as follows:

(a) Remove the $3,500 from 'accounts receivable' (if we don't do this, the account will contain a growing amount of entries for amounts that will never be collected).
(b) Remove the $3,500 from 'allowance for doubtful accounts', as, following removal of the amount from 'accounts receivable' we no longer have a need to allow for it, i.e. no need for an off-setting contra entry.

Allowance for doubtful accounts		Accounts receivable	
(3,500)			(3,500)

Step 3: Year-end adjusting entry ● ● ●

Following an appraisal of the $150,000 year-end accounts receivable balance, it is estimated that $3,200 may well prove to be uncollectible. An investigation of the books reveals that the 'allowance for doubtful accounts' has a balance of $3,000. Therefore, prior to making a year-end adjusting entry, 'net' accounts receivable is recorded at $147,000 ($150,000 – $3,000). As we expect to be able to collect $146,800 ($150,000 – $3,200), net accounts receivable is overstated by $200 and we need to make a $200 adjusting entry.

Bad debts expense		Allowance for doubtful accounts	
			3,000
(200)			(200)

The debit and credit entry made here is the same as the 'step 1' entry. The need for the year-end adjusting entry has arisen because the 'step 1' entries during the year had not been sufficient to create the requisite year-end balance on the 'allowance for doubtful accounts'. If at the year-end it is found that there is an over-provision in 'allowance for doubtful accounts', we would need to reverse the above entry by crediting 'bad debts expense' and debiting 'allowance for doubtful accounts'.

Adjusting entry type 7: Depreciation

Depreciation refers to the process of allocating the cost of a fixed asset (i.e. an asset with a useful life greater than one year) across the years in which the asset's owner can be expected to derive benefit from owning the asset. If depreciation accounting entries were not made, the type of scenario outlined in Box 4.2 could arise.

Main depreciation methods • • •

There are several distinct approaches to determining the timing of the fixed asset cost write-off. In the following description of three methods, it will be assumed that a fixed asset has been purchased for $1,200,000, and that it has been estimated that the asset can be salvaged in five years' time for $200,000.

(a) Straight line method: This widely used method involves apportioning the net cost of the fixed asset (purchase price – salvage value) equally across the life of the asset.

$$\text{Annual depreciation charge} = \frac{\text{Purchase price} - \text{salvage value}}{\text{Estimated number of years asset will be owned}}$$

$$= \frac{\$1,200,000 - \$200,000}{5} = \$200,000$$

Box 4.2
A scenario highlighting the need for depreciation

The following hypothetical discussion between a user of accounting information prepared by SouthPark, a hotel with an untrained accountant, and one of SouthPark's managers highlights the need for depreciation.

Accounting information user (e.g. a prospective shareholder):
'How come the SouthPark Hotel had a healthy profit for the last five years except for 20X1, when you reported a huge loss?'

SouthPark manager:
'Oh, 20X1 just so happened to be the year in which we bought our most expensive fixed asset. We received delivery of it on 28 December and in fact didn't get around to using it until 20X2. We had expected the delivery to be made a week later, in which case you would have seen 20X2 as having the big loss.'

Accounting information user:
'So what you're saying is that the profit figure reported for 20X1 is misleading. It doesn't really reflect SouthPark's underlying performance relative to other years. You know this means that your profit for 20X1 is understated and your profit in the other years is really overstated. While 20X1 took a big hit, it's as if the subsequent years have had use of the asset for free.'

(b) Reducing balance method: Under this method, each year a fixed percentage of the asset's net book value (the net book value is the cost of the asset minus the accumulated depreciation charged on the asset since its purchase) is expensed as depreciation. This will result in a reducing depreciation charge as the net book value (NBV) will be reducing. In the following example, suppose 40% has been identified as the annual percentage rate.

	$
Opening net book value – year 1	1,200,000
1st year dep'n charge (NBV × 40%)	480,000
Opening net book value – year 2	720,000
2nd year dep'n charge (NBV × 40%)	288,000
Opening net book value – year 3	432,000
3rd year dep'n charge (NBV × 40%)	172,800

(c) Usage based method: This is not a widely used method. To demonstrate how it can be applied, imagine that the asset purchased is a small airplane and that it has been estimated that the plane will fly 1 million kilometres in its life with the company.

If 200,000 kilometres were flown in 20X1, 20X1 depreciation charge =

(200,000 ÷ 1,000,000) × \$1,000,000 = \$200,000

If 300,000 kilometres were flown in 20X2, 20X2 depreciation charge =

(300,000 ÷ 1,000,000) × \$1,000,000 = \$300,000

Recording depreciation • • •

Similar to the contra account set up for doubtful accounts, when depreciating, we set up an 'accumulated depreciation' account, which acts as a contra account off-setting the balance in the fixed asset account.

For the 20X2 depreciation charge of \$300,000 in the airplane example above, the 20X2 year-end depreciation entry would be as follows:

Depreciation expense	Accumulated depreciation
(300,000)	200,000
	(300,000)

As the depreciation expense account and the accumulated depreciation account have somewhat similar names it is vital that their very different roles are clearly understood. The depreciation expense account is closed off to the P&L account at the year-end. The fact that it is closed off in this manner should be evident from the word 'expense' appearing in its title.

The accumulated depreciation account is reported in the balance sheet as a contra account that off-sets the fixed asset account. The fact that it is an account that accumulates across accounting periods suggests that it is a balance sheet account. Note how, by the end of 20X2, the accumulated depreciation account has increased from the $200,000 depreciation expensed in 20X1 to $500,000, as a result of the $300,000 expensed in 20X2. The fixed asset section of the company's balance sheet at the end of 20X2 would appear in a format such as that presented below:

	$	$
Fixed assets at cost	1,200,000	
Less Accumulated depreciation	500,000	
Net Book Value of Fixed Asset		700,000

Summary

Through the use of worked examples, this chapter has outlined the nature of closing and adjusting entries. At the end of each financial year, closing entries are made to all accounts relating to a period of time, i.e. revenue, expense and dividend accounts. If these accounts are not closed at the end of a year, they would not have a zero balance at the start of the new financial year. Adjusting entries need to be made in advance of preparing the year-end statements in order to update some accounts. For example, as depreciation is a function of time, periodically an adjusting entry has to be made to update all depreciation accounts.

Having read the chapter you should now know:

- That all revenue, expense and dividend accounts have to be closed at the end of the financial year
- That costs paid for but not yet incurred represent prepaid expenses and are treated as assets
- That expenses incurred but not yet paid for represent accruals and are treated as liabilities
- That if a customer pays for a service in advance of receiving the service, the receipt is referred to as unearned revenue and is treated as a liability
- The difference between perpetual and periodic inventory accounting procedures
- How to account for bad debts
- How to account for depreciation.

References

Carnegie, G., Jones, S., Norris, G., Wigg, R. and Williams, B. (1999) *Accounting: Financial and Organisational Decision Making*, Irwin/McGraw-Hill, New York, Chapter 7.

Coltman, M. M. and Jagels, M. G. (2001) *Hospitality Management Accounting*, 7th edition, John Wiley, Chichester, Chapter 1.

Kotas, R. and Conlan, M. (1997) *Hospitality Accounting*, 5th edition, International Thomson Publishing, London, Chapters 11 and 12.

Owen, G. (1994) *Accounting for Hospitality, Tourism & Leisure*, 1st edition, Pitman Publishing, Chapter 4.

Schmidgall, R. F., (1997) *Hospitality Industry Managerial Accounting*, 4th edition, Educational Institute – American Hotel & Motel Association, East Lansing, MI, Chapter 1.

Problems

✓ indicates that a solution appears at the back of the text

✓ **4.1** Describe the difference between adjusting entries and closing entries.

✓ **4.2** Given the following information for Dunedin's CityCentre Hotel, post relevant adjusting entries to CityCentre's general ledger. Assume 30 June is the year-end.

(a) The telephone account of $500 for June is unpaid and unrecorded.

(b) Rent of $3,600 for the six-month period ending 31 August is due to be paid in arrears in October.

(c) It was estimated at the time of purchasing a car two years ago for $6,000 that the car would be salvaged five years later for $1,000. The company uses straight line depreciation for all fixed assets. This year's depreciation entry for the car is still to be made.

(d) The next fortnightly pay date for the company's employees is 7 July. The fortnightly payroll is $140,000.

(e) On 2 March received $1,600 cash from a client. This was an advance payment for services to be rendered. At the time of receipt, $1,600 was recorded as a credit to unearned revenue. On 30 June 75% of this service had been provided.

(f) On 1 May received six month's rent revenue in advance totalling $600. At the time of the receipt, this was recorded as a credit to rental revenue.

✓ **4.3** On 30 November, account balances relating to the accounts receivable management function of Minnesota's CitySlickers Hotel were as follows:

Accounts receivable	$141,500	Debit balance
Allowance for doubtful accounts	$2,400	Credit balance
Revenue	$1,320,000	Credit balance
Bad debts expense	$12,400	Debit balance

The following transactions occurred in December:

1 Cash collected from credit sale customers was $92,000.
2 Credit sales were $101,000.

On a monthly basis, the manager of accounts receivable has made an allowance of 1.25% of sales to cover the contingency of trade debts turning bad. At the hotel's year-end, on 31 December, a review of accounts receivable has revealed the following:

Year-end estimate of doubtful accounts

Age of account	Account receivable amount	% Estimated as uncollectible
0–30 days	$84,000	0.75
31–60 days	44,000	1.25
61–180 days	18,000	5
Over 180 days	4,500	100
	$150,500	

The company accountant has decided that all accounts with an age of 180 days or more should be written off from the accounts receivable ledger. In addition, the doubtful accounts balance should be revised to reflect the remaining estimated doubtful accounts following the year-end review of the accounts receivable ledger.

Required ▪ ▪ ▪
(a) Record December's credit sales and cash collected transactions in appropriately titled 'T-accounts'.
(b) Record all necessary year-end adjusting entries in appropriately titled 'T-accounts'.

4.4   Marlow's WatersEdge Hotel operates a periodic inventory system with respect to its cleaning supplies. A year-end stock-take has identified a balance of £4,200 cleaning supplies held on 31 December 20X1. The cleaning supplies stock account, which has not been adjusted since the previous year-end stock-take, reflects a debit balance of £3,400. Throughout the year, all cleaning supplies purchased have been debited to the 'cleaning supplies purchases' account which has a closing debit balance of £36,000. In addition, any returns to suppliers have been credited to a 'cleaning supplies returns' account which has a year-end closing balance of £1,020.

Required ▪ ▪ ▪
Using appropriately titled 'T-accounts', make all required adjusting and closing entries.

4.5   The accounting manager at Antwerp's TranquilStay Hotel has prepared the following profit and loss statement that pertains to the most recent accounting year.

TranquilStay Hotel
Profit and loss statement
for the year ended 30 June 20X1

	€	€
Sales revenue		420,000
less: Cost of sales		80,000
Gross profit		340,000
add: Interest revenue		11,000
		351,000
less: Expenses		
Salaries and wages expense	145,000	
Depreciation expense	82,000	
Car park rental expense	3,000	
Insurance expense	18,000	
Sundry expense	14,000	
		262,000
		89,000

The accounting manager is uncertain how to handle year-end adjusting entries and has sought your advice. Following a review of the business, you determine the following:

1. A €2,500 advance payment received in connection with a conference to be held in late July has been included in the sales revenue figure.
2. Employees have not been paid €4,000 in wages and salaries earned in the last 4 days of June.
3. Depreciation of €10,000 on a new car purchased this year has not been recorded.
4. The hotel rents a small adjoining property which it uses for patrons' car parking whenever the hotel's underground car park is full. The last rental fee paid was €900. This payment was made on 1 May and covered a three-month period. The account manager recorded this as prepaid rent and no entry has been made to adjust this account at the year-end.
5. The hotel holds an investment that earns €1,000 interest per month. June's interest, which will be received in July has not been recorded in the accounts.
6. Annual property insurance of €24,000 is paid semi-annually in advance. The last €12,000 payment, which was made on 1 April 20X1 was debited to prepaid insurance. No adjusting entry to the prepaid insurance account has been made.

Required . . .
(a) Prepare the necessary adjusting entries for the TranquilStay Hotel.
(b) Following completion of the adjusting entries, prepare TranquilStay's revised profit and loss statement for the year-ending 30 June 20X1.

4.6   Given the following information for Ottawa's Capital Hotel, prepare relevant adjusting entries. Assume that 30 June is the year-end.

(a) On 1 June the hotel received $4,000 in advance for services to be rendered. This transaction was recorded on 1 June by debiting bank and crediting unearned service revenue. It was determined that by 30 June, 25% of the service paid for had been provided.
(b) On 1 May six months' insurance premium was purchased for $1,800. When the payment was made, the hotel debited prepaid insurance and credited bank.
(c) The hotel has an investment that is earning a return of $2,400 interest per annum. The last interest payment was received on 30 April. The accounting records need to be adjusted to reflect the last two months of interest accrued.
(d) In the current financial year, the hotel's supplies account had an opening balance of $600. $7,000 of supplies have been purchased during the year and debited to the supplies account. A year-end stock-take has revealed $400 of supplies in stock. During the year no accounting entries reflective of supplies usage have been made.

4.7   Given the following year-end account balances for Boston's Johnson Hotel, prepare:

(a) A profit and loss statement for the period ended 30/6/20X1
(b) A balance sheet as at 30/6/20X1.

Johnson Hotel
Account balances
as at 30 June 20X1

	Debit $	Credit $
Cash at bank	2,200	
Dividends paid	2,000	
Accounts receivable	1,500	
Closing inventory	400	
Depreciation expense	250	
Plant and machinery	11,000	
Accumulated depreciation		1,020
Sales revenue		26,500
Cost of sales	16,000	
General operating expenses	4,640	
Accrued wages		400
Accounts payable		1,900
Unearned revenue		200
Share capital		4,800
Retained profits		3,170
	37,990	37,990

Financial Information and Hospitality Management

Financial statement analysis

After studying this chapter, you should have developed an appreciation of:

1 How insights can be gained from dissecting ROI (return on investment) into its two underlying elements: profit margin and asset turnover

2 How a systematic analysis of a hotel's profit performance can be conducted through the use of ratios

3 How an analysis of a hotel's short-term and long-term financial stability can be achieved through ratio analysis

4 How operational ratios can be used as an aid to monitoring the operating performance of hotels

5 How an aged schedule of accounts receivable can assist the management of receivables

6 How it is important that an analyst develops the ability to tailor ratios with due regard to the nature of the hotel under investigation.

Introduction

This chapter moves us closer to financial management issues as it focuses on techniques that can be used to analyse the financial performance and stability of organizations. Much of the analysis can be conducted through the use of ratios, e.g. return on investment (ROI tells us the **ratio** of return to investment), and, as a consequence, we frequently refer to '**ratio analysis**' in a manner synonymous with financial statement analysis.

The results of a ratio analysis convey limited information unless they are put into some context, however. Ratio analyses are most usually conducted in the context of a comparison to one or more of the following four benchmarks:

- The hotel's ratios from prior years (a trend analysis);
- Ratios that have been set as goals (i.e. ratios underlying the hotel's budget);
- Ratios achieved by other hotels (or divisions) in the same company;
- Industry average ratios compiled by companies such as *Dun and Bradstreet* and the large accounting firms (this type of benchmarking is sometimes referred to as a cross-sectional analysis).

In this chapter's description of a systematic approach to conducting a financial analysis of the year-end accounts, two distinct perspectives will be taken:

- First, we will see how the **profit performance** of a company can be appraised.
- Second, we will see how to appraise the **financial stability** of a company.

We will conduct these analyses by drawing on the year-end financial statements of Melbourne's Celestial Hotel Ltd. These statements are presented in Exhibits 5.1 and 5.2.

Exhibit 5.1

Celestial Hotel Ltd
Profit and loss statement
for the year ending 31/12/20X1

	$000	$000
Revenue (60% of sales on credit)		100
less Cost of Sales		40
Gross Profit		60
less Expenses		
Selling	15	
General Administration	5	
		20
Earnings (profit) before interest and tax (EBIT)		40
less Interest		10
Taxable profit		30
less Taxation		15
Net Profit after Tax		15

Exhibit 5.2

Celestial Hotel Ltd
Balance sheet as at 31/12/20X1

Assets	$000	$000
Current Assets		
Cash	5	
Accounts receivable	7	
Inventory	8	
		20
Fixed Assets		
Equipment	10	
Buildings	20	
		30
Total Assets		50

	$000	$000
Liabilities		
Current Liabilities		
Accrued wages	1	
Accounts payable	4	
		5
Long-term liabilities		
Loans		15
Total Liabilities		20
Owners' Equity		
Paid-up capital (100,000 shares)	20	
Retained profits[1]	10	
		30
Total Liabilities and Owners' Equity		50

[1] The company must have started 20X1 with an accumulated loss of $5,000 (i.e. a negative retained profit account). This is apparent from the fact that the profit and loss statement for 20X1 indicates profit earned and retained during 20X1 to be $15,000, yet the retained profit at the end of the year is only $10,000 (from the information provided, it appears no dividends were declared for 20X1). Much can be gleaned from a careful review of the accounts!

Following this overview of a financially oriented analysis, the chapter will review the main ratios used to analyse a hotel's operational performance. Operational ratios focus more on day to day operating issues, e.g. room occupancy levels, restaurant covers served per employee hour worked, etc. Although many operational ratios do not involve financial measures, they represent important performance indicators as a strong operating performance is a precursor to a strong financial performance.

Profit performance

If you were to ask an investor how their investment portfolio performed in a particular year, they would likely answer by referring to their overall return on investment. This casual observation is important as it highlights the degree to which return on investment (ROI) represents a fundamental indicator of performance. If limited to one ratio in an appraisal of a company's performance, a financial analyst would most likely use ROI.

In the analysis of profit performance that follows, we will take a systematic approach by first computing ROI and then dissecting it into its underlying components. The perspective of appraising a hotel management's performance in generating a return (profit) from the assets available will be taken. This signifies that EBIT (earnings before interest and tax) is the appropriate profit level to focus on. This is because EBIT captures the operating performance of a hotel, as interest expense (the first item appearing after EBIT in the P&L statement) relates to a financing decision which is frequently outside the influence of the hotel general manager. Accordingly, we will calculate ROI in the following way:

Return on investment (ROI) = EBIT ÷ Total assets

Celestial's 20X1 ROI = 40 ÷ 50 = 0.8 (or 80%)

This 80% ROI can be broken into two elements (a profit margin and a turnover component) as illustrated in Exhibit 5.3.

The equation in Exhibit 5.3 can be verified very simply by cancelling 'revenue' in the left-hand circle (or profit margin component) with 'revenue' in the right-hand circle (or asset turnover component) to leave us with the basic ROI formula (EBIT ÷ Total assets).

This dissection of ROI into the two underlying ratios is widely referred to as the 'Dupont formula' (the formula was first observed in use in the Dupont company in the USA). The Dupont formula is highly significant as it provides the basis for a systematic analysis of ROI under two headings:

(a) profit margin
(b) asset turnover.

Profit margin

Following our first step in the ratio analysis, we found Celestial's ROI to be 80%. While this may appear to represent a healthy return, imagine it is down from last year's figure of 85%. Management would want to know what lies behind this

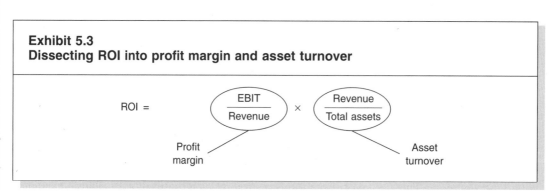

Exhibit 5.3
Dissecting ROI into profit margin and asset turnover

$$ROI = \frac{EBIT}{Revenue} \times \frac{Revenue}{Total\ assets}$$

Profit margin   Asset turnover

decline. By using the Dupont formula we can determine whether the decline stems from a decrease in the company's profit margin or its asset turnover (or a combination of both). If the profit margin is down from last year, we can work systematically through the profit & loss statement, picking up all profit figures provided and comparing them to revenue. In the Celestial example, the first profit figure in the P&L statement is gross profit. Paralleling the approach taken to compute profit margin in Exhibit 5.3, we compute gross profit margin (GPM) as follows:

Gross profit margin (GPM) = Gross profit ÷ Revenue

Celestial's 20X1 GPM = 60 ÷ 100 = 0.6 (or 60%)

If this 60% GPM is similar to last year's GPM, we would be able to conclude that the lower overall margin has not resulted from a change in the ratio of selling price to cost of sales. It would be apparent that the decline in the ratio of EBIT to Revenue must have resulted from a relative increase in selling and general administration costs, as these represent the two expense categories appearing after gross profit and before EBIT in the P&L statement. By taking this approach of progressively moving down the P&L statement, comparing every level of reported profit to Revenue, we are able to isolate the category of expense that has caused a change in the overall profit margin. If we had originally used net profit margin (net profit after tax ÷ revenue) in the ROI computed above, we could have computed more profit margins in the course of systematically progressing through the P&L statement. Published accounts of large companies generally provide data sufficient to allow the calculation of several profit margins.

Asset turnover

Returning to the Dupont formula in Exhibit 5.3, now imagine that we have noted that a decline in the total asset turnover ratio has occurred and that this decline lies behind the lower ROI. This observation would lead the analyst to look into those ratios that feed in to the total asset turnover ratio.

Similar to the approach of working systematically through the P&L statement when exploring for factors resulting in a changed profit margin, we can work through the balance sheet looking for that group of assets that lie behind a changed asset turnover ratio.

Whenever the term 'turnover' is used, it signifies we are comparing an asset to revenue (or, in the case of inventory, cost of sales). Consistent with the total asset turnover ratio computed above as part of the Dupont formula, for each turnover ratio we divide revenue (or, in the case of inventory, cost of sales) by the particular asset grouping under investigation.

Each 'turnover' ratio tells us how 'hard' the particular asset has 'worked' to generate revenue. For this reason, the turnover ratios are frequently referred to as 'efficiency' ratios. Widely computed 'turnover' ratios include:

- Accounts receivable turnover
- Inventory turnover
- Fixed asset turnover.

Accounts receivable turnover

Accounts receivable turnover = Credit sales ÷ Accounts receivable

Celestial's 20X1 A.R. turnover = $(100 \times 0.6) \div 7 = 8.57$

Many managers find it difficult to conceptualize the meaning of the 8.57 computed above. For this reason the information is commonly converted into 'number of days' by dividing the number of days in a year by the turnover.

$$\text{Average number of days to collect accounts receivable} = \frac{365}{AR\ turnover}$$

$$\text{Celestial's average number of days to collect accounts receivable} = \frac{365}{8.57} = 42.6\ days$$

If the accounts receivable turnover ratio is decreasing, the average number of days to collect accounts receivable will be increasing.

Inventory turnover

Calculation of inventory turnover and also the 'number of days inventory held' parallel the approach just taken for accounts receivable. There is one key difference, however. Unlike all the other 'turnover' ratios, we divide inventory into cost of sales and not revenue. The reason for this difference is that inventory is recorded at cost price and not selling price. If we were to compare inventory to revenue and during the year selling prices doubled, we would see the inventory turnover ratio computed also double. The doubling of the ratio would be the result of a changed selling price and not a changed stocking policy, however. The potential for this misinterpretation is avoided if we compute inventory turnover using a consistent valuation basis, i.e. cost for the denominator (inventory) and cost for the numerator (cost of sales).

Inventory turnover = Cost of sales ÷ Inventory

Celestial's 20X1 inventory turnover = $40 \div 8 = 5$

Similar to accounts receivable turnover, inventory turnover can be converted into a measure of the average number of days that inventory is held by dividing 365 by the inventory turnover.

$$\text{Celestial's average number of days inventory held} = \frac{365}{5} = 73\ days$$

When analysing a hotel's inventory turnover performance, it is desirable that beverage inventory be treated separately from the inventory of food supplies. This is because there might be differing stocking policies in the two areas. Drawing this distinction is particularly important where different personnel exercise stock making decisions in the two areas. Failure to distinguish between the two types of inventory might mask the existence of a low turnover in one area due if there is a high turnover in the other area.

Fixed asset turnover

Fixed asset turnover = Revenue ÷ Fixed assets

Celestial's 20X1 fixed asset turnover = $100 \div 30 = 3.33$ days

Fixed asset account balances do not tend to be as volatile as accounts receivable and inventory account balances. Nevertheless, due to the large relative size of fixed assets in hotels, a small percentage movement can have a significant impact on total asset turnover. The large investment in fixed assets can warrant the calculation of a turnover figure for every fixed asset sub-category identified, if such further information is available, i.e. in the Celestial example we could have computed a turnover figure for equipment as well as buildings.

General comments on turnover ratios

Except for cash, we have now computed the turnover ratio for each asset in Celestial's balance sheet. If we had noted a decline in total asset turnover, and had subsequently discovered that none of the turnovers computed above had declined, then there must have been a decrease in the ratio of revenue to cash. Consistent with the other ratios, we could compute a 'cash turnover ratio' by dividing 'revenue' by 'cash'. Due to the relatively small nature of the cash account, however, this ratio is seldom calculated. If we found that the problem lay in a declining cash turnover ratio, we would know that relative to revenue, the business is now holding more cash. We would then need to turn to question whether this development is desirable.

While it might appear from Exhibit 5.3 that we would like to see increasing turnover ratios (a higher asset turnover will increase ROI), the downside implication of turnover ratios becoming too high should also be appreciated. If inventory turnover becomes very high, we might experience stock-outs, which could result in lost sales and loss of customer goodwill. If the accounts receivable turnover increases, we are on average extending less credit to our customers. If other hotels are extending longer periods of credit, this could result in the loss of some sales.

In the worked example presented above, we took year-end balances of the asset accounts when computing the turnover ratios. A preferred approach, however, would be to take the average balance of the asset account throughout the year. It could be that the year-end inventory balance is at an all-time temporary low and that Celestial normally holds twice this amount of inventory. If this is the case, the turnover computed will be a poor reflection of reality, i.e. the inventory holding period computed will be half the year's average holding time for inventory. If the asset in question is subject to high seasonal volatility, the average asset balance throughout the year should be sought. This could be done by calculating the average of the 12 month-end balances for the year. While using an average asset balance provides a better picture of the asset's average turnover over the whole year, a new inventory manager who has been in place for only three months would be justified in arguing that her inventory turnover performance should be assessed by appraising average inventory balances since she took up her position, and not inventory balances recorded in advance of her job commencement. The same rationale applies to a recently recruited credit manager.

The problem of defining ROI

It can be confusing trying to 'tie down' ROI. It is a generic term that is tailored to many different situations, e.g. it could be used in the sense of the interest rate you earn on a bank account, or the net after-tax return made on a portfolio of shares. Its exact calculation depends on the perspective being taken in an analysis. The following is an inexhaustive list of types of ROI that can be used to assess a company's performance:

- Return on assets employed
- Return on assets available
- Return on long-term funds
- Return on equity

'Assets employed', 'assets available', 'long-term funds' and 'equity' are all types of investment. If we wish to judge the performance of a manager who has been placed in charge of a group of assets that include some assets which, for some reason, he cannot currently employ (maybe rooms undergoing refurbishment), we might like to compare EBIT to assets employed and not assets available. If we take a shareholder's perspective, we might like to compare net profit after tax to shareholders' equity. It can thus be seen that **the definition of return and the definition of investment is dependent on the context in which the analysis is being made.**

Two share market-related performance measures

A widely used ratio when considering the total profit performance of a company from the shareholder's perspective is earnings per share (EPS). This ratio, which indicates how much company profit has been earned by each individual share, is calculated by dividing net profit by the number of ordinary shares issued by a company:

Earning per share (EPS) = Net profit ÷ Total shares outstanding

A danger with EPS arises if you attempt to use it as part of a cross-company comparison. A 20X1 EPS of $4 in ABC Company does not signify a better performance than a 20X1 EPS of $2 for XYZ Company. Imagine that during 20X1, shares in ABC traded for around $50 while shares in XYZ traded for $10. The earnings when stated as a return on the owner's investment (this is sometimes called the earnings yield and is calculated by dividing EPS by the share price) is 8% for ABC (4 ÷ 50 × 100), and 20% for XYZ (2 ÷ 10 × 100). EPS can be used, however, as part of a trend analysis of a single company (assuming the number of shares issued remains constant), and is particularly useful when combined with share price to give us the price/earnings ratio (PE ratio). The PE ratio is computed as follows:

Price/Earnings (PE) ratio = Market price per share ÷ Earnings per share

Unlike EPS, the PE ratio can be used as part of a cross-company analysis. A high PE for a company relative to its competitors in the same industry can be caused by either of the following factors:

1 The investing community expects an increase in the company's EPS in the future and this has resulted in increased demand for the share which, in turn, has increased the share price (past earnings are only of interest to the investor to the extent that they provide an indication of expected future earnings).
2 The investing community perceives relatively low risk in the company. As investors are averse to risk, increasing levels of risk will result in decreasing demand for the share which, in turn, results in a decreased share price.

Financial stability

Analysis of financial stability (sometimes referred to as solvency, i.e. the ability to repay liabilities as they fall due) can be broken into short-term and long-term perspectives.

Short-term

Appraisal of a company's short-term financial stability is sometimes referred to as a 'liquidity analysis'. Analysis of liquidity concerns assets that in the normal course of business will be converted to cash, sold or consumed within a year (current assets) and also liabilities that are due for payment within a year (current liabilities). One indicator of liquidity is 'working capital' (current assets – current liabilities), however this indicator does not provide a sound basis for comparison across companies of varying sizes. More widely advocated measures of liquidity are the current asset ratio and the quick asset ratio (sometimes called the 'acid test ratio'). The current asset ratio is calculated as follows:

Current asset ratio = Current assets ÷ Current liabilities

Celestial's current asset ratio as at $31/12/X1 = 20 \div 5 = 4$

This signifies that Celestial's 'close to cash' assets cover its liabilities that will fall due for payment in the next 12 months by four times. This suggests a highly liquid situation.

If inventory is held for some time in the business prior to conversion to cash, a case can be made for its exclusion from current assets. This approach is taken in the acid test ratio, a liquidity measure which also excludes prepaid expenses from current assets. Prepaid expenses are excluded because in the normal course of business they will not be converted to cash. The acid test ratio is calculated as follows:

$$\text{Acid test ratio} = \frac{\text{Current assets} - \text{Inventory} - \text{Prepaids}}{\text{Current liabilities}}$$

Celestial's acid test ratio as at $31/12/X1 = 12 \div 5 = 2.4$

In the hotel sector, due to the relatively 'liquid' nature of most inventory, it is usual to base an appraisal of short-term liquidity on the current ratio rather than the acid test ratio. If a hotel had a large inventory of slow-moving wine, however, it would be appropriate to calculate a tailored liquidity ratio by deducting the wine inventory from current assets. Tailoring ratios in this manner can be justified if they result in a more accurate insight into the particular aspect of the company that is under investigation.

While we would certainly be concerned to see the current ratio or the acid test ratio fall below '1', it is difficult to provide an optimal current or acid test ratio. Much will depend on hotel-specific factors. A lender to the hotel would like to see high liquidity ratios as this would indicate a high ability to pay short term debts. In fact, some lenders seek to protect themselves by requiring the borrower to maintain liquidity indicators, such as the current ratio, above a certain level. A loan provision can be drafted to this effect, and if the borrower's current ratio falls below what is stipulated in the loan provision, the lender can require the borrower to immediately repay the loan. If a business experiences liquidity problems, a variety of rectification options can be considered. For instance:

- Some fixed assets could be sold, maybe under a sale and lease-back agreement (increase to cash, no effect on current liabilities).
- A long-term loan could be sought (increase to cash, no effect on current liabilities).
- Further equity could be sought (increase to cash, no effect on current liabilities).

Caution needs to be exercised in liquidity management, however, as high liquidity ratios do not signify astute management. High liquidity ratios signify sub-optimal use of funds, as funds invested in short-term assets do not provide a high rate of return to owners. If funds can be freed up from current assets, greater investment can be made in long-term assets which can be seen to represent the engine room from which owners derive profits. Further discussion of working capital management issues is provided in Chapter 11.

Long term

Over the long term we are concerned with a firm's ability to pay all its debts, not merely short-term debt.

The long-term indebtedness of the firm is generally referred to as financial leverage or gearing. Two of the most commonly cited financial leverage measures are debt to assets and debt to equity. Debt to assets (sometimes called the 'debt ratio') is calculated as follows:

Debt to assets = Total debt ÷ Total assets

Celestial's 31/12/X1 debt to assets ratio = 20 ÷ 50 = 0.4 (or 40%)

Debt to equity is calculated as follows:

Debt to equity = Total debt ÷ Total equity

Celestial's 31/12/X1 debt to equity ratio = 20 ÷ 30 = 0.667 (or 66.7%)

Lenders like to see a low level of financial leverage (low level of debt) as this signifies that there is a relatively low likelihood of insolvency resulting from an inability to honour debt obligations. While owners would also be concerned by the insolvency implications of high levels of debt, their returns can increase as a result of increased levels of leverage. The way financial leverage can be used to increase returns to owners is demonstrated in financial decision making case 5.1.

Case 5.1

Financial Decision Making in Action – The Financial Controller and financial leverage

Imagine Nottingham's RobinHood hotel chain has £2 million of assets and a debt to assets ratio of 40% (£800,000 in debt and £1,200,000 of equity). It pays 10% annual interest on its debt, currently achieves an EBIT of 15% on assets employed, and pays company tax at the rate of 40%. The management of RobinHood is considering a £1 million expansion in capital which, consistent with existing assets, is projected to earn a 15% return. The management is deliberating whether to fund the £1 million expansion through arranging a further loan at 10% annual interest or to finance the expansion through raising more equity capital. Management believes that issuance of debt will not result in insolvency problems and is primarily focusing on its desire to maximize the hotel owners' return. The impact on the owners' return resulting from the issuance of debt (financing option 1) versus the issuance of further equity capital (financing option 2) are detailed in the schedule presented below.

	Financing option 1 (debt) £	Financing option 2 (equity) £
Projected return on assets: 15% of £3 m	450,000	450,000
Less interest on debt [a]	180,000	80,000
Profit before Tax	270,000	370,000
Less 40% Tax	108,000	148,000
Profit after Tax	162,000	222,000
% Return on owners investment[b]	13.5%	10.1%

[a] For financing option 1: 10% of £1,800,000; for financing option 2: 10% of £800,000.

[b] For financing option 1: £162,000 ÷ £1,200,000 × 100; for financing option 2: £222,000 ÷ £2,200,000 × 100.

From this example, it is apparent that a greater return on owners' investment results from taking the debt financing option. This highlights how the hotel finance function can use debt financing to 'lever' or 'gear' up returns to equity holders. As a result, the terms 'leverage' and 'gearing' are used when talking of a company's level of debt financing.

The Financial Controller must be careful not to raise too much debt, however, due to risk implications. High perceived risk will reduce the value of the hotel's equity. Relative to many other industries, the hotel sector has fairly high business risk due to relatively volatile sales and a relatively high proportion of fixed costs. As a result, hotel financial controllers tend to be averse to taking on high levels of financial leverage.

Again, it is difficult to identify an optimal leverage ratio. However, these ratios do provide a means for comparing a firm's long-term liquidity position relative to that of its competitors. In addition, a trend analysis could highlight an alarming trend of increasing levels of indebtedness.

A final ratio can be computed as a further indicator of a firm's capacity to meet its long-term debt obligations. While the above ratios might suggest an insignificant level of leverage for a company, the company may be experiencing problems servicing its outstanding debt due to a low level of profitability. Such a situation would be highlighted by using the following ratio:

$$\textit{Times interest earned} = \textit{EBIT} \div \textit{Annual interest payment}$$

$$\textit{Celestial's 31/12/X1 times interest earned ratio} = 40 \div 10 = 4$$

The times interest earned ratio is sometimes referred to as a 'coverage' ratio, i.e. it indicates the extent to which interest charges are covered by the company's level of profit. The above times interest earned ratio of 4 signifies that Celestial is currently experiencing little problem servicing its debt.

Ratios using operational measures

Performance ratios that have more of an operational focus than the financial ratios presented above are grouped below according to whether they relate primarily to rooms or restaurant activities.

Rooms-related performance measures

Occupancy level is a widely quoted performance indicator in the hotel industry. It has become such an established performance indicator that hotels competing in the same geographical area frequently share information on each others' occupancy levels.

$$\textit{Room (or bed) occupancy} = \frac{\textit{Number of rooms (beds) let in hotel}}{\textit{Total rooms (beds) in hotel}} \times 100$$

This activity level indicator can be a little misleading in those hotels that let out a significant number of complimentary rooms. As a result, management's understanding of the exact nature of the occupancy level can be enhanced by modifying the room occupancy measure to provide 'paid occupancy' and also 'complimentary occupancy' activity indicators. These two indicators are nothing more than adaptations of the room occupancy performance indicator. They again highlight the importance of modifying ratios to fit the particular circumstance of the hotel under investigation.

$$\textit{Paid occupancy \%} = \frac{\textit{Number of rooms sold}}{\textit{Total rooms in hotel}} \times 100$$

$$\textit{Complimentary occupancy \%} = \frac{\textit{Number of complimentary rooms let}}{\textit{Total rooms in hotel}} \times 100$$

A high paid occupancy percentage does not necessarily signify a high revenue from rooms, however. Not all room sales are made at the rack rate (the rack rate can be defined as the maximum price that will be quoted for a room). Similar to the airline industry that sells seats in the same class and flight for a range of discounted prices, discounting room prices below the rack rate is a key characteristic of the hospitality industry. Accordingly, a performance measure that indicates the average room rate charged needs to be computed. This can be achieved via the 'average room rate' (sometimes called the average daily rate or 'ADR') performance indicator which is calculated as follows:

$$Average\ room\ rate\ = \frac{Day's\ revenue\ from\ room\ letting}{Number\ of\ rooms\ let\ in\ the\ day}$$

The room occupancy and the average room rate performance indicators, when considered independently, represent incomplete measures of sales performance. A higher level of total revenue from rooms will not result from an increased occupancy level if the room rate has been disproportionately dropped. Similarly, a higher level of total revenue from rooms will not result if an increase in the average room rate coincides with a disproportionate decline in the occupancy level.

There is a highly intuitively appealing performance measure that circumvents this 'incompleteness' problem. The manager interested in monitoring room sales performance can calculate the average revenue earned by every room in the hotel (both sold and unsold rooms). This 'revenue per available room' ratio is widely referred to by the abbreviation 'revpar' and can be calculated as follows:

$$Revenue\ per\ available\ room\ (Revpar)\ = \frac{Total\ daily\ room\ letting\ revenue}{Total\ hotel\ rooms\ (both\ sold\ and\ unsold)}$$

Box 5.1 demonstrates how revpar circumvents the incompleteness problem of the occupancy and average room rate performance indicators. The more comprehensive nature of revpar is apparent from the fact that it can be calculated by multiplying the occupancy level (stated as a decimal) by the average room rate. The significance of revpar as a performance measure will be further elaborated upon in Chapter 10's discussion of yield management.

The revpar dimension of room sales performance can be measured slightly differently by viewing actual revenue as a percentage of potential revenue. This ratio, which is generally referred to as 'room yield', will always run in tandem with revpar, i.e. a high revpar will signify a high room yield. Accordingly, there is no need to compute both performance indicators. Both measures are introduced here because, while most hotel managers use revpar, others also refer to room yield.

$$Room\ yield\ = \frac{Actual\ total\ room\ revenue}{Potential\ total\ room\ revenue}$$

On the expense side of a hotel's room sales activities, the efficiency of room service expenditure can be monitored by calculating the service cost per room in the following manner:

$$Service\ cost\ per\ room\ = \frac{Total\ daily\ room\ servicing\ costs}{Number\ of\ rooms\ serviced\ in\ the\ day}$$

Box 5.1
Revpar: a comprehensive indicator of room sales performance

Imagine you are comparing the room sales performance of two Canadian properties that are part of LuxuryLife's worldwide chain of hotels. Toronto's 120-room LuxuryLife property has been achieving an occupancy level of 65% and an average room rate of $100. Vancouver's 90-room LuxuryLife property has an average occupancy level of 72% and an average room rate of $80. The performance of these two properties highlights how the occupancy level and average room rate are relatively incomplete indicators of room sales performance. The Toronto property has the higher average room rate, but the Vancouver property has the higher average occupancy. The incompleteness of these two measures can be overcome by integrating the two measures into one, i.e. multiply occupancy level by average room rate to generate revenue per available room (revpar), i.e.:

Hotel	Occupancy		Average room rate		Revpar
Toronto	0.65	×	$100	=	$65.0
Vancouver	0.72	×	$80	=	$57.6

We can check that the product of occupancy and average room rate generates revpar by calculating the Toronto property's revpar using the 'total daily room revenue ÷ total hotel rooms' revpar formula as follows:

Toronto property's total daily room revenue = 120 × 0.65 × $100 = $7,800

Toronto property's revpar = $7,800 ÷ 120 = $65.

As the Toronto property is achieving the higher revpar, we would conclude it has the better room sales performance.

Restaurant-related performance measures

A measure providing insight concerning the productivity of restaurant labour is revenue per employee hour worked, and can be computed as follows:

$$Revenue\ per\ employee\ hour\ worked = \frac{Restaurant\ revenue}{Number\ of\ employee\ hours\ worked}$$

Revenue per employee hour worked can also be applied to beverage sales. If seeking to compare labour productivity across different meal times (where there can be a considerable spread in the profitability of meals served and also average spend per head), it might be more appropriate to calculate covers sold per employee hour worked in the following manner:

$$Covers\ per\ employee\ hour\ worked = \frac{Number\ of\ covers\ served\ in\ period}{Number\ of\ employee\ hours\ worked}$$

Similar to the room occupancy performance measure used to gauge the rooms activity level, in restaurants, activity can be gauged by calculating seat turnover. This provides an indicator of the number of customers served on each restaurant seat during a day and can be calculated as follows:

$$Seat\ turnover = \frac{Number\ of\ covers\ served\ per\ day}{Number\ of\ restaurant\ seats}$$

Paralleling the trade-off between room occupancy and the average room rate noted above, a trade-off exists in restaurants between seat turnover and expenditure made by each customer. If menu prices are increased, we can anticipate a decrease in seat turnover. Expenditure per customer is generally referred to as 'average spend per head' and can be calculated as follows:

$$Average\ spend\ per\ head = \frac{Total\ restaurant\ revenue}{Number\ of\ covers\ served\ in\ period}$$

Box 5.2
Revenue yield per seat: a comprehensive indicator of restaurant sales performance

Imagine that in May 20X1 'MedievalMeals', which is an 80-seat restaurant adjoining a Welsh castle, was open for 27 days and had a revenue of £67,500 from 2,700 covers sold. In May 20X2 MedievalMeals was open for 28 days and earned £75,264 from 2,688 covers sold. The table below presents the calculation of MedievalMeals' seat turnover, average spend per head, and average daily revenue yield per seat for the two periods. From these calculations, an improved sales performance in May 20X2 is apparent as the daily revenue yield per seat is £2.35 greater (£33.60 – £31.25), despite the decline in seat turnover from 1.25 to 1.2.

Period	Seat turnover		Average spend per head		Average revenue yield per seat
May 20X1	1.25[a]	×	£25[b]	=	£31.25
May 20X2	1.20	×	£28	=	£33.60

[a] Number of covers served per day = 2,700 ÷ 27 = 100
   Seat turnover = 100 ÷ 80 = 1.25
[b] $67,500 ÷ 2,700 = $25

We can check that the product of seat turnover and average spend per head generates revenue yield per seat, by calculating revenue yield per seat for May 20X1 using the 'total revenue ÷ number of restaurant seats' formula as follows:

£67,500 ÷ (80 × 27) = £31.25

Hospitality, Leisure & Tourism Series

Just as average room rate and room occupancy are incomplete measures of rooms performance, so too are average spend per head and seat turnover incomplete measures of restaurant performance. Following the approach taken to generate revpar, a more complete indicator of restaurant sales performance can be achieved by multiplying average spend per head by seat turnover. This term, which can be referred to as 'revenue yield per seat', provides an indication of the sales productivity of each restaurant seat. A simple way of computing revenue yield per seat is as follows:

$$Revenue\ yield\ per\ seat\ = \frac{Total\ restaurant\ revenue}{Number\ of\ restaurant\ seats}$$

The way in which revenue yield per seat represents a combination of the average spend per head and seat turnover performance indicators is demonstrated in Box 5.2.

Summary

This chapter has described how a systematic approach can be taken when analysing a company's profit performance and financial stability. By segregating the ROI measure into a profit margin and an asset turnover dimension and working through the elements that affect these two aspects of profitability, we can ensure a comprehensive profitability analysis is undertaken. We have also seen that a comprehensive analysis of financial stability can be undertaken by considering a company's short-and long-term degree of indebtedness. In addition to these financial analyses, the chapter has overviewed operational measures that are widely used in the hospitality industry.

Having read the chapter you should now know:

- How to take a systematic approach when analysing a company's profitability
- How to analyse a company's short-and long-term financial stability
- How to compute a range of operational measures that are widely used in the hospitality industry
- How an aged schedule of accounts receivable can assist managers involved in accounts receivable management
- That it is important to tailor ratios with due regard given to the nature of the organization being analysed.

References

Atkinson, H., Berry, A. and Jarvis, R. (1995) *Business Accounting for Hospitality and Tourism & Leisure*, International Thomson Publishing, London, Chapter 11.

Carnegie, G., Jones, S., Norris, G., Wigg, R. and Williams, B. (1999) *Accounting: Financial and Organisational Decision Making*, Irwin/McGraw-Hill, New York, Chapter 12.

Coltman, M. M. and Jagels, M. G. (2001) *Hospitality Management Accounting*, 7th edition, John Wiley, Chichester, Chapter 4.

Kotas, R. (1999) *Management Accounting for Hospitality and Tourism*, 3rd edition, International Thomson Publishing, London, Chapter 15.

Kotas, R. and Conlan, M. (1997) *Hospitality Accounting*, 5th edition, International Thomson Publishing, London, Chapter 22.

Owen, G. (1994) *Accounting for Hospitality, Tourism & Leisure*, Pitman Publishing, London, Chapter 17.

Schmidgall, R. F. (1997) *Hospitality Industry Managerial Accounting*, 4th edition, Educational Institute – American Hotel & Motel Association, East Lansing, MI, Chapter 5.

Problems

✓ indicates that a solution appears at the back of the text

✓ 5.1   HoJo and EasyRest are two companies in the American hotel and catering industry. The following financial data for 20X0 relate to their food and beverage activities:

	Hojo $m	Easyrest $m
Revenue	500	300
Cost of sales	200	220
EBIT	50	15
Total assets	250	75

Required
(a) Use the Dupont formula (based on EBIT) to compare the performance of the two companies' F&B activities.
(b) Do the two companies appear to be operating different strategies, and if so, in what way?

✓ 5.2   In the last financial year London's Enwad Hotel group achieved a revenue of £28.75 million and a gross profit margin of 40%. Its end-of-quarter inventory balances were as follows:

Quarter	Inventory
1	£ 400,000
2	£ 800,000
3	£ 900,000
4	£ 200,000

Required
(a) Calculate the firm's inventory turnover and the average age of inventory.
(b) Comment on Enwad's liquidity, assuming most of its competitors record an inventory turnover of 40.

✓ 5.3 A friend who owns a Sydney restaurant has presented the following information to you and asked you to comment on the restaurant's performance in 20X2.

	Year-end 20X1 $	Year-end 20X2 $
Current assets		
Cash	10,800	14,300
Accounts receivable	27,000	26,000
Marketable securities	7,500	7,500
Inventories	10,400	12,000
Prepaid expenses	1,500	1,600
Current liabilities		
Accounts payable	8,400	12,200
Accrued expenses	3,600	5,600
Current tax payable	4,500	3,400
Deposits and credit balances	700	400
Current portion of loan	10,700	9,500

Required ▪ ▪ ▪
(a) For both years calculate the working capital.
(b) For both years calculate the current asset ratio.
(c) For both years calculate the acid test ratio.
(d) Comment on whether the restaurant is becoming more or less liquid.

Revenue for the year 20X2 was $500,000 (55% of this was credit sales) and the cost of sales was $150,000. Calculate the following for 20X2:

(e) The accounts receivable turnover.
(f) The accounts receivable average collection period.
(g) The inventory turnover.
(h) The average age of inventory.

5.4 The following financial information highlights the profitability and financial stability in the last three years of FlyingFood, one of Heathrow Airport's restaurants:

Year	20X1	20X2	20X3
Current asset ratio	1.20	1.34	1.46
Food inventory turnover	36 times	30 times	25 times
Accounts receivable turnover	29 times	25 times	19 times
Debt to equity	2.40	2.20	1.85
Return on shareholders' equity	10.56%	9.44%	9.02%
Sales (all on credit)	£945,000	£952,000	£948,000

Required ▪ ▪ ▪
Using the above information, answer each of the following questions, including an explanation of why you answered each question in this way.

(a) On average, is the restaurant extending a shorter or longer credit period to its customers?
(b) Over the years has more or less money been invested in food inventory?

(c) During the period, has the liquidity of the restaurant improved?

(d) Do you expect the shareholders to be satisfied with their return on investment? From the shareholders' point of view, is the profitability of the operation improving or not?

(e) Imagine that in 20X3 the restaurant wants to finance a proposed expansion through a loan. Relative to its financial position in 20X1 do you think it will be easier or harder to borrow?

5.5   Imagine you are head of the food and beverage department in a large Los Angeles hotel complex. One of the hotel's restaurants is currently earning an annual ROI of 14% on the $200,000 of assets attributed to the restaurant. The average profit margin on covers served is 40%. The restaurant manager believes that if cover prices were dropped by 10% (the average cover currently provides $20 revenue), there would be a significant increase in ROI.

Required • • •
(a) Prior to the proposed price decrease, what is the restaurant's sales/total assets turnover ratio?

(b) If the proposed price decreases were implemented, what level of sales to total assets must be achieved in order to avoid a decline in ROI?

(c) Following on from part (b), how many more covers must be served in order to avoid a decline in ROI?

5.6   Imagine you are the rooms manager of Will'sWooms an 80-room hotel located in Stratford upon Avon. Demand for hotel rooms is significantly affected by the tourist season and the popularity of plays appearing in the nearby Shakespeare theatre. The General Manager has asked you to defend your decision to increase average room rates to £120 during the recent summer theatre season. Occupancy for this year's summer theatre season was 80% which is down from the previous year's summer occupancy of 90%. Average room rates charged during the previous year's summer season were £100.

Required • • •
Use revpar to defend your decision to increase room rates charged during this summer's theatre season.

5.7   A manager of a 120-seat Singaporean restaurant is interested in comparing the sales performance of two recent years. In 20X1, the restaurant achieved an average lunch spend per head of $15 and a lunchtime seat turnover of 1.4. Also in this year, its dinner average spend per head was $28 with a dinnertime seat turnover of 1.1. In 20X2 the restaurant was open for 312 days and had a revenue of $2,135,000. 37% of the revenue was earned from lunches (56,160 covers served) and 63% was earned from dinners (44,928 covers sold).

Required • • •
Provide the manager with an analysis comparing the relative sales performance of the two years.

Cost management issues

After studying this chapter, you should have developed an appreciation of:

1 How the range of decision making and control situations confronted by managers results in many different cost classifications

2 What is meant by an opportunity cost

3 What is meant by direct and indirect costs

4 Methods that can be used to allocate indirect costs to departments

5 What is meant by fixed and variable costs

6 What is meant by incremental and sunk costs.

Introduction

This chapter focuses on the different ways **costs are classified in order to support management decision making and organizational control**. When referring to costs in everyday hotel affairs, managers use terms suggesting a multitude of cost classification schemes. These classifications include: fixed and variable costs, direct and indirect costs, opportunity costs, incremental costs, sunk costs, non-controllable and controllable costs. It is not surprising that staff without any accounting background become somewhat bewildered by the existence of so many cost classifications.

It is important to recognize that the range of cost classifications used results from the wide diversity of management decision-making and control situations that can arise. Rather than attempting to memorize widely used cost classifications, however, it is recommended that you focus on common control and decision-making issues that can arise and how cost information can be tailored to suit the particular management issue at hand. This chapter provides an overview of several typical decision-making and control scenarios that can arise and the main cost classification schemes that have been developed in light of these scenarios. Before considering this range of scenarios, it is important to recognize that accountants refer to any 'thing' that is to be costed as a 'cost object'. The range of cost objects that one could confront in a career is limitless. Generally monitored cost objects in the hotel industry include: cost of cleaning a room, cost of processing a unit of laundry, and food cost in a meal. To further highlight the range of cost objects that can be encountered, five cost objects that could be referred to in restaurant management are summarized in Box 6.1.

Management's need for cost information

Accounting information is a resource that has a cost. It is important to recognize that organizational resources are expended collecting and analysing cost information. We should not spend more money on collecting and analysing cost information than the decision making or control benefit that will derive from the costing information.

Box 6.1
Exploring cost objects: examples found in large restaurants

When considering costing for different purposes, it is important that we recognize what it is that we are costing. The 'thing' that is being costed is called a cost object. For a large restaurant, possible cost objects include:

1 Cost of staffing a shift (we might be considering dropping a shift)
2 Cost of food in a meal (for the purposes of controlling costs, we might like to compare actual cost to budgeted cost)
3 Cost of providing and serving a meal (we might like this information to aid menu pricing decisions)
4 Cost of cleaning the restaurant (we might like this information if we were considering outsourcing this function to a cleaning specialist)
5 Cost of overhauling the kitchen (we might be considering replacing kitchen infrastructure).

We will begin this chapter's review of widely used cost classifications by first considering some general examples of how cost information can be used in management decision making and control.

Decision making

Cost information can be important for decisions such as:

- Should we close a shop?
- Should we outsource laundry activities?
- What rate should be charged for a room?
- Should we promote single room sales more than double room sales?

Cost classification issues that can arise in connection with decision making include the need to distinguish between fixed and variable costs. As will be seen below, we may want to distinguish between fixed costs and variable costs because in the short run it can be in the organization's interest to accept a room rate that covers only the variable cost of selling one night's accommodation.

Control

When monitoring the performance of a departmental head, it is desirable that we distinguish between controllable costs (those which the department head can influence) and non-controllable costs. If we fail to make this distinction, the performance measure used will not represent an appropriate proxy for appraising the department head's managerial judgement and effort. As department heads tend to be acutely aware of inappropriately calibrated performance measures, frustration and resentment typically result from poorly designed performance measurement systems.

The need for departmental control also raises the issue of how best to deal with those hotel costs that are not readily traceable to a department that sells services. For example, should a portion of training costs be allocated to the F&B and rooms departments? While both these departments benefit from hotel training pro-grammes provided, can a sound basis be developed for allocating training costs to other departments? As will be seen below, costs that are readily traceable to the cost object in question (in this case the F&B and rooms departments), are referred to as direct costs, and costs that are not readily traceable to the cost object are referred to as indirect costs.

Major cost classification schemes

In this section, five cost classification schemes are described:

(a) Outlay versus opportunity costs
(b) Direct versus indirect costs
(c) Variable versus fixed costs
(d) Controllable versus non-controllable costs
(e) Incremental versus sunk costs.

Box 6.2
The nature of opportunity cost

The nature of opportunity cost can be illustrated by a small worked example. Imagine London's Victoria Hotel is appraising whether to open a new restaurant that will require floor area that is currently leased out to a souvenir vendor for £5,000 per annum. If the Victoria proceeds with the proposed restaurant development, it will no longer be able to lease out the floor space and will therefore lose the £5,000 per annum revenue. This loss is described as an 'opportunity cost', as although the Victoria does not have to pay £5,000, it will have lost the opportunity of receiving £5,000.

It is important that this potential loss of the £5,000 annual lease revenue is considered at the time the restaurant development decision is taken. However, if the hotel decided to expand the restaurant, the accounting system would not continue to record the £5,000 opportunity cost. To record all opportunity costs on a continuing basis would be an impossible exercise, as every time an organization assigns a resource to a particular purpose (the resource could be cash, floor space, people, etc.), the organization has incurred the opportunity cost associated with not assigning the resource to some other purpose.

Outlay versus opportunity costs

An outlay cost is 'real' in the sense that it involves a disbursement of funds. An opportunity cost does not involve a disbursement of funds, it is, however, a cost to the organization in the sense of an opportunity that is lost. The nature of opportunity cost is illustrated via a hypothetical scenario in Box 6.2.

Direct versus indirect costs

As already noted, a direct cost is readily traceable to a particular cost object, while an indirect cost is not easily traced to a cost object. The term 'overhead cost' is also widely used and means the same as 'indirect cost'. A cost may be direct with respect to one cost object, but indirect with respect to another, e.g. the cost of a hotel's sponsorship of a local sporting event, is a direct cost with respect to the hotel's marketing department (one cost object), but will be indirect with respect to rooms and restaurant meals sold (another set of cost objects).

The direct versus indirect cost classification is significant when designing a departmental performance reporting system. Some hotel accounting systems do not allocate indirect costs to departments while others attempt allocation of some indirect costs. The manner in which indirect cost allocation can be achieved will be illustrated through the following 'HighRollers' scenario.

Imagine HighRollers, a large Chicago hotel and casino complex with three profit-making departments: F&B, rooms and casino. Since its construction ten years ago, HighRollers' performance reporting system has not allocated indirect costs to these three profit centres. This is evident from the copy of HighRollers' most recent quarterly performance report reproduced as Exhibit 6.1.

HighRollers' General Manager has had a concern that some of the complex's managers are not directing sufficient attention to indirect cost containment. In addition, he feels that some of the profit centres may be setting prices without due

Hospitality, Leisure & Tourism Series

Exhibit 6.1
HighRollers' unallocated profit and loss performance statement for the 3 months ending 31 December 20X1

	Casino $	Rooms $	Food & Beverage $	Total $
Revenue	700,000	200,000	100,000	1,000,000
Cost of sales			20,000	20,000
Labour	210,000	41,000	25,000	276,000
Other direct costs	65,000	8,000	7,000	80,000
Departmental profit	425,000	151,000	48,000	624,000
Indirect costs:				
Advertising				60,000
Senior management salaries & administrative support				120,000
General building maintenance				40,000
Training and personnel				35,000
Transportation				10,000
Total indirect costs				265,000
Profit before tax				359,000
Tax				107,700
Net profit				251,300

regard to ensuring a sufficient margin is earned to cover indirect costs as well as direct costs. He feels that if indirect costs were to be allocated to the profit centres, there would be a greater incentive for the profit centre managers to hold other staff in the complex more accountable for efficient indirect cost management. In addition, the General Manager feels that allocating indirect costs to the profit centres would result in managers setting revenue targets that result in adequate profit margins earned on all costs, not just direct costs.

As a result, the General Manager has approached the Financial Controller and asked that the performance report presented as Exhibit 6.1 be redesigned in a way that results in the allocation of the indirect costs to the three profit centres. Following this request, the Financial Controller collected information that she felt provided the basis for a rational allocation of the indirect costs. The indirect cost allocation bases used, together with the rationale for their usage, are outlined in Exhibit 6.2.

Following development of the indirect cost allocation bases, the Financial Controller produced a revised hotel performance report for the three months ending 31 December 20X1 (Exhibit 6.3). In this report, the indirect costs have been allocated to the three profit centres in a manner consistent with the rationale outlined in Exhibit 6.2.

The performance report that includes the allocation of indirect costs (Exhibit 6.3) indicates a loss of $2,000 for the F&B department. Be careful not to conclude from this that the complex would be more profitable if the F&B department were to be closed. Two factors highlight why this view is inappropriate. First, from a commercial viewpoint, it would appear naïve to suggest a casino could be operated successfully in the absence of food and beverage services. Second, closure of the F&B

Exhibit 6.2
Methods used to allocate HighRollers' indirect costs to profit centres

Indirect cost	Rationale for the indirect cost allocation basis used	Amount allocated to profit centres ($)		
		Casino	Rooms	F&B
Department-specific advertising	$20,000 of the $60,000 advertising expenditure was found to be specific to the complex's casino activities. This will all be allocated to the casino.	20,000		
General advertising	The remaining advertising expenditure ($40,000) was general, complex-wide advertising. This is to be allocated to departments based on their proportion of the complex's total sales (i.e. casino: 70%, rooms: 20% and F&B: 10%).	28,000 (0.7 × $40,000)	8,000 (0.2 × 40,000)	4,000 (0.1 × $40,000)
Senior management salaries and admin. support	Senior management have indicated that they can provide a reasonable estimate of time spent on each profit centre's affairs. On average senior management's time is distributed as follows: 50% on casino, 25% on rooms and 25% on F&B.	60,000 (0.5 × 120,000)	30,000 (0.25 × 120,000)	30,000 (0.25 × 120,000)
General building maintenance	Building maintenance is to be allocated to departments based on their relative floor space occupation. The casino occupies 15% of the complex's floor space, rooms occupies 80% of floor space and F&B occupies 5%.	6,000 (0.15 × 40,000)	32,000 (0.8 × 40,000)	2,000 (0.05 × 40,000)
Training and personnel	Most of the training and personnel department's activities are generated by staff turnover. In the last year the casino hired 50 new staff, rooms hired 20 new staff and F&B hired 30 new staff. Training & personnel costs are to be allocated based on these proportions.	17,500 (0.5 × 35,000)	7,000 (0.2 × 35,000)	10,500 (0.3 × 35,000)
Transportation	Staff transportation costs are to be allocated according to the relative number of equivalent full time staff in each department. On 31st December 20X1 the number of full time staff in each department was: Casino: 100; Rooms: 30; F&B:70.	5,000 (0.5 × 10,000)	1,500 (0.15 × 10,000)	3,500 (0.35 × 10,000)

Exhibit 6.3
HighRollers' profit and loss performance statement based on allocated indirect costs for the 3 months ending 31 December 20X1

	Casino $	Rooms $	Food & Beverage $	Total $
Revenue	700,000	200,000	100,000	1,000,000
Cost of sales			20,000	20,000
Labour	210,000	41,000	25,000	276,000
Other direct costs	65,000	8,000	7,000	80,000
Profit before indirect costs	425,000	151,000	48,000	624,000
Indirect costs:				
Advertising	48,000	8,000	4,000	60,000
Senior management salaries & administrative support	60,000	30,000	30,000	120,000
General building maintenance	6,000	32,000	2,000	40,000
Training and personnel	17,500	7,000	10,500	35,000
Transportation	5,000	1,500	3,500	10,000
Total indirect costs	136,500	78,500	50,000	265,000
Profit before tax	288,500	72,500	(2,000)	359,000
Tax				107,700
Net profit				251,300

department will not result in the elimination of all indirect costs that have been allocated to the F&B department. Note the nature of the indirect costs that have been allocated. It may well be the case that none of the costs allocated to F&B would disappear if the department were to be closed. It is more likely that following closure of the F&B department, most of the indirect costs that had been allocated to F&B would remain. This would mean that these indirect costs would then have to be allocated to the two remaining departments instead of to F&B. If the F&B department were closed, it is highly likely that the decline in the casino and rooms profits resulting from reallocating the costs that had formerly been allocated to F&B would be greater than the $2,000 loss currently recorded for the F&B department.

Most accountants argue that allocation of indirect costs is appropriate, so long as a sound basis for conducting the allocation can be identified. As was seen in the HighRollers case, advocates of overhead allocation claim that it results in a more complete picture of departmental profit and will prompt managers to set prices at levels that cover indirect as well as direct costs. Further, it can result in managers of profit centres holding other service centre managers more accountable for controlling indirect costs. If no rational basis can be found for allocating a particular overhead, however, it is generally accepted that rather than allocating the cost on a highly arbitrary basis, it is better not to attempt an allocation of the cost.

Variable versus fixed costs

A key determinant of many costs is the volume of sales achieved. If we double sales, some costs will double, e.g. food used in meals served; such costs are termed 'variable costs'. Other costs will be unaffected by the increased output (e.g. senior staff salaries, grounds maintenance, depreciation of fixed assets, etc.). Those costs that do not alter with changed levels of sales activity are termed 'fixed costs'. Some costs have a fixed and a variable component, these are termed 'semi-variable' or 'mixed' costs. A marketing manager's salary that comprises a fixed monthly amount and a commission component that varies according to the number of sales made is an example of a semi-variable cost.

There are several decision-making scenarios necessitating the classification of costs into variable and fixed. One of these is in connection with breakeven analysis, which is a particular analytical technique which will be addressed in the next chapter. Three other scenarios where the distinction between variable and fixed costs is important are:

(a) The danger of treating fixed costs as variable when considering a range of activity levels for the organization
(b) Short-term pricing decisions
(c) The decision to close a hotel during the off-season.

Following a description of how an organization can classify its costs into fixed and variable, these situations where an appreciation of the distinction between fixed and variable costs is important will be described.

Determining the variable and fixed cost functions • • •

An approximation of an organization's fixed and variable costs can be determined relatively easily using a technique generally referred to as the 'high–low' method. An example illustrating the application of this method is presented in Box 6.3.

The high–low method has the advantage of being simple to calculate and serves as a rough approximation of the cost function. However, only two observations – the highest and the lowest points – are considered and it may not always be the case that these two observations are representative of the underlying fixed and variable cost relationship throughout the year. More sophisticated approaches such as regression analysis, which is a statistical technique generally available on most statistical computer software packages, can also be used. The technical aspects of this technique are not reviewed here as the steps necessary to complete the exercise will depend on the software used. The interested reader will find further discussion of regression analysis in most introductory statistics books.

A range of activity levels and the danger of treating fixed costs as variable costs • • •

A trap that some managers and accounting students fall into relates to treating fixed costs as if they are variable costs. As can be seen from the example provided in Box 6.4, you fall into this trap if you attempt to interpret average cost per unit information in the context of a range of activity levels.

Short-term pricing decisions • • •

The distinction between fixed and variable costs is also important when considering short-term pricing situations. The example in Box 6.5 shows that in the short term it can be justifiable to accept a price that covers variable cost and not total cost.

This use of variable cost in short-term pricing is particularly pertinent to room rates charged during the off-season. If we have spare room capacity and wish to adopt a very aggressive room-pricing strategy in an effort to increase occupancy levels, an argument can be made for dropping the room rate to a level just above the variable cost associated with room occupancy. If the sale of one more room results in extra variable costs of $10 (most of this would be the cost of cleaning the room following checkout), then an argument can be made for dropping the room rate to a level just above $10. If one extra room was sold at a rate of $11 then $1 additional

---

Box 6.3
Determining fixed and variable costs using the 'high–low' method

Imagine the SqueakyClean Hotel, a fell walkers retreat located in the English Lake District. Identified below are data relating to SqueakyClean's housekeeping costs for January to June 20X1.

Month	Housekeeping costs £	Number of rooms cleaned
January	17,000	2,100
February	15,500	1,800
March	16,250	1,950
April	16,450	1,990
May	16,500	2,000
June	16,775	2,055

To use the high–low method, we compare across the organization's busiest and quietest periods. It can be seen that January is the busiest month and February is the quietest month. By determining the changed level of activity and also the change in costs across these two months, we can determine the variable cost per unit. SqueakyClean's variable housekeeping cost per room can be determined as follows:

When 2,100 rooms were cleaned (highest level of activity), cost = £17,000.

When 1,800 rooms were cleaned (lowest level of activity), cost = £15,500.

It therefore costs an extra £1,500 (£17,000 − £15,500), to clean an extra 300 rooms (2,100 − 1,800).

Therefore, the variable cost per room is £1,500 ÷ 300 = £5 per room.

Having determined that the variable cost per room is £5, determining the fixed costs is straightforward:

As Total cost = Total Variable cost + Total Fixed cost,

Total cost − Total Variable cost = Total fixed cost

SqueakyClean's total housekeeping costs for January are £17,000, and their variable housekeeping costs are £10,500 (£5 × 2,100 rooms). Fixed housekeeping costs must therefore be £6,500 (£17,000 − £10,500).

profit will result ($11 – $10). Again, significant marketing issues would arise if such an aggressive room-pricing strategy were to be adopted. Nevertheless, variable cost information can be important in the context of short-term pricing decisions. This issue is further explored in Chapter 10.

The decision whether to close during the off-season • • •

As many hotel operations experience significant seasonality, hotel managers can confront the issue of whether to close a hotel for a period of the year. As will be apparent from the following example, drawing a distinction between fixed and variable costs provides useful insight when deciding whether to close during a quiet period. Imagine the RockiesResort, a Canadian mountain lodge that has a high

---

Box 6.4
The danger of treating average cost per unit as a constant

Be careful if you are provided with total cost information and use it to determine an average unit cost. Danger awaits if you attempt to use this information in the context of different levels of activity. To demonstrate how easy it can be to fall into this trap, work through this small exercise.

Before reading any further, place your right hand over the final two columns appearing in the schedule of data at the bottom of this box (i.e. that part of the schedule relating to cleaning 100 rooms). From the schedule, which concerns room cleaning costs, you will note that cleaning 50 rooms requires $250 of labour costs and $450 of depreciation. From this we can easily determine that the average cost of cleaning a room is $14 ($700 ÷ 50). Now, are we safe to conclude that if twice as many rooms are cleaned it will cost us $1,400 (i.e. $14 × 100)? Unfortunately many managers and accounting students fall into this trap. They believe that once they have calculated average cost at one level of activity, this number can be used to determine total cost across a range of different activity levels.

You can now take your hand away from the page. Note that doubling the level of activity to 100 rooms cleaned does not result in the total cost doubling. Part of the costs have doubled, i.e. the total labour cost, as labour is variable. However, depreciation is a fixed cost and it is the same in total for each period of time, regardless of the level of activity in that period. The key to understanding this little conundrum involves recognizing that the cost of cleaning a room is $14 only when 50 rooms are cleaned. If more rooms are cleaned, the per room cost of cleaning goes down because the fixed cost of $450 is spread across more rooms, i.e. when 100 rooms are cleaned, the average cost per room is $9.5 ($950 ÷ 100). Be careful in your organization if someone quotes an average cost for making an item or performing a particular activity. If fixed costs are present (some of an organization's costs are invariably fixed), the average cost for making the item or for performing the activity will change depending on the activity level.

	Cleaning 50 rooms		Cleaning 100 rooms	
	Total	Per room	Total	Per room
Labour	$250	$5.0	$500	$5.0
Equipment depreciation	$450	$9.0	$450	$4.5
	$700	$14.0	$950	$9.5

occupancy of skiers in the winter months and a low occupancy in the summer months. During winter months a relatively high room rate is charged and average occupancy levels are 90%. During the summer months average occupancy is 30% and a lower room rate is charged. Exhibit 6.4 analyses RockiesResort's profitability in the summer and winter seasons.

Variable costs move in line with occupancy levels. With respect to the semi-variable costs, there is a fixed electricity charge of $1,000 per six-month period, and maintenance costs have a fixed cost component of $2,000 per six-month period.

Although it appears from Exhibit 6.4 that the hotel is making a loss of $28,000 during the summer months, it would be wrong to conclude from this that the hotel should be closed during this time. Closure of the hotel in the summer period would not result in the removal of the fixed costs associated with the summer period. Similar to the approach taken earlier, this type of problem can be approached by conducting an incremental analysis that identifies all factors that would change following closure in the summer. If the hotel were to close, the following changes would occur:

Box 6.5
Using variable cost as a short-term pricing threshold

Imagine that a restaurant in Turin has a monthly output of 20,000 meals which are sold for an average of €20 per meal. Variable cost per meal is €8 and fixed costs per month are €40,000. Mr Bozo, the restaurant's accountant, has worked out the average cost per meal to be:

$$€8 + (€40,000 \div 20,000) = €10$$

The restaurant currently has excess capacity that would allow it to serve a further 5,000 meals per month, and during a local senior citizens' convention that is running for a month, the restaurant has received a one-off offer to provide 4,000 meals for €9.50 per head. Bozo believed that the offer should be rejected as it fails to cover the cost per meal. Is he right?

An easy way to tackle a problem such as this involves taking an incremental perspective, i.e. identify all changes that will occur if the offer is accepted. If the offer is accepted, changes that will occur are:

	€	Profit impact
Increased total variable cost (4,000 × €8)	32,000	Negative
Increased fixed cost	0	
Increased revenue (4,000 × €9.50)	38,000	Positive
Net impact on profit	6,000	Positive

On the basis of a short-term profit impact appraisal, the offer could be accepted as it will increase profit by €6,000 (€38,000 – €32,000). It should be acknowledged, however, that this represents a short-term profitability impact analysis only. The analysis has not considered longer-term marketing issues such as whether the convention organizer might return and bargain hard for a discounted price again in the future, and also whether there is a likelihood that existing clients will become dissatisfied and start seeking lower prices if they become aware of the rates charged to the senior citizens.

Exhibit 6.4
RockiesResort profit and loss analysis

	November–April $	May–October $	Total $
Sales	500,000	100,000	600,000
Variable costs	90,000	30,000	120,000
Semi-variable costs			
Electricity	10,000	4,000	14,000
Maintenance	8,000	4,000	12,000
Fixed costs	90,000	90,000	180,000
Total costs	198,000	128,000	326,000
Net profit	302,000	(28,000)	274,000

	$	Impact on annual profit
Lost revenue	100,000	Negative
Reduction in variable costs	30,000	Positive
Reduction in electricity ($4,000 – $1,000)	3,000	Positive
Reduction in maintenance ($4,000 – $2,000)	2,000	Positive
Net impact on profit	65,000	Negative

From this analysis we can conclude that closing the hotel in the summer would reduce profit for the year by $65,000. As a result, the hotel should be kept open during the summer months.

Controllable versus non-controllable costs

In responsibility accounting, managers should only be held accountable for costs that they can control. In a manager's performance report, an attempt should be made to segregate controllable costs from non-controllable costs. The issue of responsibility accounting is explored in greater detail in Chapter 8.

Incremental versus sunk costs

In some decision-making situations, the distinction between incremental and sunk costs can be important. As can be seen from financial decision making Case 6.1, sunk costs are irrelevant in many decision-making situations. This is because 'sunk' is the term used to describe a cost that has been incurred in the past and is now irreversible. A good example of a sunk cost is depreciation. This is because it is a cost that relates to the purchase of an asset at an earlier time. As the fixed asset purchase cannot be reversed, the depreciation charge cannot be avoided.

Case 6.1

Financial Decision Making in Action – The F&B Manager and the decision to outsource

It is important that decision makers appreciate that cost information has to be tailored to suit the particular circumstances of each decision confronted. Imagine an F&B manager is considering outsourcing pastry production. A local baker has offered to supply pastries at a cost of $7.50 per tray. Data pertaining to the F&B department's pastry-making activities for last year follows:

Direct materials	$20,000
Direct labour	$110,000
Variable overhead	$10,000
Fixed overhead	$90,000
Trays of pastry produced	20,000

The direct materials, labour and variable overhead can all be expected to be incremental (i.e. will change if pastry production is ceased). If fixed overhead comprises depreciation on ovens used in pastry production, the $90,000 can be treated as a sunk cost (non-incremental) and not relevant to the decision. We will assume the ovens cannot be sold due to prohibitively high removal costs. Based on these data, it appears undesirable to purchase outside as the incremental cost of continuing to make the 20,000 trays of pastries is $140,000 ($20,000 + $110,000 + $10,000) which is less than the $150,000 (7.5 × 20,000 trays) it would cost to buy outside.

Qualitative and behavioural factors in management decisions

All the issues addressed above have been approached by conducting quantitative analyses. The financial data provided by the accounting system frequently play a powerful information role as they carry an air of 'objectivity'. Despite this, it is important to remember that qualitative factors must also be appraised. In the outsourcing decision-making scenario outlined above, it might be that the cost saving associated with purchasing outside would have to be very significant before the F&B manager is willing to sacrifice a position of being able to guarantee continued availability of pastries. In addition, quality issues are obviously important in the context of an outsourcing decision, and marketing issues are obviously important in decisions such as what price to charge and whether a hotel should close during the off-season. Clearly, an astute manager will always attempt to strike an appropriate balance between quantitative and qualitative analyses when making decisions.

Summary

In this chapter we have reviewed different ways that costs can be classified. The reason that several cost classification schemes exist is that there is a wide diversity of decision-making and control situations that can arise. Decision-making situations requiring a particular analysis of cost information include the setting of prices, the decision whether to close during the off season as well as the decision whether to outsource a function or activity.

Having read the chapter you should now know:

- Cost analysis has to be designed in accordance with the specific needs of each decision-making scenario at hand
- When opportunity costs should be appraised
- The distinction between direct and indirect costs
- Methods that can be used to allocate indirect costs to departments
- The importance of distinguishing between fixed and variable costs
- The significance of distinguishing between incremental and sunk costs.

References

Atkinson, H., Berry, A. and Jarvis, R. (1995) *Business Accounting for Hospitality and Tourism & Leisure*, International Thomson Publishing, London, Chapter 13.

Carnegie, G., Jones, S., Norris, G., Wigg, R. and Williams, B. (1999) *Accounting: Financial and Organisational Decision Making*, Irwin/McGraw-Hill, New York, Chapter 23.

Coltman, M. M. and Jagels, M. G. (2001) *Hospitality Management Accounting*, 7th edition, John Wiley, Chichestar, Chapter 7.

Kotas, R. (1999) *Management Accounting for Hospitality and Tourism*, 3rd edition, International Thomson Publishing, London, Chapter 3.

Kotas, R. and Conlan M. (1997) *Hospitality Accounting*, 5th edition, International Thomson Publishing, London, Chapters 17 and 18.

Owen, G. (1994) *Accounting for Hospitality, Tourism & Leisure*, Pitman Publishing, London, Chapter 11.

Schmidgall, R. F. (1997) *Hospitality Industry Managerial Accounting*, 4th edition, Educational Institute – American Hotel & Motel Association, East Lansing, MI, Chapter 6.

Problems

✓ indicates that a solution appears at the back of the text

✓ 6.1 Why do so many different classifications of cost arise in accounting?

✓ 6.2 The conference department of the MerryWeather hotel in Inverness, Scotland has fixed costs of £360 per day. A local university is seeking a quote in connection with a conference it is planning to hold next year. The university would like the hotel to provide morning coffee, lunch, afternoon tea and to prepare conference materials to be distributed to all conference attendees. The hotel's cost of providing food and drink during the day is £7 per attendee. In addition, preparing the conference materials would cost the hotel £6 per attendee. The university has estimated that the conference will be attended by between 80 and 120 people.

Required ● ● ●
(a) What is the total average cost per attendee if the conference has an attendance of 80 people?
(b) What is the total average cost per attendee if the conference has an attendance of 120 people?
(c) Explain why the cost per attendee is affected by the number of people that attend the conference.
(d) If 120 people attend the conference and the hotel wants to earn a profit of 20% on revenue, what price per person should be charged?
(e) There are several other local hotels that provide conference facilities. The university, which holds several conferences per year, has always used a venue provided by MerryWeather's main competitor. MerryWeather's conference manager is exceedingly keen to develop a working relationship with the University and has received permission from the General Manager to provide a very aggressively priced quote to the University. To help in his deliberations on this matter, the conference manager has approached MerryWeather's accounting department and asked them to determine what is the lowest price that can be charged per attendee without the conference adversely affecting this year's hotel profit. If you were an accountant at MerryWeather, what advice would you give to the conference manager?

✓ 6.3   Darwin's HighFlyer Hotel has spare laundry capacity and is considering offering a laundry service to the Luigi Brothers who own three Italian restaurants. To aid deliberations concerned with what rate should be quoted when offering the service, the Laundry Manager has asked for your assistance in analysing the Laundry department's fixed and variable costs.

From her departmental records, the laundry manager has extracted the following schedule of cost information.

Month	Laundry costs $	Kilograms of laundry processed
July	22,000	20,000
August	21,600	19,500
September	21,800	19,750
October	20,800	18,500
November	20,720	18,400
December	20,400	18,000

Required ● ● ●
(a) Use the high–low method to determine the laundry department's fixed and variable cost structures.
(b) Provide an estimate of the total cost if 25,000 kilograms of laundry were processed in a month.

6.4   Hawaii's SurfingViews Hotel has three selling departments: rooms, restaurants and bars. Some of SurfingViews' indirect operating expenses are allocated to the three departments in the following manner.

Indirect expense	Allocation basis	Total expense to be allocated
Rent	Floor space	$90,000
Advertising	Sales	$20,000
Depreciation	Net book value of assets	$45,000
Personnel department	Salaries and wages	$100,000

The hotel's accountant has collected the following information in connection with the hotel's indirect cost allocation exercise.

	Rooms	Restaurants	Bars
Floor space in square metres	350	100	50
Sales	$1,150,000	$250,000	$100,000
Net book value of fixed assets	$900,000	$200,000	$100,000
Salaries and wages	$250,000	$210,000	$40,000

Required • • •
Calculate the amount of indirect expense to be allocated to each department.

6.5   The Santa Fe is a Californian hotel with three revenue-generating departments. One of these is a foyer shop that has recorded a loss in each of the last three years. In the most recent year, the shop's profit performance schedule was as follows.

	$
Sales	300,000
Cost of goods sold	185,000
Gross profit	115,000
Other expenses	126,000
Net loss	(11,000)

Included in other expenses is an allocated hotel electricity expense of $7,500. This overhead is allocated to the shop according to a complicated formula that recognizes floor space as well as the hours that the shop is open. Of the $7,500 allocated, it is estimated that if the shop were to close, $3,000 in electricity would be saved. The other expenses also include $12,000 of allocated overheads pertaining to rent of the building and also maintenance of the hotel's physical infrastructure. All of the remaining 'other expenses' are directly traceable to the shop and would be eliminated if the shop were to close.

Required • • •
Prepare a financial analysis that demonstrates whether the shop should be closed.

6.6 The HeavensAbove Hotel in Auckland has three revenue-generating departments: rooms, restaurant/bar and disco. The following schedule provides the most recent profit performance statement for the hotel.

HeavensAbove unallocated profit and loss performance statement for June 20X1

	Rooms $	Restaurant/bar $	Disco $	Total $
Revenue	375,000	100,000	25,000	500,000
Cost of sales		22,000	8,000	30,000
Labour	80,000	31,000	4,200	115,200
Other direct costs	35,000	6,000	4,000	45,000
Departmental profit	260,000	41,000	8,800	309,800
Indirect costs:				
Marketing				34,000
Facility Maintenance				21,000
General Administration				40,000
Depreciation				32,000
Insurance				6,000
Total indirect costs				133,000
Profit before tax				176,800
Tax				40,000
Net profit				136,800

The hotel's new accountant believes that significant further performance insights could be gained if the indirect expenses were allocated to the hotel's three revenue departments. He has determined that marketing expenses should be allocated based on the relative level of sales made by each department. Facility maintenance is to be allocated based on floor space, general administration is to be allocated according to the number of employees in each department, and depreciation and insurance is to be allocated according to the book value of depreciable assets held in each department. The accountant has compiled the following information to aid in the allocation of indirect expenses.

	Rooms	Restaurant/bar	Disco
Square metres of floor space	800	120	80
Number of employees	25	20	5
Book value of assets	$8.5 m	$1 m	$0.5 m

Required • • •

(a) Prepare a profit and loss statement that allocates the indirect costs to the three sales-generating departments and shows each departments' profitability subsequent to this allocation exercise.

(b) Imagine that following the allocation of indirect expenses to the revenue-generating departments it has been found that one of the departments is recording a loss. Explain whether from this analysis one can conclude that the loss-making department should be closed down.

6.7 The General Manager of Nova Scotia's Trenton Hotel is concerned that in January and February her hotel is running at a loss. She has decided to hold a senior management meeting to consider whether the hotel should be closed during these two months. Prior to the meeting she has asked the chief accountant to prepare an analysis of profit that compares the hotel's performance in January and February with the performance in the remainder of the year. The accountant has produced the following schedule.

Trenton Hotel – profit performance

	January–February $	March–December $	Total $
Revenue	8,000	150,000	158,000
Cost of sales	2,000	37,500	39,500
Gross profit	6,000	112,500	118,500
Other expenses			
Salaries & Wages	6,800	45,000	51,800
Electricity	340	6,000	6,340
Advertising	800	4,000	4,800
Maintenance	300	1,600	1,900
Depreciation	7,000	35,000	42,000
Insurance	200	1,000	1,200
Total expenses	15,440	92,600	108,040
Net profit (loss)	(9,440)	19,900	10,460

In addition, the accountant has produced the following information pertaining to the proposed two-month closure.

Salaries and Wages: $3,000 of this cost is fixed per month as it relates to long-term salaried staff.

Electricity: Even if closed, $50 of electricity would be used per month.

Advertising: The hotel has been conducting advertising that costs $400 per month. The cost of two months' advertising would be saved if closed for January and February.

Maintenance: It is estimated that $200 of maintenance would be saved if the hotel closed for two months.

Depreciation: The accountant applies depreciation on a time basis, i.e. 20% per annum depreciation is being charged on the hotel's assets that have a gross book value of $210,000.

Insurance: If closed, the hotel would save $40 per month in insurance.

Required ● ● ●
Prepare an analysis that shows the financial implication of closing the hotel for January and February.

Cost–volume–profit analysis

After studying this chapter, you should have developed an appreciation of:

1 What is meant by 'contribution margin' and 'contribution margin ratio'

2 The benefits that derive from using the contribution margin format when preparing a profit and loss statement

3 How breakeven can be determined

4 How the level of sales required to achieve a before- or after- tax target profit can be determined.

Introduction

When considering a decision to enter a new commercial activity (e.g. open a restaurant), questions frequently posed by managers include: 'How many units will we need to sell in order to break even?' and 'How much will we need to sell in order to achieve our target profit level?' Other questions that sometimes arise in connection with existing activities include: 'What will happen to profit if we manage to increase sales volume by 10%?' and 'If we increase advertising by 15%, how much more would we have to sell in order to maintain our current level of profit?' This chapter outlines an analytical approach that will enable you to answer these types of questions. This approach is generally referred to as 'cost–volume–profit' (CVP) analysis.

Contribution margin

The primary focus in CVP analysis concerns projecting future levels of profitability. Projecting profit requires an understanding of how much costs and profits will fluctuate following a change in sales volume. The conventional profit and loss statement, such as that presented as Exhibit 7.1, is unfortunately not well designed to support such an analysis.

When a profit and loss statement is presented in this conventional format, costs are classified according to business function (e.g. administration, marketing, etc.). An alternative to this approach involves classifying costs according to whether they are variable or fixed. Total revenue minus total variable costs is generally referred to as 'contribution margin'. Accordingly, a profit and loss statement that distinguishes between variable and fixed costs is generally described as presented in a contribution margin format. DapperDrake's profit and loss statement for the period ending 30 June 20X1 is restated using the contribution margin format in Exhibit 7.2.

Exhibit 7.1
The DapperDrake Resort Profit and loss statement for the year ending 30 June 20X1 (conventional format)

	$	Percentage
Sales revenue	2,000,000	100
less Cost of sales	300,000	15
Gross Profit	1,700,000	85
Operating expenses		
Administration	400,000	20
Marketing	380,000	19
Human resources	120,000	6
Engineering	260,000	13
Financial expenses	220,000	11
Other	100,000	5
	1,480,000	74
Net Profit	220,000	11

Exhibit 7.2
The DapperDrake Resort Profit and loss statement for the year ending 30 June 20X1 (contribution margin layout)

	$	Percentage
Sales revenue	2,000,000	100.0
Variable costs		
Variable cost of sales	300,000	15.0
Variable operating expenses	200,000	10.0
Contribution margin	1,500,000	75.0
Fixed costs		
Administration	380,000	19.0
Marketing	350,000	17.5
Human resources	70,000	3.5
Engineering	210,000	10.5
Financial expenses	220,000	11.0
Other	50,000	2.5
	1,280,000	64.0
Net Profit	220,000	11.0

Note that the only difference between the two statements is the cost classifications used. The revenue and the net profit figures are the same in the two statements.

The advantage of the contribution margin layout is that it highlights what proportion of revenue is consumed by variable costs. In the case of DapperDrake, this is 25% (i.e. variable cost of sales comprise 15% of revenue, and variable operating expenses comprise 10% of revenue). It is important to recognize that because variable costs move in line with revenue, this relationship is constant. By implication, as 25% of DapperDrake's sales revenue is consumed by variable costs, 75% of its sales revenue remains as a contribution towards covering fixed costs. Once revenue achieves a level that is sufficient to cover all fixed costs, additional sales will contribute to the earning of profit. As the contribution is 75% of revenue, once fixed costs are covered, profit will accumulate at the rate of 75% of every additional dollar of sales. Note the use of the words 'contribution' and 'contribute' in the previous two sentences. This highlights why the term 'contribution margin' is used when referring to sales revenue minus variable costs. 'Contribution margin ratio' refers to the percentage of sales that is not consumed by variable costs. It is found as follows:

Contribution margin ratio = Contribution margin ÷ Revenue × 100

DapperDrake's contribution margin ratio is:

$1,500,000 ÷ $2,000,000 × 100 = 75%

The contribution margin format is useful as it enables us to quickly answer questions such as 'What will happen to DapperDrake's profit if revenue increases by $200,000?'. As DapperDrake's contribution margin ratio is 75%, we know that increased revenue of $200,000 will add $150,000 (0.75 × $200,000) to profit. Viewed slightly differently, as revenue and variable costs move in tandem, a 10% increase in sales, i.e. $200,000, will result in a 10% increase in contribution, i.e. $150,000. These quick observations can be made due to the way that the information is provided in Exhibit 7.2, and they underline the value of using a contribution margin format when preparing profit and loss statements.

Breakeven analysis

Breakeven analysis can be applied in different scenarios that signify varying degrees of complexity. In the light of this, the technique will be described in several stages. Initially, the basic situation of calculating breakeven when only one service is sold is outlined. This basic situation will then be extended by considering the sale of more than one service. Following this, the question of how many units need to be sold to achieve a target level of profit is described.

Calculating breakeven when one service is sold

By distinguishing between fixed and variable cost, we can determine the volume of sales necessary to achieve breakeven (i.e. that level of sales where profit is $0). To conduct a breakeven analysis, we need to consider contribution at the unit level. In the context of hospitality management, by 'unit' we usually mean rooms (if appraising room sales necessary to break even), or covers (if appraising what level of restaurant sales are necessary to break even). As contribution margin refers to total revenue minus total variable cost, it follows that contribution per unit is calculated as follows:

Contribution per unit = Unit sales price – Unit variable cost

In Case 7.1, the calculation of breakeven is illustrated in the context of a rooms division manager attempting to determine what level of occupancy must be achieved if his hotel's rooms division is to avoid recording a loss.

Case 7.1	
	Financial Decision Making in Action – **The Rooms Division Manager and breakeven analysis**

Imagine the Rooms Division Manager of Glasgow's BudgetStay Hotel is due to meet with the hotel's Marketing Director to discuss next year's promotion activities. The Rooms Division Manager is concerned by a recent drop in occupancy, and prior to meeting the Marketing Director he would like to ascertain the level of occupancy necessary to reach breakeven. The Rooms Division Manager knows that £2,190,000 of annual fixed costs are charged to his division. The hotel has 200 rooms and the average room rate charged is £67. As the variable cost associated with providing one night's accommodation is £7, average contribution per room night sold is £60 (£67 – £7).

At the beginning of the year, the BudgetStay can be described as £2,190,000 'in the hole', due to the £2,190,000 fixed costs that will be incurred regardless of the number of room nights sold. Following the sale of the first room night, the degree to which the hotel is 'in the hole' will have declined by £60, as £60 will have been contributed to covering the £2,190,000 fixed costs. Now, how many room nights with a contribution of

£60 have to be sold to cover all the hotel's £2,190,000 annual fixed costs? As 36,500 contributions of £60 provide £2,190,000 (i.e. £2,190,000 ÷ £60), we can conclude that once the BudgetStay sells 36,500 rooms, it will have achieved breakeven. This line of logic has taken us through the following widely quoted formula for determining breakeven:

Breakeven number of units to be sold = Fixed costs ÷ Contribution per unit

BudgetStay's breakeven point of 36,500 rooms sold per annum can also be stated in terms of the occupancy level required to achieve breakeven. If the hotel is open for 365 days per annum, it would have 73,000 room nights available per annum (365 days × 200 rooms). 36,500 rooms represents 50% of BudgetStay's annual available room nights (36,500 ÷ 73,000 × 100). We can therefore conclude that an occupancy rate of 50% will result in BudgetStay achieving breakeven. The occupancy breakeven formula can be stated as:

Number of room sales necessary for breakeven ÷ Room nights available × 100

If the Rooms Division Manager develops a basic grasp of breakeven, he will quickly recognize that the breakeven level of room sales would be lowered if he can achieve any of the following:

- Increase the average room rate above £67
- Reduce the variable costs per room night sold below £7
- Reduce the level of fixed costs below £2,190,000.

Exhibit 7.3 presents a graphical representation of breakeven. In this graph, sales activity is shown on the horizontal axis with dollars on the vertical axis. If we draw in the total sales revenue line and also the total cost line for all levels of activity, we can determine the breakeven level of sales. As breakeven occurs at that activity level where total cost equals total sales, breakeven is represented by the point where the sales and total cost lines intersect. In the graph, this breakeven point is highlighted by the vertical dotted line. Any level of sales to the right of the dotted line will result in a profit. Any level of sales to the left of the line will result in a loss. Some managers find that breakeven graphs represent useful visual aids to considering the profit implications of different levels of sale activity.

One further extension to the basic breakeven analysis that some managers find useful concerns the safety margin concept. This concept arises when managers raise the question 'By how many sales are we surpassing breakeven?' Alternatively, a manager might ask 'How much could our level of occupancy decline before we would record a loss?' Calculation of safety margin is illustrated in Box 7.1.

Calculating breakeven when more than one service is sold

Finding breakeven when more than one service is sold will be considered initially in a scenario of a hotel selling two types of room with different contribution margins. Following this, the case of different contribution levels arising from two different room types and also restaurant sales is explored.

In Box 7.2 an approach to calculating breakeven when selling two services is outlined.

Exhibit 7.3
Graphing breakeven

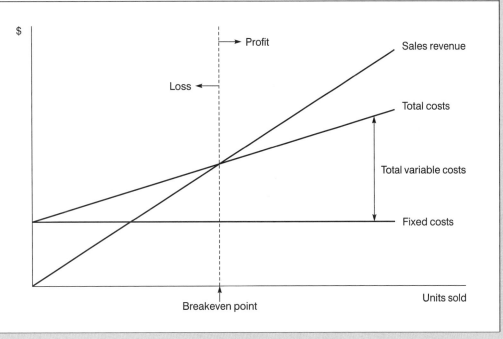

Box 7.1
Calculating safety margin

To illustrate how the safety margin can be calculated, let us continue with the BudgetStay breakeven scenario developed in the earlier financial decision-making case. Imagine that BudgetStay has current annual sales revenue of £3,668,250. We have already determined that BudgetStay must sell 36,500 rooms to break even, i.e. revenue must be £2,445,500 (36,500 × £67). Annual sales could therefore fall by £1,222,750 (£3,668,250 − £2,445,500) before the hotel would incur a loss. £1,222,750 of sales represents 18,250 room nights (£1,222,750 ÷ £67). As a result, we can also state that annual room nights sold could fall by 18,250, or 25% of occupancy (18,250 ÷ 73,000 × 100), before the hotel enters loss-making levels of sales activity.

Following this rationale, it can be seen that margin of safety can be stated in any of the following ways:

Margin of safety in £ sales = Current £ sales − £ sales required to break even.

Margin of safety in unit sales = Current unit sales − unit sales required to break even

% occupancy safety margin = Current occupancy % − occupancy % required to break even.

Box 7.2
Calculating breakeven: the case of two room types with different contribution margins

Assume that BudgetStay's sister hotel, the BudgetRest, is in Toronto and has 110 single and 90 double rooms. Past experience indicates that sales occur in the ratio of 4 single room sales for every 3 double room sales. BudgetRest's single rooms sell for an average of $67 per night and a $7 variable cost is incurred cleaning the rooms. The double rooms have an average rate of $86 and cost $9 to clean. BudgetRest has annual fixed costs of $2,072,400.

As with the BudgetStay example, we commence the calculation of breakeven by determining the contribution earned from a room sale:

BudgetRest's contribution earned per single room night sold $= \$67 - \$7 = \$60.$

BudgetRest's contribution earned per double room night sold $= \$86 - \$9 = \$77$

One way of dealing with the fact that BudgetRest sells two types of room that earn differing contribution levels involves viewing the hotel as selling packages. In light of the mix of rooms sold in the past, we will view each package as comprising 4 single room sales and 3 double room sales. We now determine the contribution earned from selling one package:

Contribution from sale of 1 package =

Contribution from 4 single rooms + Contribution from 3 double rooms =

$(4 \times \$60) + (3 \times \$77) = \$240 + \$231 = \$471.$

Now, using the basic breakeven formula, we can determine how many packages need to be sold to break even:

Breakeven in packages = Fixed costs $\div$ Contribution per package

$\therefore$ BudgetRest's breakeven in packages $= \$2,072,400 \div \$471 = 4,400$

As BudgetRest has to sell 4,400 packages to break even, and each package comprises 4 single rooms and 3 double rooms, we can conclude that the hotel must sell 17,600 single room nights per annum ($4,400 \times 4$) and 13,200 double room nights per annum ($4,400 \times 3$) in order to break even. The accuracy of this breakeven solution can be verified by checking whether this level of sales results in a zero level of profit.

Check to see if breakeven solution is correct:

Contribution from single room sales:	$17,600 \times (\$67 - \$7)$	$1,056,000
Contribution from double room sales:	$13,200 \times (\$86 - \$9)$	$1,016,400
Total Contribution		$2,072,400
less Fixed costs		$2,072,400
Profit		$0

As profit is $0 when 17,600 singles and 13,200 doubles are sold, this represents breakeven.

The case of two room types as well as restaurant sales • • •

Some readers will have found the computation in Box 7.2 somewhat challenging. Unfortunately, in this sub-section the breakeven analysis becomes still more complicated, as we introduce a further dimension. For some this might represent one straw too many, and enough to break the camel's back. The task becomes easier, however, if you remember to view sales as comprising packages that consist of more than one type of room and, in this case, restaurant meals as well.

We will illustrate an approach that can be taken to determine breakeven when contribution is earned from two types of room as well as restaurant sales by extending the BudgetRest scenario developed in Box 7.2. Assume that BudgetRest's management is considering converting an under-utilized lounge area into a facility that will provide buffet breakfasts. It has been estimated that breakfasts will have an average selling price of $8 and an average variable cost of $3. It has also been estimated that the provision of breakfasts will increase the hotel's annual fixed costs by $416,170 to $2,488,570. The existing ratio of single to double room sales is expected to continue. All double room sales result in two guests and it is estimated that 20% of these guests will purchase a breakfast. Single room sales are only made to individuals and it is estimated that 50% of single room guests will eat breakfast at the new facility.

The total contribution earned for each single room night sold now has to include 50% of the $5 contribution earned per breakfast sold, as 50% of single guests will eat their breakfast at the restaurant. Accordingly, total contribution per single room can be calculated as follows:

$$(\$67 - \$7) + (0.5 \times \$5) = \$60 + \$2.5 = \$62.5$$

The total contribution earned for each double room night sold now has to include 20% of the contribution earned from two breakfasts as 20% of double room night sales will result in two breakfasts sold. Accordingly, total contribution per double room can be calculated as follows:

$$(\$86 - \$9) + (0.2 \times 2 \times \$5) = \$77 + \$2 = \$79$$

As rooms are sold in the ratio of 4 singles for every 3 doubles, we will again refer to units as packages. As before, each package is viewed as comprising 4 single room nights and 3 double room nights.

Contribution earned from sale of a package =
$$(4 \times \$62.5) + (3 \times \$79) = \$250 + \$237 = \$487$$

Number of packages to be sold to break even =
Fixed costs ÷ contribution per package = $2,488,570 ÷ $487 = 5,110

As each package comprises 4 single rooms and 3 double rooms, 5,110 packages comprise 20,440 single rooms (5,110 × 4) and 15,330 double rooms (5,110 × 3).

∴ Need to sell 20,440 single rooms and 15,330 doubles in order to break even.

Box 7.3   Determining the sales necessary to achieve a targeted profit

To illustrate how to calculate the sales level necessary to achieve a targeted before-tax profit, let us return to the basic breakeven scenario outlined in Case 7.1. Recall that the BudgetStay Hotel had annual fixed costs of £2,190,000, and offered one type of room. The average room rate was £67 and a variable cost of £7 was incurred for each room night sold. Now imagine that BudgetStay's management wants to determine how many room sales are necessary to achieve an annual profit of £328,500.

If you were able to grasp the rationale for the approach taken in the basic breakeven situation, understanding how we determine the level of sales necessary to achieve a target profit will be relatively straightforward. In the breakeven formula, we found that 36,500 £60 room night contributions were necessary to cover the fixed cost of £2,190,000. Now we are concerned with not only covering £2,190,000 of fixed costs, we must also generate enough sales to provide £328,500 profit. We could determine that beyond the breakeven point, a further 5,475 room nights would have to be sold (i.e. £328,500 ÷ £60). Alternatively, we can find the sales required to achieve the profit target by simply adding £328,500 to the fixed costs in the breakeven formula. Accordingly, the target profit formula can be stated as:

(Fixed cost + Target profit) ÷ Contribution per unit

Applying this formula to the BudgetStay scenario we find:

Room sales to achieve £328,500 profit = (£2,190,000 + £328,500) ÷ £60 = 41,975

Now imagine that BudgetStay revised its £328,500 before-tax profit target to a £328,500 after-tax profit target, and that the hotel is subject to 40% tax. Note that until now we have been dealing exclusively with before-tax amounts. The easiest way to deal with an after-tax amount is to convert it to its before-tax equivalent. If a 40% tax applies, £100 before tax is equivalent to £60 after tax, i.e. £100 (1 − 0.4). As we multiply by '1 − tax rate' to convert a before-tax amount to its after-tax equivalent, we divide by '1 − tax rate' when reversing the conversion. Accordingly, £60 after tax is equivalent to £100 before tax, i.e. £60 ÷ (1 − 0.4). We can incorporate this line of logic to the target profit formula to develop the following formula for finding the level of sales necessary to achieve a targeted after-tax profit:

$$\frac{\text{Fixed costs + (After-tax target profit} \div \text{'1 − tax rate')}}{\text{Contribution per unit}}$$

Applying this formula to the BudgetStay example, we find that room sales necessary to generate an after-tax profit of £328,500 =

$$\frac{£2,190,000 + [£328,500 \div (1 − 0.4)]}{£60} = (£2,190,000 + £547,500) \div £60 = 45,625 \text{ rooms}$$

Check to see if solution is correct:

		$
Contribution from single room sales	20,440 × ($67 – $7)	1,226,400
Contribution from double room sales	15,330 × ($86 – $9)	1,180,410
Contribution from breakfasts sold to single room guests	20,440 × 0.5 × $5	51,100
Contribution from breakfasts sold to double room guests	15,330 × 2 × 0.2 × $5	30,660
Total Contribution		2,488,570
Less Fixed costs		2,488,570
Profit		0

As profit is $0 when 20,440 single and 15,330 double rooms are sold, this level of sales represents breakeven for the hotel.

Calculating the level of sales necessary to achieve a target level of profit

Some managers are interested in determining the level of sales necessary to achieve a profit target. A profit target can be stated in terms of a before-tax, or after-tax, amount. The worked example in Box 7.3 demonstrates how the level of sales necessary to achieve a profit target stated in both before- and after-tax terms can be determined.

The assumptions of cost–volume–profit analysis

It should be noted that several assumptions are made when applying CVP. The main assumptions are:

(a) Selling price is constant. In reality we may need to drop the price in order to sell more.
(b) Fixed costs are constant. This assumption is reasonable if the analysis is restricted to a range of sales activity levels that could be supported by the current level of fixed costs. This signifies that CVP analysis should be used in the context of the short term, i.e. the period of time in which fixed costs will not alter.
(c) Total variable cost varies directly in proportion with sales volume. This relationship will break down if higher levels of sales activity results in the hotel securing volume discounts on purchases, or any economies of scale.

Summary

In this chapter we have reviewed how distinguishing between fixed and variable costs enables contribution margin to be determined. Contribution margin represents the key to appraising profit implications of changed levels of activity. In addition, we have seen how breakeven analysis can be conducted. It is relatively straightforward to calculate breakeven when only one service or product is sold. When more than one service or product is sold, however, the analysis becomes more challenging. We have also seen how to determine the volume of sales necessary to achieve a before- or after-tax target profit level.

Having read the chapter you should now know:

- How to compute contribution margin and also the contribution margin ratio associated with the sale of a particular product or service
- How to present a profit and loss statement using the contribution margin layout
- How to compute breakeven when one or more products and services are sold
- How to determine the level of sales necessary to achieve a before- or after-tax profit target.

References

Atkinson, H., Berry, A. and Jarvis, R. (1995) *Business Accounting for Hospitality and Tourism & Leisure*, International Thomson Publishing, London, Chapter 13.

Carnegie, G., Jones, S., Norris, G., Wigg, R. and Williams, B. (1999) *Accounting: Financial and Organisational Decision Making*, Irwin/McGraw-Hill, New York Chapter 25.

Coltman, M. M. and Jagels, M. G. (2001) *Hospitality Management Accounting*, 7th edition, John Wiley, Chichester, Chapter 8.

Harris, P. (1999) *Profit Planning*, Butterworth-Heinemann, Oxford, Chapter 5.

Kotas, R. (1999) *Management Accounting for Hospitality and Tourism*, 3rd edition, International Thomson Publishing, London, Chapter 4.

Kotas, R. and Conlan, M. (1997) *Hospitality Accounting*, 5th edition, International Thomson Publishing, London, Chapter 18.

Owen, G. (1994) *Accounting for Hospitality, Tourism & Leisure*, Pitman Publishing, London, Chapter 13.

Schmidgall, R. F. (1997) *Hospitality Industry Managerial Accounting*, 4th edition, Educational Institute – American Hotel & Motel Association, East Lansing, MI, Chapter 7.

Problems

✓ indicates that a solution appears at the back of the text

✓ 7.1   (a) Describe the benefits that derive from preparing a profit and loss statement using the contribution margin format.

      (b) In what ways might a manager use cost–volume–profit analysis?

✓ 7.2   Paul Hulse, the owner of the Hulsey Restaurant in West Auckland, recently attended a management training seminar in which he was shown the benefits of using the contribution format to prepare profit and loss statements. He now wants to see his restaurant's profit and loss statement prepared using the contribution margin format. In the year ending 31 December 20X1, the restaurant sold 20,000 covers with an average cover price of $25. Variable food and drink costs average $5 per cover and the head chef's salary includes a performance-related component giving him a commission of $0.8 per cover sold. All the hotel's remaining costs can be viewed as fixed. The restaurant's profit and loss statement presented in conventional format for the year ended 31 December 20X1 is as follows:

**The Hulsey Restaurant
Profit and Loss statement
for the year ending 31 December 20X1**

	$
Sales revenue	500,000
less Cost of sales	100,000
Gross Profit	400,000
Operating expenses	
Salaries and wages	160,000
Marketing	10,000
Rent	48,000
Maintenance	5,000
Other	10,000
Total operating expenses	233,000
Net Profit	167,000

Required ▪ ▪ ▪
(a) Using the contribution margin format, prepare the Hulsey Restaurant's profit and loss statement for the year ending 31 December 20X1.
(b) What is the restaurant's current breakeven point?
(c) If the volume of sales were to increase by 10%, by how much would the restaurant's profit increase?
(d) If revenue next year reached $600,000, what would the restaurant's profit be?
(e) If the restaurant were to increase average menu prices by 10% but was able to maintain the current volume of covers sold, what would be the impact on profit?

✓ 7.3   A 60-room hotel near Land's End in Cornwall incurs annual fixed costs of £360,000. The hotel is open for 365 nights in the year and charges an average room rate of £68. The variable costs associated with room occupancy are £8 per room night.

Required ▪ ▪ ▪
(a) At what room occupancy level would the hotel break even?
(b) At what level of sales would the hotel make a before-tax profit of £60,000?
(c) If the hotel pays 40% tax, how many rooms must be sold in order to make an after-tax profit of £72,000?

7.4   Tim Stokes recently invested $325,000 to acquire the RockOyster, a restaurant on Vancouver Island. RockOyster meals sell for an average of $30 and the average variable cost per meal is $8. Tim believes that by reducing newspaper advertising, he can reduce fixed costs by 10% from their current level of $12,000 per annum. Other fixed costs amount to $100,000 per annum.

(a) What will be the restaurant's breakeven level of sales in units and dollars subsequent to the reduced advertising?
(b) Assuming the reduced level of advertising, determine how many meals must be sold if Tim wants to earn a 20% after-tax annual rate of return on his investment. Assume the restaurant's profits are subject to a 35% tax rate.

Hospitality, Leisure & Tourism Series

7.5 Vermont's PineCrest hotel has a restaurant and 90 double rooms and 60 single rooms. The average room rate for double rooms is $88 and the variable cost per double room night sold is $8. Single room nights sell for $56 and the variable cost per single room night sold is $6. The average occupancy for both types of room is 70%. The hotel has annual fixed costs of $1,998,000.

Past records indicate the following:

- 90% of guests staying in single rooms purchase breakfast in the hotel's restaurant, and 50% of single guests buy their dinner in the restaurant.
- 70% of guests staying in double rooms purchase breakfast in the hotel's restaurant, and 30% of double room guests buy their dinner in the restaurant.
- The average contribution per breakfast cover sold is $8 and the average contribution per dinner sold is $20. The restaurant serves only hotel guests.
- For every 3 double rooms sold, 2 single rooms are sold.
- A double room sale signifies two guests and a single room sale signifies one guest.

Required • • •

(a) What is the volume of double room and single room sales that must be achieved in order for the hotel to break even (assume the 3 double rooms to 2 single rooms ratio is maintained)?

(b) What is the hotel's current level of profit? Assume the hotel is open for 365 days per year.

7.6 Mercury Hotel, a large hotel complex that operates a divisionalized management structure, is located in South East Queensland, Australia. The director of accommodation has been called into the marketing director's office. The marketing director tells the director of accommodation that he has just been approached by a Japanese tour operator who is looking to book accommodation in a South East Queensland hotel for 800 guests. All guests would stay in double rooms for one of four consecutive weeks (200 guests per week booked into 100 rooms). The four-week period falls within the hotel's quiet season. Consistent with its competitors, the hotel has never sold more than 40% of its 300 double rooms at this time of the year.

Mercury's accounting department has estimated that the full cost per double room sold per week is $300 and that the variable cost is $180. A recent analysis of past behaviour of Japanese guests indicates that in the course of a one-week stay, each guest will purchase, on average, 2 dinners and 3 breakfasts at one of the hotel's restaurants. Average contribution per dinner cover is $25. Average contribution per breakfast served is $7.

The marketing director has informed the director of accommodation that the Japanese tour operator knows the Queensland hotel market well and the fact that it is the quiet season. He also believes that the tour operator will be seeking quotes from other hotels to secure a low price.

Required • • •

(a) As the director of accommodation, concerned with maximizing reported profit for your department, what is the lowest conceivable weekly rate you would be willing to quote for a double room in the off-season?

(b) The marketing director has been charged with the responsibility of maximizing profit of the entire hotel. What is the lowest price the marketing director should be willing to accept, for a double room booked during an off-season week by a 'typical Japanese guest'?

(c) How could the accounting system be modified in order to motivate the director of accommodation to act in a manner consistent with the maximization of total hotel profit and not just his own department's profit?

7.7　　Saturn Ltd, a large American hotel organization, has purchased a small rooming house on a property adjacent to one of its main hotels. The acquisition was made with a view to demolishing much of the existing structure and building a custom-designed health club that could be used by hotel guests. Building of the new health club is not due to start for at least a year.

Saturn has been approached by Reg Norman, a contact of the property's vendor. Norman specializes in arranging golfing holidays. In keeping with the last 5 years, Norman wants to use the building for 30 weeks to house a particular niche market of 'economy golfers'. Norman says that he can provide between six and fifteen guests per week. Under the proposed arrangement, Norman will pay Saturn $200 for each guest provided with lodging and morning and evening meals for a week.

Saturn's accountant has developed the following cost data which he believes relevant to the decision of whether to accept Norman's offer.

Weekly cost incurred by Saturn per guest:
Food	$70
Electricity	$6
Laundry, cleaning etc.	$10

Casual staff to provide cleaning and other services for 30 weeks:
For 6 to 10 guests per week:	$22,000
For 11 to 15 guests per week:	$34,000

Other incremental costs if building occupied for 30 weeks:
Maintenance and security:	$12,000

Required . . .

(a) From Saturn's perspective what is the breakeven number of guests per week?

(b) Calculate the change to Saturn's total profit if 10 guest rooms are sold per week throughout the 30-week period.

(c) Calculate the change to Saturn's total profit if 12 guest rooms are sold per week throughout the 30-week period.

CHAPTER 8

Budgeting and responsibility accounting

After studying this chapter, you should have developed an appreciation of:

1 How organizations are subdivided into responsibility centres

2 The four main types of responsibility centre

3 How to compute residual income as an alternative to using ROI when measuring the performance of an investment centre

4 The importance of budgeting

5 The organizational roles that are served by budgeting

6 The behavioural implications of budgeting

7 How a purchases, production and labour budget schedule can be prepared.

Introduction

This chapter focuses on **responsibility accounting** and **budgeting**. The underlying theme of these two topics is **organizational control**. Responsibility accounting involves sub-dividing an organization into **units of accountability**. It is fundamental to control as it involves holding managers accountable for the performance of their respective units. Closely associated with responsibility accounting is budgeting. This is because budgeting involves allocating resources to an organization's sub-units. In addition, the budget highlights benchmarks that are used when appraising a unit manager's performance.

Budgeting is an exceedingly important yet challenging exercise as it requires managers representing the full range of an organization's activities to commit themselves to the **same co-ordinated plan**. Emmanuel *et al.* (1990) highlight the budget's importance in the following way:

> Budgetary planning and control is the most visible use of accounting information in the management control process. By setting standards of performance and providing feedback by means of variance reports, the accountant supplies much of the fundamental information required for overall planning and control. (p.160)

The extent to which the budget provides information that is fundamental to planning and control becomes particularly evident if you try to envisage a large organization without a budget. If a hotel had no budget, management would have no sense of what they should be striving for in terms of sales, costs, cash flow, etc. Without a sense of what we are trying to achieve, we cannot pass judgement on the adequacy of our performance. It follows that the budget is a critically important instrument required for maintaining organizational control.

The importance of the budget is also apparent when we consider its all-encompassing nature. If a General Manager of a hotel were asked for a model of what his organization will be doing over the next year, in responding he would most likely refer to the hotel's budget. The budget's comprehensive nature underlines how it serves as a common point of reference for managers drawn from all levels and representing all functions within the organization.

Just as each division's profit and loss statement feeds into a comprehensive profit and loss statement for a company, so the budget comprises many schedules that feed into an overarching schedule that is widely referred to as the master budget. The master budget comprises the hotel's forecast profit and loss statement for the forthcoming period (typically a year), and also the forecast balance sheet at the end of the budgeted period. These statements do not provide sufficient detail when seeking to control the hotel's many different departments, however. We need a budgeted profit and loss statement for F&B (maybe broken down by restaurants and kitchens), a budgeted profit and loss statement for the rooms division, plus many other budget schedules to facilitate planning and control of the range of activities undertaken in a large hotel (e.g. budget schedules relating to labour cost, food preparation, training, advertising, cash flow, etc.).

The remainder of this chapter is structured as follows. The next two sections describe issues associated with responsibility accounting and the four main types of responsibility centre found in organizations. From this overview of responsibility accounting, it will become apparent that the scope of a manager's influence should determine what he or she can be held accountable for (many organizations get this fundamental principle wrong). Following this, the different roles performed by budgets and behavioural aspects of budgeting are described. In the final section, the manner in which production, purchases and labour cost budget schedules can be prepared is illustrated via a worked example.

Responsibility accounting

The term 'responsibility centres' is used when talking of an organization's sub-units, as each unit is concerned with a particular aspect of an organization's affairs and the manager (or management team) overseeing a sub-unit will be held responsible for its performance. Segmenting an organization into responsibility centres can be achieved on the basis of function, e.g. F&B, rooms, training, accounting, engineering, laundry, gardening, conference and banqueting, etc., or it can be geographically based, e.g. a senior manager in a large multinational hotel chain may be held accountable for the performance of hotels in a designated region of a country, a whole county or a region of the world. For the purposes of this chapter, we are mainly concerned with responsibility accounting issues arising within a single hotel. For this reason, we are primarily concerned with functional segmentation.

A hotel's responsibility accounting system is inextricably linked to its organization structure. An example of how an organization structure is generally depicted appears as Figure 8.1. This extract of an organizational chart has been prepared from the perspective of the F&B department. You should note that that each of the responsibility centres identified in the chart is focused on a particular activity.

Most responsibility centres consume inputs (e.g. labour and materials). Some will produce outputs that can be measured monetarily and some will have an identifiable asset base that represents invested capital. The relationship of inputs,

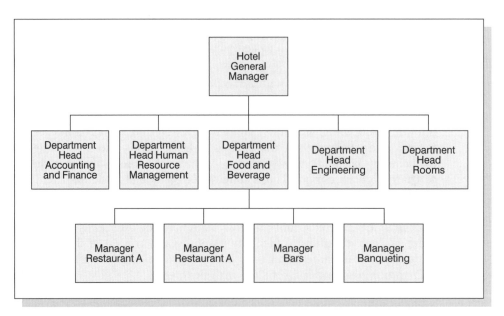

Figure 8.1 An example of a hotel's organization chart

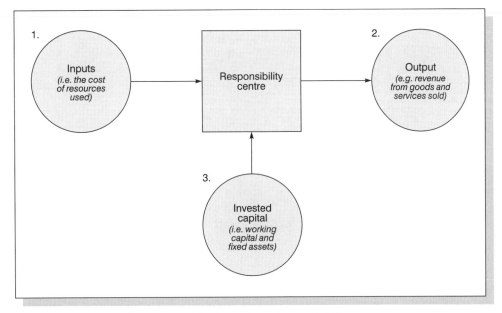

Figure 8.2 A responsibility centre and its dimensions of accountability

outputs and assets to a responsibility centre is depicted in Figure 8.2. In this figure inputs and invested capital are depicted as flowing into the responsibility centre, and outputs are depicted as flowing out of the centre.

The distinction between inputs, outputs and assets is important. These three aspects of accountability provide a checklist when determining a manager's scope of influence. If we can identify which of these three areas can be affected by a responsibility centre's manager (in many cases it is more than one), we can determine what he or she should be held accountable for. Applying this approach to determining scope of accountability results in four main types of responsibility centre:

1 Cost centres
2 Revenue centres
3 Profit centres
4 Investment centres.

A cost centre refers to a responsibility centre where the scope of the manager's influence is limited to inputs (i.e. cost as depicted by circle 1 in Figure 8.2). A revenue centre is the term used for a responsibility centre where the scope of the manager's influence is limited to outputs that can be monetarily measured (i.e. revenue as depicted by circle 2 in Figure 8.2). A profit centre is the term used to describe a responsibility centre where the manager's influence spans both costs and revenues (i.e. circles 1 and 2 in Figure 8.2). Finally, an investment centre is the term used for a responsibility centre where the manager's influence includes costs and revenues (i.e. profit) as well as the asset base employed to generate profit (i.e. all three circles in Figure 8.2).

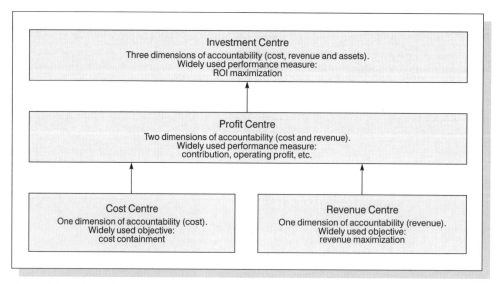

Figure 8.3 A hierarchical perspective of responsibility centres' accountability

In order to highlight their differing scope and degree of accountability, these four generic types of responsibility centre are presented hierarchically in Figure 8.3. In this figure, cost centres and revenue centres appear at the lowest level, as each is accountable for only one of the three dimensions of accountability depicted in Figure 8.2. A profit centre appears at the intermediary level as it is accountable for two of the circles in Figure 8.2. Investment centres appear at the top of Figure 8.3 as managers of investment centres are accountable for all three dimensions of accountability.

Issues of cost, revenue, profit and investment centre design

This section provides an overview of issues arising in connection with the design of these four generic types of responsibility centre. When reading this section, it is important to remember that a responsibility centre's sphere of influence determines whether it is a cost, revenue, profit or investment centre. We will see that some organizational units lend themselves better to accounting control than others. For example, we will see that accounting is well equipped to monitor the efficiency of room servicing, it is not, however, well equipped to monitor the performance of administrative support departments such as the personnel, training or accounting departments of a hotel.

Cost centres

There are two main types of cost centre: engineered cost centres and discretionary cost centres. An engineered cost centre is a centre where an output can be quantitatively measured and there is a reasonably good understanding of the input/output relationship, i.e. the level of costs that should be incurred to achieve a specified level of output is known. Examples of engineered cost centres in hotels include housekeeping (the average cost of cleaning a room can be predetermined), and laundry (the cost of processing a specified amount of laundry can be also predetermined). In a discretionary cost centre, however, more subjective judgement must be exercised when budgeting. For example, as training results in no readily measurable output, setting the training budget is bound to involve a high degree of discretion. How many hours should be spent training a new staff member? Should recruiting the highest quality (expensive) trainers be given high priority? Considerable subjective judgement is bound to be invoked when answering these questions. Even if an output is relatively measurable, a poor understanding of the input/output relationship will signify high judgement exercised when determining the budgeted expenditure level. For example, in the case of a marketing department, the level of sales may well be seen as a reasonably objective measure of output, however as appreciation of the input/output relationship between advertising expenditure and sales revenue is weak (many factors such as competitor actions affect sales), budgeting for advertising expenditure is bound to involve a relatively high degree of discretion.

In discretionary cost centres, the primary role of the budget is to restrict expenditure to a predetermined amount. This is a relatively incomplete form of control, however, as reference to the budget provides little insight as to whether resources have been expended efficiently. Accordingly, a report comparing actual expenditure to budgeted expenditure in a discretionary cost centre should be viewed differently from a report prepared for an engineered cost centre. When considering the performance of an engineered centre, efficiency (i.e. the ratio of inputs to outputs) can be monitored. In a discretionary cost centre, however, if performance measurement places too much emphasis on cost minimization, the discretionary cost centre manager will simply reduce expenditure. Such reduced expenditure does not signify improved efficiency or performance, however. For example, cutting advertising expenditure by half may well carry long-term adverse implications for the whole organization.

Discretionary cost centres in hotels can be classified according to two main types: administrative centres and marketing centres. Administrative centres include all administrative support centres such as human resources, legal, training and accounting. The accounting system does not represent a strong tool to objectively measure performance in such centres. A major problem when managing these centres concerns a potential for goal incongruence (i.e. the goal of the centre may significantly differ from the goal of the whole organization). An example of goal incongruence is where a department is seeking to expand in order to help it reach its internal goal of providing an excellent service, despite the fact that the benefits of further expansion in the department do not exceed the costs. In this type of situation we have empire building, i.e. expansion is for the benefit of the head of the department, but not for the benefit of the organization as a whole.

With respect to marketing responsibility centres, two significant control issues arise:

1 A key performance indicator for marketing is the achievement of company sales targets. This might be an inappropriate indicator of performance, however, due to the fact that sales are affected by many factors outside the marketing manager's sphere of influence (e.g. actions taken by competitors). In addition, hotel sales are particularly affected by the health of the economy, and hotels in tourist locations

are affected by factors such as international exchange rates and the changing nature of a tourist destination's image. These factors that affect sales all fall outside a marketing manager's sphere of influence.

2 Although most marketing managers would agree that marketing activities result in increased sales, many marketing budgets are set in a manner suggesting the reverse. When sales and profit increase, more money tends to be made available for marketing. This 'sales-led marketing' rather than 'marketing-led sales' phenomenon underlines the discretionary nature of budget setting with respect to marketing expenditure.

Revenue centres

Revenue centres are not widely found in the hotel industry. They generally arise in sales departments where sales quotas are set for staff (e.g. in real estate and car retail operations). Unlike the case for inputs, it is often quite hard to measure outputs in terms of money. For example, we generally do not attempt to attach a dollar value to the outputs of departments such as accounting, training or public relations simply because these outputs do not lend themselves to financial measurement.

Profit centres

Profit is clearly an important performance indicator as it is widely used by investors when monitoring company performance. It is a broader measure of performance than the indicators used in revenue and cost centres as it encompasses both revenue and cost. Despite its considerable appeal, it is a less than perfect measure because:

(a) Monetary measures do not exactly measure all aspects of input or output.
(b) Standards used as a basis of performance evaluation can only be estimates.
(c) Profit measures are used predominately in the context of one year or less, i.e. they tend to have a short-run achievement bias.
(d) Rarely are all factors that determine profitability controllable by the profit centre head.

Some cost centres exert a degree of influence over revenue, however it becomes a judgement call as to whether this is sufficient to make them a profit centre. A restaurant kitchen is a responsibility centre where this dilemma arises frequently. Kitchen staff can affect the profitability of a restaurant due to the time taken to prepare a meal, the quality of food prepared, and willingness to extend and vary the menu. In order to motivate kitchen staff to act in a way that is consistent with increasing revenue, consideration can be given to treating the kitchen as a profit centre.

A significant problem in profit centre accountability concerns what definition of profit should be used. Care should be taken to adhere to the golden rule of only holding a manager accountable for factors that he or she can influence. The exact boundary of a particular manager's sphere of influence is not always clear-cut, however. For example, with respect to insurance, a manager may affect the premium paid due to the level of care taken ensuring adequate security is exercised over an asset held in his or her area. The selection of the insurance policy purchased tends to be a decision taken at the level of head office, however. Who, therefore, should be held accountable for insurance premium expense? Should it be the manager in charge of the asset insured, or the head office official responsible for negotiating and purchasing the insurance premium? This is but one example of many where it is not easy to trace responsibility for a particular expense to a single functional area.

Possible measures of profit that can be used to gauge a profit centre's performance include:

(a) Gross profit – this is appropriate if the profit centre manager's main sphere of influence is limited to sales and cost of sales.
(b) Contribution margin – this is appropriate where the majority of fixed costs are relatively uncontrollable by the profit centre's manager. Over the long term, most fixed expenses are partially controllable, however.
(c) Profit before tax – this measure of profit will frequently include expenses that lie beyond the profit centre manager's scope of influence. Its use can be defended on the ground that it focuses the head of the profit centre on maintaining revenues at a level that cover all expenses, not merely those which he or she can directly influence.

Investment centres

Several particular issues arise in connection with investment centre accountability. In this section, the issues surrounding the scope of an investment centre's account-ability are initially outlined. Following this, performance measures that may be used in investment centres are described.

Scope of investment centre accountability • • •

It is evident from Figure 8.3 that of the four generic types of responsibility centre, investment centres encompass the greatest span of accountability (note how all three dimensions of accountability referred to in Figure 8.2 are captured in an investment centre). The more comprehensive nature of an investment centre's accountability becomes particularly apparent when we recognize the incomplete nature of measuring profit without regard to the investment base that generates profit. If your bank account earned you $200 interest last year, you would not be able to make an informed comment on whether this represents a good rate of return unless you knew what you had deposited in the account, i.e. how big an investment you had made. Imagine a hotel with two restaurants, a large restaurant earning an annual profit of $500,000 and a small restaurant earning an annual profit of $100,000. Due to its higher profit, there may be a tendency to view the large restaurant as the high performer. If, however, the restaurants were established as investment centres and the large restaurant had assets of $10 million (return on investment = 5%), and the small restaurant had assets of $1 million (return on investment = 10%), it becomes apparent that the small restaurant has the better financial performance.

In the above discussion of profit centres, it was noted that a degree of subjectivity tends to be exercised when defining the level of profit that a profit centre head is to be held accountable for. This problem is also present in investment centres, however it becomes exacerbated as judgement has to also be exercised with respect to which hotel assets are to be included in the investment centre's scope of accountability. Again, the golden rule of only holding managers accountable for factors that they can influence should be applied. This signifies that heads of investment centres should only be held accountable for an asset where they can influence whether it is purchased or sold. A further issue concerns the value that should be assigned to assets. This issue can be challenging as there can be a wide discrepancy between the book and market value of a fixed asset. This problem is discussed at some length in advanced management accounting texts, and it is beyond the scope of this text. Nevertheless, it is noteworthy that the vast majority of companies use the book value of assets when monitoring the performance of investment centres.

Performance measures used in investment centres ● ● ●

- *Return on investment*   The most widely used performance measure in investment centres is return on investment (ROI). It is normal to state ROI as a percentage, i.e. Profit ÷ Assets × 100. As noted in Chapter 5, ROI can be sub-divided into a profit margin and an asset turnover component. This signifies that an investment

---

Box 8.1
Highlighting a problem with ROI accountability

Consider the case of GlobalHotels, a large international company. The General Managers of the company's European hotels have been told by the director of European operations to maximize the ROI of their respective hotels. GlobalHotels has a corporate long-term ROI target of 10%. Information relating to last year's performance in its Madrid and Barcelona hotels appears below.

	Madrid hotel	Barcelona hotel
Profit	€20,000	€90,000
Investment	€500,000	€500,000
ROI	4%	18%

Imagine the General Manager of the Madrid Hotel has identified an asset that she believes will provide an annual profit of €18,000 and can be purchased for €200,000. She wants to purchase the asset as it will increase her hotel's ROI to 5.4% [(€20,000 + €18,000) ÷ (€500,000 + €200,000)].

Meanwhile, the General Manager of the Barcelona hotel wants to sell one of his hotel's lower-performing assets for its book vale of €180,000. The sale of this asset will reduce his hotel's annual profit by €21,600. The Barcelona hotel's General Manager has justified his decision to sell on the basis that it will increase his division's ROI from 18% to 21.4% [(€90,000 − €21,600) ÷ (€500,000 − €180,000)].

While the heads of the two divisions are following the Managing Director's directive of maximizing their respective hotel's ROI, the presence of sub-optimal decision making is clear. GlobalHotels is preparing to buy an asset that will provide an ROI of 9% (€18,000 ÷ €200,000) and at the same time to sell an asset that provides an ROI of 12% (€21,600 ÷ €180,000), i.e. it is proposing to buy an asset that earns less than the company's target 10% ROI, and sell an asset that is currently earning a return greater than the company's target 10% ROI. This example highlights how a General Manager who is motivated by a desire to maximize divisional ROI may be acting in a manner that is contrary to corporate interests. This particular problem is avoided if residual income (explained in Box 8.2) is used in the place of ROI.

centre's ROI performance can be further analysed by considering its profit margin performance as well as its asset turnover performance.

There is a particular shortcoming that can arise when managers are encouraged to maximize their investment centre's ROI, however. Managers in high-performing centres might be motivated to sell relatively high-performing assets while managers in low-performing divisions may be motivated to purchase relatively low-performing assets. A scenario outlining how this can occur is presented in Box 8.1.

- *Residual income*   Residual income is calculated as follows:

Investment centre profit – Capital charge
(The capital charge is: Investment centre's assets × Required rate of return)

Residual income can be used instead of ROI to evaluate the performance of an investment centre. Increasing an investment centre's residual income signifies increased performance. An example that shows the calculation of residual income is presented in Box 8.2.

Roles of the budget

It was noted in this chapter's introduction that the budget plays an important role in organizational control as it provides a set of benchmarks used in the appraisal of responsibility centres' performance. Control is somewhat multidimensional, how-ever, and a different facet of control is evident in each of the budgetary roles outlined below. As you read through these budgetary roles, it would be helpful to consider how each role contributes towards maintaining control in a hotel. The main roles of budgets are:

(a) *Authorization*: The budget sets the limit on what a department can spend. This budgetary role is particularly evident in connection with departments that have a high proportion of discretionary expenditure (as noted earlier, this is expenditure where there is no strong cause/effect relationship that can inform management deliberations on how much should be spent). Hotel departments with a high proportion of discretionary expenditure include marketing (the amount of funds allocated to the advertising budget is highly discretionary) and personnel (the amount allocated to training is highly discretionary). Managers in these cost centres can be heard to say 'my budget is $200,000'. What they mean by this is, the budget authorizes $200,000 of expenditure for their cost centre in the current year.

(b) *Forecasting*: The annual budgetary cycle represents a discipline requiring the sales and marketing departments to provide sales estimates for the forthcoming year. These estimates require a forecast of trends and developments in the hotel's relevant commercial environment. Factors to be considered in forecasting include the general economic climate, the timing of significant local events that will affect occupancy levels (e.g. large conventions), and also competitive developments such as the opening date of a new competing hotel.

(c) *Planning*: The budget represents a plan. Managers should ensure that the forecast commercial environment informs their planning. The importance of planning is captured by the adage:

'No business plans to fail. Many that flop, failed to plan'.

Box 8.2
Calculating residual income

The GlobalHotels scenario developed in Box 8.1 will now be used to show the calculation of residual income. The schedule below calculates the residual income for the two hotels prior to the proposed sale and purchase of assets using the formula:

Investment centre profit − Capital charge

(The capital charge is: Investment centre's assets × Required rate of return)

Residual income prior to proposed purchase and sale of assets

Profit	€20,000	€90,000
minus Capital charge	€50,000[a]	€50,000[a]
Residual income	(€30,000)	€40,000
[a]10% × €500,000		

Residual income will now be used to demonstrate that the changes proposed by the General Managers in the two hotels should not be made.

Residual income following proposed purchase and sale of assets

	Madrid hotel	Barcelona hotel
Profit	€38,000	€68,400
minus Capital charge	€70,000[a]	€32,000[b]
Residual income	(€42,000)	€36,400
[a]10% × €700,000		
[b]10% × €320,000		

Note how the residual income of both hotels would decline if the proposed sale and acquisition of assets were to take place. The Madrid hotel's residual income would decline from − €30,000 to − €42,000, and the Barcelona hotel's residual income would decline from €40,000 to €36,400. If the Director of European operations were to use maximization of residual income rather than maximization of ROI as the performance target for the hotels, the two hotel general managers would be motivated to act in a manner that is more consistent with the hotel group's overall interests. This highlights how using residual income as a performance measure can result in better outcomes than using ROI to motivate managers. Despite this, ROI is much more widely used than residual income in investment centres. This may be because managers find it more intuitively appealing to conceive of return as a percentage of assets.

(d) *Communication and coordination*: Preparation of a budget requires extensive negotiation between members of the organization. This negotiation comprises vertical communication (superiors discussing appropriate budgetary targets with subordinates), and also horizontal communication (cross-departmental discussion). Communication is important as the information shared can signify a key learning phase for management. It is also a process that requires compromise between different parts of the organization holding incompatible aspirations. Without the discipline imposed by the annual budgetary cycle, different areas of the hotel might increasingly pursue irreconcilable objectives (e.g. marketing seeking a significant increase in occupancy in a year of restricted room availability due to the rooms division's plans to conduct room refurbishments). This highlights how horizontal communication triggered by the budgetary cycle facilitates improved organizational coordination.

(e) *Motivation*: The budget provides a quantified performance target to be strived for. An enduring finding of psychological research suggests that a quantified target provides management with a point of focus and greater motivation than when a manager has no target other than being told to 'Do the best you can'.

(f) *Performance evaluation*: As already noted, the budget represents an important vehicle generating benchmarks that can be used as a basis for assessing performance.

(g) *Attention directing*: If something is monitored and recorded in the budget, it is more likely to be regarded as important. The adage 'What gets measured gets managed' is pertinent here. Imagine that a hotel has decided to analyse its restaurant activity in a manner that distinguishes between sales made to hotel guests and sales made to customers not staying at the hotel. When budgeting for restaurant sales, two factors would drive projected sales to hotel guests, the projected number of guests staying at the hotel and the projected proportion of hotel guests that dine in the hotel's restaurant. If the budget were to be prepared in this manner, it would direct management's attention to a dimension of performance that may have hitherto not been accounted for, i.e. the proportion of hotel guests that dine in the hotel's restaurant. A reference in the budget to the proportion of hotel guests that dine at the hotel's restaurant, will likely result in managers focusing more attention on this dimension of performance.

This range of budgetary roles highlights the degree to which there are a host of ways that hospitality managers are affected by budgeting. To illustrate one particular example of a manager's interaction with the budget, Case 8.1 shows how a human resource manager will draw on budget information when determining staffing needs.

Case 8.1

Financial Decision Making in Action –
Human Resource Managers' use of budgets when planning staffing levels

Imagine a manager in a hotel's human resource department is attempting to determine staffing needs in housekeeping in the first quarter of a year. Staffing level plans are based on the hotel's sales department's estimates of daily room sales which are developed in connection with each year's budget (it is normal for these forecasts to be updated during the year as events affecting demand occur).

For several years, the hotel's human resource department has applied the standard that housekeeping maids should clean 20 rooms in a standard 8-hour working day. By dividing the projected daily room sales by the 20 rooms per day standard, the human resource manager can determine the number of staff necessary to complete the projected room cleaning workload. Once projected staffing needs have been determined, the human resource manager can identify those times when the hotel is likely to experience a surplus or shortage of labour.

This calculation procedure is outlined in the schedule below. The 'room sales' column lists the projected daily room sales, and the 'performance standard' column records the number of rooms a maid should clean in a day. The 'labour days required' is calculated by dividing 'room sales' by the 'performance standard'. The 'full-time staff available' column records the hotel's projected supply of maids. Finally, the 'adjustment needed' column highlights when there is a projected surplus or shortage of labour (brackets highlight a shortage).

Day	Room sales	Performance standard	Labour days required	Full-time staff available	Adjustment needed
Monday	150	20	7.5	9	1.5
Tuesday	150	20	7.5	9	1.5
Wednesday	160	20	8.0	9	1.0
Thursday	160	20	8.0	9	1.0
Friday	220	20	11.0	9	(2.0)
Saturday	220	20	11.0	9	(2.0)
Sunday	180	20	9.0	9	0

From the information developed, the human resource manager will note a projected surplus of staff on Mondays to Thursdays and a shortage on Fridays and Saturdays. This information would be used when developing staffing rosters. Attempts could be made to encourage staff to take any planned days off work on Mondays to Thursdays. In addition, the human resource department may feel it necessary to schedule some overtime or for more casual staff to be recruited to cover the projected labour shortage on Fridays and Saturdays.

Behavioural aspects of budgeting

Traditionally, the behavioural aspects of control systems have been given little attention, and accountants have tended to be viewed as technocrats with little interest in the behavioural implications of control systems. More recently, however, there appears to be a growing awareness of the behavioural implications of budgetary control. Consistent with this development, the following four major budget-related behavioural issues are now discussed:

(a) Budgets as targets
(b) Budgets and performance evaluation
(c) Manager participation in budget setting
(d) Politically charged nature of budgeting.

Budgets as targets

We noted above that one of the roles of the budget is to motivate. Setting budgetary targets in a manner consistent with stimulating high motivation requires considerable managerial judgement. Psychological researchers suggest that higher motivation results when targets are just beyond reach, but not so hard that the manager views them as unreasonable (i.e. the budgetary target is perceived as challenging but not unfair). If budgetary targets are set too high, managers might view them as unreasonable and will lose motivation. This view on the appropriate degree of difficulty in budgetary targets raises two issues:

(a) As we all differ in the way we respond to challenging targets, senior managers responsible for setting budgetary targets should consider each subordinate manager's psychological nature and likely reaction to a challenging goal.

(b) If the desire to set high targets results in some targets not being achieved, the budget will lose some of its value as a coordinating device. For example, if the desire to set challenging targets results in budgeted sales levels set 5% above management's sales forecasts, there is a high likelihood that the budgeted sales levels will not be achieved. The budgeted level of sales drives operational plans, however, and areas such as F&B, rooms and laundry use the sales budget as a basis for planning their staffing and purchasing needs. Accordingly, failure to achieve a budgeted sales level can compromise planning and result in wasted resources. This problem, which stems from two competing roles of the budget (i.e. the motivation and coordinating roles), is diagrammatically depicted in Figure 8.4.

In Figure 8.4, the diagonal line labelled 'budget difficulty level' shows how an increasingly difficult budget signifies the setting of increasingly high performance standards. The 'actual performance' line is positively sloping as a result of the

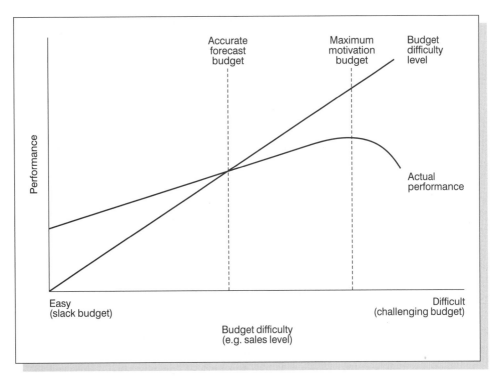

Figure 8.4 Budget difficulty and management performance (adapted from Emmanuel *et al.*, 1990)

motivating effect of the increasingly challenging budget. After a critical point, however, the actual performance will decrease. This is because if the budget is set at exceedingly challenging levels, it will lose its power to motivate (managers feel like 'throwing in the towel'). From the perspective of stimulating maximum management performance, the budget should be set at the level identified as 'maximum motivation budget'. From the perspective of optimizing the budget's use as a coordinating vehicle, however, it should be set at the level identified as 'accurate forecast budget', i.e. the point at which the 'budget difficulty level' and 'actual performance' lines intersect.

There is no easy answer as to whether the budget should be set at the 'accurate forecast' or the 'maximum motivation' level, as the nature and priorities of each business unit need to be considered. If high emphasis is attached to accounting performance measures in a hierarchical organization, failure of a subordinate to achieve a budgetary target will carry unfavourable budgetary performance implications for the subordinate's superior. As a result, in this situation we can expect the 'accurate forecast' budget to predominate over the 'maximum motivation' budget.

Budgets and performance evaluation

Budgets represent an important basis for monitoring the performance of managers. Management rewards that result from achieving budgetary targets include salary increments, promotion, and enhanced peer and self-esteem. In the light of the significance of budgets, managers frequently find budget setting to be a highly emotionally charged organizational activity. To the extent possible, it is important that managers are set equally difficult budgets, as perceived inequity can be disruptive and adversely affect morale.

Budgets cannot always serve as a strong basis for appraising performance, however. Before the budget is used in this manner, the factors outlined in Box 8.3 should be considered.

Manager participation in budget setting

Participation refers to the degree to which managers are involved in setting the budgetary targets for which they will be held accountable. Three benefits derive from greater participation:

(a) It can give rise to a more informed budgetary process, e.g. a manager working in a particular restaurant may well have a more intimate understanding of operational factors in the restaurant than the director of F&B.
(b) Greater participation in target setting is likely to result in a manager feeling greater commitment to achieving the target set (i.e. internalizing the budget goal).
(c) Participation in budget setting facilitates organizational learning as it provides managers with the opportunity to better understand the rationale for the organization's direction.

A danger arises with high budget participation, however, as it provides managers with an opportunity to influence the setting of targets in a way that makes them relatively easy to achieve. When the budget contains easy targets, it is described as containing 'slack'.

Box 8.3
Factors affecting the accountability of a department's performance

Before a manager attempts to use the budget to appraise the performance of a department, the following factors should be considered:

(a) Does the key dimension of a manager's work lend itself to accounting measurement? The manager of a restaurant can be held accountable for restaurant profit, and the manager of housekeeping held accountable for the average cost of cleaning a room. In discretionary cost centres such as personnel, public relations and accounting, however, it is difficult to determine a key dimension of performance that lends itself to accounting measurement.

(b) To what extent is the performance of the responsibility centre in question affected by the actions of managers in other business units? Consider the case of a laundry manager. Laundry is a service department providing clean laundry to other hotel departments. Laundry managers frequently complain that a particular department's low inventory of linen necessitates the provision of fast turnarounds. Maintaining a fast turnaround time can require laundering in uneconomic batch sizes, i.e. starting a washing cycle before the washing machine is filled to capacity. If departments such as F&B and rooms have the ability to require fast laundry turnarounds, the laundry department's independence is compromised, and part of its cost structure will be driven by the actions of other hotel responsibility centres. Where this type of situation exists, it is inappropriate to place emphasis on budget achievement as a performance indicator. High interdepartmental dependency is often evident in restaurant management where sales can be affected by the hotel's occupancy levels. In fact, restaurant sales can be affected more by the hotel's effectiveness in marketing rooms than the restaurant manager's actions.

(c) Is the hotel activity in question relatively new and therefore difficult to budget for? Imagine that a new tennis facility has been opened in a hotel that emphasizes the achievement of budgetary targets. As it will be difficult to forecast the expected court usage in the first year, care should be taken not to place too much emphasis on the budget when appraising the performance of the tennis complex manager. This highlights the fact that achievement of a budgeted target can be affected as much by forecasting accuracy as good performance.

In addition to securing an appropriate level of participation from subordinates when setting budgets, it is also important that senior managers are involved. The involvement of senior managers facilitates vigilance over any tendency for budgetary slack creation. In addition, it provides senior managers with the opportunity to develop their understanding of management issues confronting subordinates and to enhance the general perception of the budget's importance. If the budgetary process is not perceived to be important, its power as a vehicle of organizational control will be adversely affected.

Political aspects of budgeting

Budget setting represents a major process of negotiation that affects the entire organization. This negotiation can be seen as vital to effective organizational functioning. The budget is the most powerful vehicle driving the reconciliation of potentially conflicting aspirations held by managers representing the many disparate parts of the organization. When we consider the degree of compromise that has to be achieved, it is not surprising that managers frequently comment on frustration experienced during the budget-setting process. In its capacity of reconciling differences within functions, across functions, divisions and the corporate office, the budget department will have to frequently return budgets to initiators for revision. During this process, many managers will discover that some organizational aspirations that they may have held for some time will not materialize. It is therefore not surprising that budget setting can become highly political. Political aspects of budgeting include individuals competing for resources in a manner designed to gain the best outcome for themselves, and managers informally developing coalitions in order to increase their bargaining strength.

This potential for politics in the budget-setting process is exacerbated when we recognize that for many managers the budget identifies the upper limit for their expenditure. The size of a manager's budget is frequently related to the manager's perceived organizational importance and power. Accordingly, ambitious managers can be expected to be focused on securing large budgets for their departments. Conflicting ambitions of managers provide further scope for a wide range of political game playing during the budget-setting process.

Technical aspects of budget preparation

In this section, the preparation of budget schedules will be illustrated by means of a worked example. This demonstrates preparation of the purchases, production and labour cost budget schedules in a restaurant setting.

Before considering these specific budget schedules, it is important to note that from a technical stand-point, the most important element of the budget is the budgeted sales level. This is because the sales estimate drives much of the remainder of the budget. In the following worked example, note how budgeted sales information is a prerequisite to the preparation of the budget schedules. It should not be forgotten, however, that as sales are affected by environmental factors that are external to the organization, projecting next year's sales is perhaps the most difficult aspect of forecasting in the budgetary cycle. Further, the degree to which sales are volatile in the hotel industry was noted in the first chapter.

When we think of a production setting such as a kitchen, we tend to think of activities as they occur. Figure 8.5 depicts this sequence, i.e. food ingredients are purchased, kitchen staff then use these ingredients in the preparation of meals, and finally the meals produced are sold in the restaurant.

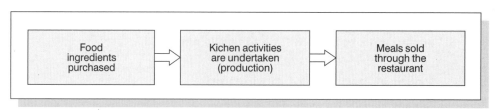

Figure 8.5 Kitchen and restaurant physical sequencing of events

When producing a budget, however, we need to conceive of these events in reverse order. This is because the amount of food ingredients purchased will be driven by the projected kitchen production activity, and the amount of kitchen production activity is determined by food sales made in the restaurant. As restaurant sales drive kitchen production activities, and kitchen production activities drive food ingredients purchased, if we are attempting to prepare a budget for food ingredients purchased we must first prepare a sales budget and then prepare a kitchen production budget. This sequencing of the preparation of budget schedules relating to the kitchen is depicted in Figure 8.6.

The remainder of the chapter works through an example that demonstrates how budgeted schedules for purchases, production and labour costs can be prepared. In this example, note how certain budget schedules can only be prepared once other budgeted schedules have been completed.

Imagine a large New Orleans hotel complex 'the JazzFest' which makes its own pastries. The JazzFest hotel sells the pastries in its three restaurants and coffee shop bar. In addition, an outside baker purchases any excess pastries for cost price + 10%.

Ingredients required for pastry production include flour, fruit, margarine, salt and water. 1 kilogram of flour is used per tray of pastries produced. Flour costs $1.50 per kilogram. At the end of the month, the pastry chef likes to always maintain in stores enough flour to support 10% of the following month's production.

Following preparation of the pastry dough, pastries are baked on trays, with each tray containing 25 pastries. To cater for any unexpected increases in demand, at the end of any month, the chef likes to have 5% of the following month's projected demand for pastries stored in the freezer (freezer storage is handled on a rotating basis with no pastries held in the freezer for more than 10 days). On 1 April it is anticipated that 125 pastries will be held in the freezer.

The head chef has developed two schedules, the first providing details of pastry production labour costs (Exhibit 8.1), and the second providing information on anticipated demand for pastries over the next four months (Exhibit 8.2).

This information is sufficient to allow preparation of:

1 The budgeted pastry production schedule for April, May and June
2 The budgeted purchase of flour schedule for April and May
3 The budgeted pastry labour cost schedule for April, May and June.

It is evident from Figure 8.6 that the purchases budget cannot be prepared until the production budget has been prepared. In addition, as the labour cost information

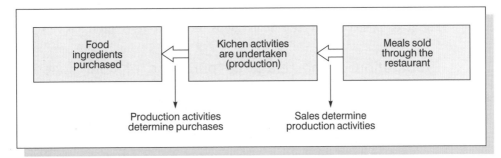

Figure 8.6 The sequence in which budget schedules relating to kitchen activities are prepared

Exhibit 8.1
JazzFest pastry production labour costs

	Hourly rate	Time taken to produce 10 trays of pastries
Pastry chef	$22	5 hours
Junior kitchen staff	$14	2 hours

Exhibit 8.2
JazzFest projected sales demand for pastries

	April	May	June	July
Projected pastry sales	2,500	3,000	3,000	2,500

provided in the chef's first schedule relates to hourly production costs, the budgeted labour cost schedule can only be prepared once the pastry production budget schedule has been finalized. As will be seen, preparation of the budgeted production and purchase schedules becomes somewhat complicated by movements in the opening and closing balances of inventory.

Preparation of the budgeted pastry production schedule

An easy way to prepare a budgeted production schedule involves adding the inventory balance required at the end of the period to the production throughput required to support the period's sales (this aggregated figure can be referred to as 'number of pastries to be made available'). The amount of pastries that must be produced in the period can then be determined by deducting the number of pastries held at the beginning of the period (i.e. we do not need to produce what is already available at the beginning of the period). Note that the number of pastries at the end of a particular month (closing inventory required) is the same as the number of pastries at the beginning of the next month (opening inventory balance). JazzFest's budgeted pastry production schedule is presented as Exhibit 8.3.

Preparation of the budgeted purchase of flour schedule

Having determined the monthly production of pastries, we are now in a position to prepare the budgeted purchases of flour schedule. Projected purchases for June cannot be determined as we are unable to budget July's production of pastries (we do not know August's projected sales and this figure is needed to determine July's closing inventory required), which is necessary to determine the flour inventory required at the end of June. When preparing the budgeted purchases schedule we

Exhibit 8.3
JazzFest budgeted production of pastries

	April	May	June
Closing inventory required (5% of following month's sales)	150	150	125
+ Sales	2,500	3,000	3,000
Number of pastries to be made available	2,650	3,150	3,125
− Opening inventory balance	125	150	150
Production of pastries	2,525	3,000	2,975

Exhibit 8.4
JazzFest budgeted purchase of flour schedule (in kilograms)

	April	May
Closing inventory of flour required (following month's production ÷ 25 × 0.1)	12.0	11.9
+ Flour necessary to support production (this month's production ÷ 25)	101.0	120.0
Amount of flour to be made available	113.0	131.9
− Opening inventory balance (current month's production ÷ 25 × 0.1)	10.1	12.0
Flour purchased in kilograms	102.9	119.9
Flour purchased in $ (kg purchases × $1.50)	$154.35	$179.85

can follow the approach taken to prepare the budgeted production schedule. Determining the closing kilograms of flour required involves dividing the number of pastries to be produced in the following month by 25 (there are 25 pastries per tray) and then multiplying by 0.1 (enough flour to support 10% of next month's demand must be held in stock at the month end). Once the kilograms of flour to be purchased in the month has been determined, this amount can be multiplied by $1.50 to determine the cost of flour to be purchased. JazzFest's budgeted purchase of flour schedule is presented as Exhibit 8.4.

Preparation of the budgeted labour cost for pastry production schedule

Compared to the budgeted production and purchases schedules, preparation of the budgeted labour cost schedule is relatively straightforward. From Exhibit 8.1 we can see that it takes a pastry chef 5 hours to produce 10 trays of pastries, therefore 1 tray requires half an hour of pastry chef labour. As these chefs are paid $22 per hour, it costs $11 of pastry chef labour to make 1 tray of pastries. As 2 hours of junior kitchen staff labour is involved in the production of 10 trays of pastries, 1 pastry tray requires 0.2 hours of junior kitchen staff labour. The preparation of 1 tray of pastries therefore costs $2.80 of junior kitchen staff labour ($14 × 0.2). JazzFest's budgeted labour cost for pastry production schedule is presented as Exhibit 8.5.

Exhibit 8.5
JazzFest budgeted labour cost for pastry production

	April	May	June
Number of pastry trays produced (pastry production ÷ 25)	101	120	119
Pastry chef labour cost ($11 per tray)	$1,111.0	$1,320	$1,309.0
Junior kitchen staff labour cost ($2.8 per tray)	$282.8	$336.0	$333.2
Total labour cost	$1,393.8	$1,656.0	$1,642.2

Summary

In this chapter we have reviewed responsibility accounting and budgeting. Responsibility accounting refers to the way that different managers are held accountable for different aspects of an organization's activities. The main types of responsibility units are cost, revenue, profit and investment centres. We noted the importance of budgetary control in light of the many organizational roles performed by budgeting. In addition, we considered behavioural implications of budgeting and reviewed how to prepare a restaurant's purchases, production and labour cost budget schedules.

Having read the chapter you should now know:

- What issues need to be considered when deciding whether a responsibility centre should be a cost, revenue, profit or investment centre
- How to compute residual income as an alternative to using ROI when measuring the performance of an investment centre
- The main organizational roles of budgeting
- Behavioural issues that need to be considered when using budgetary controls
- How to produce a purchases, production and labour cost budget schedule.

References

Atkinson, H., Berry, A. and Jarvis, R. (1995) *Business Accounting for Hospitality and Tourism & Leisure*, International Thomson Publishing, London, Chapters 15 and 16.

Carnegie, G., Jones, S., Norris, G., Wigg, R. and Williams, B. (1999) *Accounting: Financial and Organizational Decision Making*, Irwin/McGraw-Hill, New York, Chapter 25.

Coltman, M. M. and Jagels, M. G. (2001) *Hospitality Management Accounting*, 7th edition, John Wiley, Chichester, Chapter 9.

Drury, C. (1992) *Management and Cost Accounting*, 3rd edition, Chapman and Hall, London, Chapters 16 and 20.

Emmanuel, C., Otley, D. and Merchant, K. (1990) *Accounting for Management Control*, 2nd edition, Chapman and Hall, London, Chapter 7.

Hansen, D. R. and Mowen, M. M. (1996) *Management Accounting*, 4th edition, South-Western, Cincinnati, OH, Chapter 8.

Harris, P. (1999) *Profit Planning*, Butterworth-Heinemann, Oxford, Chapter 8.

Kotas, R. (1999) *Management Accounting for Hospitality and Tourism*, 3rd edition, International Thomson Publishing, London, Chapter 12.

Kotas, R. and Conlan, M. (1997) *Hospitality Accounting*, 5th edition, International Thomson Publishing, London, Chapter 24.

Owen, G. (1994) *Accounting for Hospitality, Tourism & Leisure*, Pitman Publishing, London, Chapter 14.

Schmidgall, R. F. (1997) *Hospitality Industry Managerial Accounting*, 4th edition, Educational Institute – American Hotel & Motel Association, East Lansing, MI, Chapter 10.

Problems

✓ indicates that a solution appears at the back of the text

✓ 8.1 Describe the way in which a responsibility accounting system is closely linked to an organization's budgeting system.

✓ 8.2 Joe Smith is the stores and purchasing manager for the Pristine Waters hotel and golfing complex located on one of Australia's Whitsunday Islands. Joe receives purchase requisitions from other department heads in the organization. When he took the job, Joe was informed that he had responsibility for servicing the purchasing needs of other department heads. In the case of rarely purchased items, it is customary for Joe to be provided with specifications from the department initiating the request.

In June last year, the hotel secured the contract for a large conference to take place in February this year. As a result of September and October meetings with the conference organizers, it was decided that the conference would include a high-tech 'real-time' link-up to a similar conference being held at the same time in the USA. This live link-up was given significant prominence in the conference's promotional material. To facilitate the link up, the hotel needed to buy a particular computer accessory. Maxine Bromwich, the head of the hotel's banquet and conference department, informed Joe of the need to purchase this computer accessory in late November last year. At that time she also informed him that it would be needed for the February convention. Following initial inquiries, Joe discovered that his regular supplier of computer equipment did not stock the part. He called many other potential suppliers and finally found a computer specialist located in Perth that agreed to supply the required accessory. Joe mailed the purchase order to the chosen supplier in mid-December. In mid-January, following his annual three week holiday, Joe telephoned the supplier to ensure that all was well with the shipment. At that time the supplier informed him that the computer part was on its way. A week before the conference, the part had not arrived so Joe called again, and again he was told not to worry and that the part had left on time. Two days before the conference start date the part had still not arrived. Joe called again and it was discovered that the part had been mailed to the wrong address.

At the commencement of the conference, Maxine Bromwich informed delegates that due to a technical hitch, the forum that was to involve the link up to the US conference had been cancelled. This caused considerable ill-feeling among delegates and as part of a damage limitation exercise, they were reimbursed with $145. This represents the price charged to delegates for one night's accommodation at the hotel. This damage limitation exercise signified a loss of $60,900 ($145 × 420 delegates) for the hotel.

Explain in one page or less, how this $60,900 loss should be accounted for. Your answer should include an appropriately reasoned justification for the answer you provide. Should it be charged to Joe Smith's purchasing department, or should it be charged to Maxine Bromwich's banquet and conference department? Maxine Bromwich has complained that if it is to be charged to her department, she will be unable to meet her department's budgeted profit for the year.

✓ 8.3   The 'Dreaming of Stars' company owns a chain of large hotels. Its hotel located on America's eastern seaboard is its largest and comprises a casino, four restaurants, extensive conference facilities, and a health club.

Over the last month, business activity at the hotel has been significantly down following a radical political group's terrorist threat to blow up a plane while in flight over American airspace. The terrorist threat has been taken very seriously by air aviation authorities and the matter has received considerable attention from the news media.

Senior management at the hotel feel this is a largely uncontrollable setback, but that demand should return to normal levels in a couple of months' time. In the meantime, many unskilled workers have been temporarily laid off. Highly skilled chefs, however, are likely to find alternative employment if laid off and the director of F&B has argued convincingly that it would be to the long-term detriment of Dreaming of Stars if they were to be allowed to leave. As a result of this stance, the highly skilled chefs have been employed in various menial facility maintenance tasks such as maintaining gardens, building storage racks in the store rooms and painting some of the hotel rooms.

Upon receipt of his most recent performance report, the head of the maintenance department was left fuming. The performance report indicated a 70% adverse variance compared to budgeted expenditure for the month. He went straight to the accounting office and complained:

> This just isn't fair. The reason I'm 70% over budget this month is I'm using that elitist bunch of pastry cutters to do work that is going to get their fingernails dirty. I normally pay my boys $9 per hour, this crowd comes in at $13.50 per hour. These guys know I can't lay them off. They're treating work in my department likes it's a joke, and once they've gone back behind revolving doors I'm going to have to work my boys overtime in order to meet our scheduled maintenance for the year.

Required • • •
This is a fine example of how the accounting system can give rise to undesirable ill-feeling within a company. What do you see as the best course of action for the accountant?

8.4   As part of a consulting assignment you have been asked to review the appropriateness of a hotel's responsibility accounting system. In the course of conducting your review, you become aware of a degree of dissatisfaction felt by the head of the hotel's facility maintenance department.

The facility maintenance department was established as a cost centre a number of years ago. In recent years the department has experienced problems containing costs within limits established by the budget. One particular area of concern to the head of the department is the cost of repairs to the hotel's three staff buses which have recently been involved in a series of minor accidents. Most of these accidents have been no more serious than bodywork dents resulting from reversing into one of the concrete pylons that surround the hotel car park's perimeter. Consistent with repairs to most of the hotel's assets, bus repairs are managed by the facility maintenance department. In light of this, the cost of performing the repair work is charged to the facility maintenance department. It is generally accepted that this department contains the greatest expertise and local contacts to effectively oversee asset repairs.

Three part-time employees are employed by the hotel to drive the staff buses. As their pick-up schedules are determined by the residential location of rostered staff, the drivers report to the head of personnel. This arrangement facilitates the flow of paperwork as the personnel department maintains staff roster records and also the database containing staff members' addresses.

The head of the facility management cost centre has complained to you that he has asked the bus drivers to take more care when driving the buses. He believes, however, that the drivers take little notice of him as they feel primarily accountable to the head of personnel.

Required . . .
What recommendation would you make in your consulting report concerning the specific lines of accountability uncovered by this case?

8.5 The Sea Breeze is a 200-room family resort hotel in Blackpool, Northern England that is open 7 days per week. It has one restaurant and restaurant sales are only made to hotel guests. During the next quarter beginning 1 April, the rooms manager anticipates an average occupancy of 70% and an average of 2.5 people in each occupied room. Restaurant records indicate that 90% of guests eat breakfast, 30% each lunch and 60% eat dinner at the restaurant. The average contribution earned from covers served in the restaurant is £4 for breakfast, £8 for lunch and £12 for dinner.

Required . . .
Calculate the estimated contribution (revenue – variable costs) that will be earned at Sea Breeze's restaurant in the next quarter beginning 1 April.

8.6 One of the kitchens in a large Las Vegas hotel complex produces fresh local fruit jam. The jam is placed into expensive jars moulded with the hotel's logo, a depiction of tumbling dice. The jam is labelled 'Lucky Dip'. For several years a jar of 'Lucky Dip' has been given as a complimentary gift to all guests staying in the hotel, and the marketing department feel that this promotion has been well received by guests. Some jam is also sold through the hotel's gift shop.

The company accountant has provided the head chef with the following schedule that outlines the anticipated demand for jam in the next four months.

	Complimentaries	Shop sales
October	1,000 jars	100 jars
November	800 jars	80 jars
December	1,200 jars	120 jars
January	700 jars	70 jars

The chef likes to have 10% of next month's jam demand already produced and in stock by the month end. On 30 September, 120 jars of 'Lucky Dip' were held as inventory.

The chef runs a fruit-stocking policy of holding 5% of next month's fruit needs in inventory. On 30 September, 20 kg of fruit was held in inventory. Each jar of 'Lucky Dip' requires 0.5 kg of fruit. It has been estimated that the fruit will cost $2 per kg during the year's final quarter.

Required • • •

Prepare a purchases budget for fruit for October and November.

8.7   The manager of Ritzy Rooms, a small 40-room Saskatchewan roadside motel, is seeking a $90,000 bank loan bearing a 10% annual rate of interest. Mr Scroogy, the manager of the bank considering the loan application, requires the motel to produce a budgeted profit and loss statement for next year, 20X1. Mr Scroogy requires this information to help him assess Ritzy Rooms' credit risk.

Ritzy Rooms' accountant has assembled the following schedule of information to facilitate preparation of 20X1's budgeted profit and loss statement.

Number of single rooms	10
Estimated occupancy of single rooms	70%
Single rooms' projected average room rate	$50
Average contribution earned on single rooms	85%
Number of double rooms	30
Estimated occupancy of double rooms	40%
Double rooms' projected average room rate	$70
Average contribution earned on double rooms	90%
Operating fixed costs per annum (not including loan interest)	$180,000
Tax rate levied on profit after deduction of interest expense	40%

Required • • •

(a) Assuming the motel is open for 360 days in the year, prepare the budgeted profit and loss statement for 20X1. Include the interest on the $90,000 loan in the budgeted statement.

(b) Mr Scroogy has a policy of not lending to any business that cannot demonstrate a projected times interest earned ratio greater than 3 (the times interest earned ratio is described in Chapter 5). Based on the budgeted figures, does Ritzy Rooms satisfy the bank manager's loan approval requirement?

Flexible budgeting and variance analysis

After studying this chapter, you should have developed an appreciation of:

1 The value of using flexible budgets

2 A systematic approach that can be used when preparing variance analyses

3 The insights resulting from variance analyses

4 The nature and merits of benchmarking.

Introduction

This chapter builds on some of the budget and responsibility accounting issues introduced in the previous chapter. First, we examine **flexible budgeting**, a technique that represents a slight refinement of the static budgeting approach described in the previous chapter. In a static budgeting system, a budget is rigid in the sense that it is not modified once the actual volume of sales is known. While this approach is used extensively, some managers find it helpful to flex budgets up or down in line with the actual volume of sales achieved. Failure to accurately predict the volume of sales is a major factor causing many significant differences between the static budget and actual performance. Under flexible budgeting, however, the effect of a hotel selling more or less than was originally projected is excluded from differences between the actual and budgeted performance. Exclusion of this factor is significant because, by definition, managers in cost centres exert little influence on sales volumes. If managers in cost centres cannot affect sales, why should the effect of selling more than anticipated be included in a variance used to gauge their performance?

A second technique introduced in this chapter is **variance analysis**. 'Variance' is the accounting term for any difference between an actual and budgeted amount. Variance analysis relates to the responsibility accounting issues introduced in the previous chapter as it involves the isolation of factors contributing to variances. Greater appreciation of what factors lie behind a particular variance supports responsibility accounting through enhanced accountability. The chapter concludes with a description of benchmarking, a technique that has commanded increasing attention as a financial management tool in the last few years.

Flexible budgeting

As just noted, the budget schedules developed in the previous chapter were based on a single set of estimated levels of monthly activity, i.e. the projected sales demand for pastries. A shortcoming of this static approach to budgeting is that invariably the actual level of activity achieved will differ from the budgeted activity level. Can you think of a situation where a restaurant manager is able to exactly predict the number of covers that will be sold in a year? Discrepancies between budgeted and actual activity levels result in variances for revenue and variable costs. These variances are not necessarily reflective of performance, however. A part of each observed variance would be attributable to the fact that, in most businesses, it is almost impossible to predict exactly the volume of sales in a forthcoming accounting period.

To illustrate this issue with an example, imagine that a restaurant budgeted $8,000 for food costs in a period when it was estimated that 1,200 covers would be sold. If the restaurant actually incurred food costs of $8,400 and 1,320 covers were sold, is it reasonable to conclude there has been poor food cost management? A static budget would highlight that the cost of food for the period was $400 over budget ($8,000 – $8,400). This suggestion of poor food cost management is highly misleading, however. Food costs are variable (they increase in line with the volume of sales achieved), therefore we need to recognize the impact of the restaurant selling more covers than anticipated. In reality, the restaurant has been 10% busier than anticipated ([1,320 – 1,200] ÷ 1,200 × 100), yet food costs are only 5% above budget ([$8,400 – $8,000] ÷ $8,000 × 100). To overcome this problem of potentially misleading variances that can arise when using static budgets, we can prepare a flexible budget.

Exhibit 9.1
The Poplars Hotel Rooms Department
Flexible budget performance report – month ended 30 April 20X1

	Actual	Static budget	Flexible budget (90% of static budget)	Flexible budget variance[a]
Room sales	1,800	2,000	1,800	
	$	$	$	$
Revenue (sales)	207,000	220,000	198,000	9,000 (F)
Variable Costs:				
Labour	12,015	12,000	10,800	1,215 (U)
Cleaning materials	5,200	6,000	5,400	200 (F)
Contribution Margin	189,785	202,000	181,800	7,985 (F)
Fixed Costs	49,000	50,000	50,000	1,000 (F)
Operating Profit	140,785	152,000	131,800	8,985 (F)

[a]The difference between the actual and the flexible budget amounts.
U denotes unfavourable variances; F denotes favourable variances.

Flexible budgeting can be achieved by preparing a series of budgets for different levels of sales activity. More usually, however, once the actual volume of sales is known, the static budget is proportionately 'flexed' up (if the actual volume of sales is above the budgeted amount), or down (if the actual volume of sales is below the budgeted amount). The resulting flexible budget will show what costs and revenues should have been for the actual level of activity achieved. Any unfavourable cost variances between actual performance and the flexible budget will be attributable to inefficient use of resources (e.g. labour or material inefficiencies, etc.) or purchasing resources at prices above what was estimated when the budget was originally set.

Exhibit 9.1 provides an illustration of a flexible budget and also the computation of flexible budget variances. To understand how the flexible budget was prepared, initially focus on the first two data columns, i.e. the actual and static budget information. As the 1,800 actual room sales achieved are 90% of the 2,000 room sales projected when the static budget was prepared, the flexible budget is set at 90% of the static budget. This signifies that all budget items that move with sales volume (i.e. revenue and variable costs) are recorded in the flexible budget at 90% of the amounts in the static budget.* Fixed costs in the flexible budget are unaltered from the value in the static budget as fixed costs are assumed to be unaffected by varying

* Alternatively, the unit price or cost for each line of the static budget could have been determined. These amounts could then be multiplied by the actual sales volume achieved to derive the flexible budget amount. For example, the unit price of sales in the static budget must be $110, as $220,000 revenue was budgeted for 2,000 rooms sold. Multiplying $110 by the actual activity level, i.e. 1,800 rooms sold, we find that the budgeted revenue to be included in the flexible budget is $198,000 ($110 × 1,800).

levels of activity. Once the flexible budget has been prepared, the flexible budget variances for each line can be determined by calculating the difference between the actual results and the flexible budget amounts (final column in Exhibit 9.1). These variances are labelled 'U' (unfavourable) if the direction of the variance carries a negative impact on the actual profit level relative to the budget, and 'F' (favourable) if the direction of the variance carries a positive impact on the actual profit level relative to the budget.

The following observations can be made with respect to this flexible budget performance report:

- The $9,000 flexible budget revenue variance signifies that average actual room rates charged exceeded the budgeted room rate. If actual revenue is compared to the revenue in the static budget, we find an unfavourable variance of $13,000 ($220,000 – $207,000). This variance stems primarily from the fact that the number of room sales is below the static budget and masks the fact that the average room rate achieved of $115 ($207,000 ÷ 1,800) compares favourably with the budgeted room rate of $110 ($220,000 ÷ 2,000). It could be that setting the average room rate above the budgeted room rate has contributed to the number of rooms sold being below budget.
- Variable labour costs have a $1,215 unfavourable flexible budget variance. This signifies that the labour has performed inefficiently and/or labour's actual hourly rate of pay is greater than what was budgeted for. It could be that in light of the static budget (2,000 room sales predicted) more than the required amount of staff were rostered. The extent of labour's unfavourable performance is not highlighted if the actual performance is compared to the static budget as this reveals only a small $15 unfavourable variance.
- The cleaning materials have a $200 favourable flexible budget variance. This signifies that the materials have been used efficiently and/or they have been purchased at an average price below the budgeted price.
- As noted above, fixed costs are not 'flexed' when producing a flexible budget. This is because they do not vary with levels of activity over the short term. The $1,000 favourable fixed cost variance signifies that fixed-cost activities have been conducted efficiently and/or items have been bought for prices below what was budgeted for. As staff salaries can represent a significant proportion of fixed costs, it might be that annual salary rates of pay are below what was budgeted for, or a salaried position was vacant for some of the month.
- Overall, there is a favourable flexible budget operating profit variance of $8,985. The primary factor driving this favourable variance is the $9,000 favourable flexible budget revenue variance (rooms sold at above the budgeted rate).

Variance analysis

We have just seen that a cost's variance between actual and flexible budget may be attributable to more than one factor. For example, the $1,215 unfavourable flexible budget variance for labour in Exhibit 9.1 could be due to inefficient labour performance and/or labour's actual hourly rate being above the budgeted hourly rate. In this section, we explore variance analysis, which is a technique that moves us closer to identifying the cause of a variance. The technique will be illustrated by considering it in the context of two specific types of cost variance: direct labour cost variance and direct materials variance. In addition, an approach that can be taken to analysing the variance between actual revenue and revenue identified in the static budget will be shown.

Direct labour variance

The variance between actual labour cost and labour cost in the flexible budget comprises two main elements: the labour rate variance and labour efficiency variance. A labour rate variance arises when the actual wage rate differs to the budgeted wage rate. A labour efficiency variance results when more or less than the budgeted time is taken to complete a particular task.

Direct labour variance worked example • • •

To illustrate the analysis of labour variance, we will return to the Poplars Hotel example presented in Exhibit 9.1. We can see that in April the hotel was 200 rooms short of selling its budgeted target of 2,000 rooms. Imagine that the budgeted cost of labour was based on an anticipated $10 per hour wage rate and an expectation that each room sold would generate 36 minutes of work. In addition, assume accounting records indicate that in April labour worked 1,350 hours at a rate of $8.90 per hour.

This provides us with enough information to determine Poplars' labour rate and efficiency variances for April. We can take a systematic approach to calculating these variances by using the matrix presented as Exhibit 9.2. A particular strength of this approach will become evident as you progress through this section, as the same matrix format is used in all the variance analyses described in this chapter.

The matrix comprises three columns. In the first column we multiply actual hours worked by the actual hourly pay rate to give us the actual total cost of labour, i.e. 1,350 × $8.90 = $12,015. In the second column we make just one modification, replacing the actual rate of pay with the budgeted rate of pay to give us 1,350 × $10 = $13,500. Moving to the final column, we make one further change, replacing actual

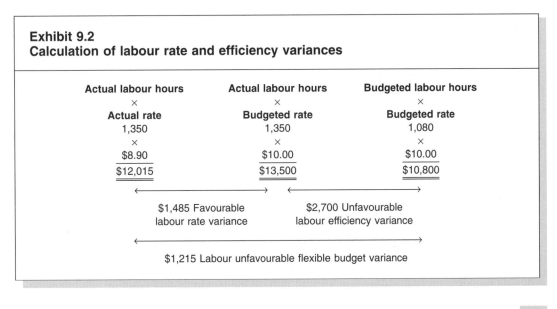

Exhibit 9.2
Calculation of labour rate and efficiency variances

Actual labour hours	Actual labour hours	Budgeted labour hours
×	×	×
Actual rate	Budgeted rate	Budgeted rate
1,350	1,350	1,080
×	×	×
$8.90	$10.00	$10.00
$12,015	$13,500	$10,800

← $1,485 Favourable labour rate variance → ← $2,700 Unfavourable labour efficiency variance →

← $1,215 Labour unfavourable flexible budget variance →

hours with the hours that it should have taken to complete the output achieved. As it was budgeted that each room sold should result in 36 minutes (0.6 hour) of direct labour and 1,800 rooms have been sold, we can conclude that 1,080 hours should have been worked (0.6 × 1,800). The data compiled in column three provides us with the flexible budget for labour which is $10,800 (1,080 × $10). It is important to note that only one change was made when we moved from column one to column two, and again when moving from column two to column three.

Now let us consider the nature of the information provided by the matrix. Moving from column one to column two we substituted budgeted rate of pay for actual rate of pay. This signifies that the difference between the totals of these two columns is attributable to a pay rate differential. Accordingly, the term 'labour rate variance' is used to describe the $1,485 variation between the first two columns. This is a favourable variance as the actual hourly pay rate is below the budgeted pay rate. When moving from column two to column three, we changed actual hours worked to the hours that should have been worked given the number of rooms sold. This signifies that any variation between these two columns arises due to labour's level of efficiency. As we have found that actual labour time exceeds budgeted labour time, we conclude that the $2,700 unfavourable variance has resulted from labour performing inefficiently. Combining the $1,485 favourable rate variance and the $2,700 unfavourable efficiency variance gives us the $1,215 unfavourable labour flexible budget variance noted earlier in Exhibit 9.1. The significance of what this analysis reveals is discussed in Case 9.1.

Case 9.1

Financial Decision Making in Action – The Rooms Division Manager and variance analysis

The $1,215 labour cost flexible budget variance is the largest cost variance identified in Exhibit 9.1. We can expect that the rooms division manager would want to find out what lies behind this variance, not least because senior management is likely to hold him accountable for it.

Requesting a variance analysis such as that presented in Exhibit 9.2 can be seen as representing a first step to securing a greater understanding of what lies behind the unfavourable flexible budget variance for labour. Once the rooms division manager sees that labour has been recruited at a rate below the budgeted rate, he may question whether this was due to the recruitment of untrained personnel. If it was, he may have determined a major factor that has contributed to the unfavourable labour efficiency variance and conclude that continued recruitment of untrained labour represents a false saving.

If the labour rate variance arose as a result of lower than expected labour rates established in a company-wide enterprise agreement, then it would be appropriate for the rooms division manager to regard the responsibility for the labour rate variance as resting with the department that was influential in formulating the enterprise agreement (most probably human resources). This is significant as it highlights how the variance analysis has enabled the rooms division manager to trace some of the responsibility for one of 'his' variances to a manager in another department. If, however, the labour rate variance has resulted from the head of housekeeping deciding to recruit labour on a pay scale below the budgeted pay scale, then clearly the responsibility for the labour rate variance rests with housekeeping.

In light of the relatively large unfavourable labour efficiency variance uncovered by the variance analysis, the rooms division manager can be expected to want some explanations from the staff member in charge of housekeeping. It could be that the variance was due to an excessive number of staff rostered by human resources following the sales estimates fed into the budget by the marketing department (remember that the actual volume of sales was 10% below the sales level projected in the static budget). If this was the case, it would again highlight how the variance analysis has enabled the rooms division manager to determine that a causal factor for the labour cost flexible budget variance lies largely beyond his control.

Direct material variance

The direct material variance comprises two elements: materials price variance and materials efficiency variance. The price variance shows the impact of not purchasing materials at the budgeted price. The efficiency variance shows the impact of not using the budgeted standard amount of materials to produce the actual volume of output achieved.

Direct material variance worked example • • •

Imagine that a restaurant kitchen makes trays of lasagne and it has been determined that each tray should contain 0.5 kilogram of meat at a cost of $5 per kilogram. Accounting records indicate that during last month, 1,000 trays of lasagne were produced and 600 kilograms of meat was used at a total cost of $2,700.

The materials purchase price and materials efficiency variances can be calculated using a very similar approach to that taken in calculating the labour variances (as noted earlier, the beauty of this approach is that it can be used in a range of variance analyses). The direct material variance analysis is presented in Exhibit 9.3. Exhibit 9.3 parallels Exhibit 9.2, the only differences are materials replace labour hours, and we talk of 'price' rather than 'rate' in connection with materials. Note how in both tables we calculate actual cost in the first column, in the second column we substitute budgeted price (rate) for actual price (rate), and in the final column we substitute budgeted materials (labour hours) for actual materials (labour hours). From the information provided, we can determine that the actual per kilogram cost of meat is $4.50 (i.e. $2,700 ÷ 600). In the interest of completeness, the actual per kilogram cost has been calculated and included in column one, however it is not actually needed as the total actual cost of meat (i.e. the total for column one) was provided in the scenario information outlined above. It is again important to note that 'budgeted amount of materials' in column three refers to the amount of materials that should have been used to produce the volume of output actually achieved.

From Exhibit 9.3 it can be seen that a $300 difference appears between columns one and two. As actual price in column one is replaced by budgeted price in column two, it is evident that this $300 difference is attributable to the material's price. The actual price is less than the budgeted price so the materials price variance is favourable.

There is a $500 difference between columns two and three. As the only difference between these columns relates to the amount of materials actually used and the

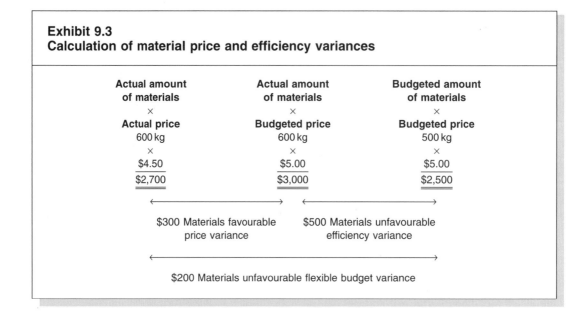

Exhibit 9.3
Calculation of material price and efficiency variances

Actual amount of materials × Actual price	Actual amount of materials × Budgeted price	Budgeted amount of materials × Budgeted price
600 kg	600 kg	500 kg
×	×	×
$4.50	$5.00	$5.00
$2,700	$3,000	$2,500

$300 Materials favourable price variance $500 Materials unfavourable efficiency variance

$200 Materials unfavourable flexible budget variance

amount of materials that should have been used to produce the 1,000 lasagne trays, this variance is referred to as the 'materials efficiency variance'. The actual amount of materials used were above the amount that should have been used, therefore this variance is unfavourable.

Upon further investigation, we might find that the quality of the meat purchased was below the normal standard and that this has resulted in the favourable price variance. If this were the case, the low-quality meat might in turn account for the unfavourable efficiency variance, due to a larger than normal proportion of meat being discarded. The restaurant official responsible for food purchasing should be held accountable for the price variance. This could be the chef, or if the restaurant is in a large hotel containing several other restaurants, it could be a purchasing manager. The chef that oversees the preparation of lasagne should be held accountable for the efficiency variance.

A potential problem can arise when one manager is held accountable for food purchasing and a different manager is held accountable for food preparation. In their pursuit of favourable price variances, there may be a tendency for purchasing managers to compromise on the quality of materials purchased. This will carry negative implications for those managers responsible for overseeing efficient use of materials, as a significant proportion of substandard materials may have to be scrapped. High scrap rates will increase the volume of materials used, and this will result in an unfavourable materials efficiency variance.

This scenario represents a good example of how accounting systems can provide incentives that counter the development of a team culture by placing managers in adversarial positions. If this type of problem becomes significant, an attempt can be made to introduce quality standards for meats purchased. Alternatively, if this is not workable, consideration can be given to moving the purchasing function under the control of the manager responsible for production (i.e. the chef in the lasagne example just outlined).

Revenue variance

Analysis of the variance between budgeted revenue and actual revenue can be applied to any of a hotel's sources of revenue (food & beverage, accommodation, etc.). In the following example, revenue variance analysis is illustrated in the context of a banqueting department.

Revenue variance worked example

Imagine that for a hotel's most recent quarter, the banqueting department had budgeted to serve 9,500 guests at an average price of $20 per person. From accounting records it has been determined that 8,000 guests were served at an average price of $21 per person. From this information we can determine that there is an unfavourable revenue variance of $22,000, i.e. (8,000 × $21) – (9,500 × $20). However, two underlying revenue variances can be uncovered by again applying the matrix that was used in the labour and materials variance analyses. The analysis of revenue variance is presented in Exhibit 9.4 which shows how the selling price and the sales volume variance can be isolated from one another.

Determination of the selling price and sales volume variances may well increase the banqueting manager's understanding of factors behind the $22,000 unfavourable revenue variance. Accountability for the two variances will depend on a hotel's organizational structure, as the scope of a banqueting manager's influence varies significantly across hotels. If the setting of banqueting prices and the marketing of banquets are influenced by different functional heads, care must be taken to recognize the degree of inter-dependency between these two aspects of a banqueting department's performance. For example, the setting of higher prices will likely result in a lower sales volume.

Exhibit 9.4
Calculation of the selling price and sales volume variances

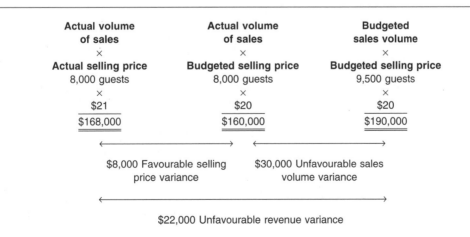

Actual volume of sales × Actual selling price	Actual volume of sales × Budgeted selling price	Budgeted sales volume × Budgeted selling price
8,000 guests	8,000 guests	9,500 guests
×	×	×
$21	$20	$20
$168,000	$160,000	$190,000

$8,000 Favourable selling price variance

$30,000 Unfavourable sales volume variance

$22,000 Unfavourable revenue variance

Other variance analyses

The materials, labour and revenue variance analyses just outlined can be regarded as three of the most widely used forms of variance analysis. They do not represent a complete listing, however, as there are other aspects of a hotel's performance that can be investigated using variance analysis. These other aspects include variable and fixed overheads, sales mix (e.g. the proportion of F&B to accommodation sales), market share and market size. All of these analyses can be conducted using a similar approach to that outlined above. The question of which variance analyses should be conducted can only be answered by appraising the nature and context of a particular hotel's business. If a hotel is located in a well-defined market segment and significant resources are assigned to the maintenance and development of market share, a variance analysis of market share and size could be warranted. In such an analysis, the profit implication of a variance between actual and budgeted market size is isolated from the profit implication of actual market share varying from budgeted market share. While a detailed review of the techniques to be used in an extensive range of variance analyses is beyond the scope of this book, such reviews can be found in many advanced management accounting texts.

When should a variance warrant further investigation?

There is no hard generalizable rule with respect to when a variance is deserving of further investigation. Senior managers see the need to conduct further investigation of variances in the context of factors pertinent to a hotel at a particular time. A small unanticipated variance might warrant a senior manager's attention more than a larger anticipated variance. For items critical to a hotel's overall performance, a small variance might be viewed as important. For example, as room sales frequently affect the sales levels of other hotel activities, a small room sales volume variance might be significant. For other items, senior management might choose to follow up variances that are above a certain percentage of the budgeted amount, or above a certain dollar size. Obviously a 3% variance in labour costs of $30,000 may warrant greater scrutiny than a 10% variance in miscellaneous costs of $2,000. Consequently, rules such as 'investigate all variances greater than $4,000 or 10% of budget' are frequently applied in practice.

Benchmarking

In variance analysis we are concerned with identifying underlying factors that account for differences between a hotel's actual performance and its budgeted performance. Widespread use of variance analysis clearly highlights the importance of the budget as a performance benchmark. Recent years have seen this benchmarking philosophy broadened to include non-budgetary and also non-financial benchmarks of performance. A significant non-financial benchmark that has been used extensively in the hospitality industry for many years is occupancy rate. This is a key performance indicator and some competing hotels have been observed to share their occupancy level information on a nightly basis.

For the many hotel managers that work in a large chain organization, data provided by high-performing hotels within the chain can provide a valuable performance benchmark. In fact the term 'benchmarking' is frequently used in the sense of comparing to best practice. The hotel with the best performance for a given activity is the one that provides the standard for that activity. Such benchmarking can become a highly formalized process with high-performing hotels sharing information on how their performance levels have been achieved. In order for such a benchmarking process to work, it is obviously important that consistent accounting methods and measures are used within each hotel. In addition, if it is important that managers in high-performing hotels participate fully in the benchmarking process by sharing the secrets of their success, care must be taken not to attach significant management rewards to relative performance levels. If high rewards are attached to relative performance, managers in high-performing units will be reluctant to share information that could improve the standing of low performers, as this would reduce the high performers' margin of superiority.

Benchmarking can also involve making comparisons with competitors. While such benchmarking might provide the basis for improved performance, competitor benchmarking is frequently compromised by the problems of accessing information and also inconsistent accounting practices applied across hotels (e.g. different depreciation methods, central administration cost allocation, procedures, etc.). One way around this problem is to purchase industry average data compiled by organizations such as Dun and Bradstreet and large accounting firms such as PricewaterhouseCoopers. These companies collect data from hotels and produce aggregated hotel profit and loss and balance sheet statements and also key performance indices. The information is generally categorized according to three-, four- and five-star properties and presented on a percentage basis, i.e. the reader can determine ratios such as cost of sales as a percentage of sales, labour costs as a percentage of sales, etc.

It is important to put the role of variance analysis and benchmarking into context. These approaches to performance monitoring represent little more than attention-directing activities of the accounting function. Determining what course of action needs to be taken in light of observed discrepancies is an issue requiring managerial judgement. The importance of establishing an effective attention-directing system should not be underestimated, however. Failure to detect a fire will always result in failure to put out a fire. The accounting system can frequently aid fire detection, but managerial judgement is required when determining how the fire is to be extinguished.

Summary

In this chapter we have reviewed flexible budgeting, variance analysis and benchmarking. Flexible budgeting involves adjusting the beginning of year budget in line with the actual volume of sales achieved. This approach is particularly justified when a large proportion of reported variances between actual and budgeted performance result from the challenging nature of correctly predicting sales volume. Flexible budgeting is also particularly pertinent in cost centres, as cost centre managers are not in a position to influence sales levels. Variance analysis is a technique that helps a manager to identify underlying factors giving rise to variances. We saw how a systematic approach can be taken in variance analysis. In addition, the chapter described how managers are increasingly using the performance of other hotels as a benchmark when appraising their own hotel's performance.

Having read the chapter you should now know:

- How to produce a flexible budget and the merits of flexible budgeting
- How a hotel manager can use variance analysis as a useful complement to budgetary controls
- The role of benchmarking in performance management.

References

Atkinson, H., Berry, A. and Jarvis, R. (1995) *Business Accounting for Hospitality and Tourism & Leisure*, International Thomson Publishing, London, Chapter 16.

Coltman, M. M. and Jagels, M. G. (2001) *Hospitality Management Accounting*, 7th edition, John Wiley, Chapter, Chapter 9.

Drury, C. (1992), *Management and Cost Accounting*, 3rd edition, Chapman and Hall, London, Chapter 18.

Hansen, D. R. and Mowen, M. M. (1996) *Management Accounting*, 4th edition, South-Western, Circinnati, OH, Chapter 9.

Harris, P. (1999) *Profit Planning*, Butterworth-Heinemann, Oxford, Chapter 9.

Horngren, C. T., Foster, G. and Datar, S. M. (2000) *Cost Accounting: A Managerial Emphasis*, Prentice Hall International, Englewood Cliffs, NJ, Chapter 7.

Kotas, R. (1999) *Management Accounting for Hospitality and Tourism*, 3rd edition, International Thomson Publishing, London, Chapter 12 and 13.

Schmidgall, R. F. (1997) *Hospitality Industry Managerial Accounting*, 4th edition, Educational Institute – American Hotel & Motel Association, East Lansing, MI, Chapter 10.

Problems

✓ indicates that a solution appears at the back of the text

✓ 9.1 Karen Brady, the general manager of the Curbside Motor Lodge in Central England, has approached you for advice in connection with her most recently quarterly performance report. The summarized version of the report is as follows:

The Curbside Motor Lodge
Financial performance report
for the quarter ended 30 September 20X1

	Actual	Budget	Variance
Room nights sold	12,420	10,800	
	£	£	£
Sales Revenue	1,179,900	1,080,000	99,900 (F)
Variable Costs:			
Labour	84,456	75,600	8,856 (U)
Room amenities	5,216	5,400	184 (F)
Contribution Margin	1,090,228	999,000	91,228 (F)
Fixed Costs	241,000	235,000	6,000 (U)
Operating Profit	849,228	764,000	85,228 (F)

The lodge has produced this type of quarterly internal financial report for several years now. Karen has heard that some hospitality businesses are using flexible budgeting, a technique that she has not encountered before in her career. She is wondering what insights can derive from preparing flexible budgets and whether it is a technique that she should introduce at the lodge.

Required • • •

(a) Prepare a flexible budget for the Curbside Motor Lodge for the quarter ending 30 September 20X1. Also record all flexible budget variances, and indicate whether they are favourable or unfavourable.

(b) In connection with the flexible budget performance report you have prepared for the Curbside Motor Lodge, prepare a brief statement for Karen Brady that summarizes the benefits of flexible budgeting.

✓ 9.2 With respect to the previous problem concerned with the Curbside Motor Lodge, imagine you have conducted a detailed review of accounting records and found the following.

- The budgeted wage rate was £14 per hour and the budgeted allowance for cleaning rooms was half an hour per room night sold. The actual average wage rate paid was £15 per hour and 5,630.40 hours were worked cleaning rooms in the quarter ended 30 September 20X1.
- Room amenities were provided in guest bathrooms in small transparent plastic packs comprising shampoo, conditioner and a bar of soap. The lodge budgeted on each amenity pack costing £0.50 and the provision of one amenity pack per room night sold. It appears, however, that the rate of one pack per room night was exceeded as 13,040 amenity packs were issued from stock during the quarter. These amenity packs actually cost £0.40 each.

Required • • •

(a) Calculate the room cleaning labour rate and efficiency variances.
(b) Calculate the room amenity price and efficiency variances.
(c) Calculate the selling price and sales volume variances.

✓ 9.3 Tiff's Bordeaux restaurant serves breakfasts, lunches and dinner. In June it was budgeted that 500 covers would be served. The budgeted revenue and variable cost per cover is presented in Schedule 1 below. In addition, the restaurant manager budgeted that June's fixed costs would be €800.

Schedule 1: Tiff's Restaurant
June budgeted volume of covers, average revenue
and variable cost per cover served

	Covers served	Average revenue per cover	Variable cost per cover
Breakfasts	100	€7	€2.5
Lunch	150	€14	€5.0
Dinner	250	€25	€10.0

Actual results achieved in June are detailed in Schedule 2. Fixed costs actually incurred in June were €740.

Schedule 2: Tiff's Restaurant
June actual volume of covers served, average revenue
and variable cost per cover served

	Covers served	Average revenue per cover	Variable cost per cover
Breakfasts	110	€6.9	€2.20
Lunch	100	€17.0	€5.40
Dinner	300	€22.0	€9.50

Required ▪ ▪ ▪

(a) Produce a flexible budget performance schedule for June that presents the flexible budget revenue variances and also the flexible budget variable cost variances for each of the three restaurant sittings.

(b) Comment on any variances that might warrant further management investigation.

9.4   In the face of increasing local competition, the financial director of a large Canadian hotel complex convened a task force with the express purpose of identifying potential cost-saving initiatives. One of the participants on the task force, the head of engineering, aired the view that water consumption in the complex had risen considerably over the last couple of years and that this had occurred during a time of increasing water rates. The head of engineering felt that, as a result of minimal real accountability in this area, little was being done to ensure efficient water usage. He recommended that the hotel's five restaurants should be separately metered in order to monitor water consumption and that an appropriate accounting analysis be made of performance with regards to water consumption. The task force agreed that this was an initiative worth pursuing. In the following month, all restaurants were metered for water consumption and monthly water expense budgets developed.

The 'Niagra Falls' restaurant's monthly water expense budget was set at $600. This was set based on an estimated monthly consumption of 60,000 litres of water at a rate of $10 per 1,000 litres. In formulating this budget it had been agreed that water can be viewed as a variable cost, i.e. when restaurant activity doubles, water consumption would double.

Niagra Falls' performance in the first month of 'water accountability' was as follows:

Covers served:	10% above budget
Water consumed:	90,000 litres
Cost per 1,000 litres:	$9.50

Required ▪ ▪ ▪

(a) Calculate water price and efficiency variances for Niagra Falls in the first month of 'water accountability'.

(b) Who should be held accountable for the water efficiency variance, and who should be held accountable for the water price variance?

9.5   The kitchen of the Ambience Hotel in Australia's Gold Coast has developed a strong local reputation for its pastries. It sells the pastries to carefully chosen bakeries and also through one of its restaurant outlets. At the beginning of the current financial year, the company's management established the standard that it should take half an hour of labour time to produce 1 tray of pastries. It was also budgeted that labour should be paid at the rate of $14 per hour.

At the end of the January, the performance report for the kitchen revealed that 120 hours had been worked by the pastry chefs. They were paid $1,440 and had produced 220 trays of pastries.

Required • • •
(a) Calculate the labour rate and efficiency variances. Indicate whether each variance is favourable or unfavourable.
(b) Comment on any adverse implications that may arise from a head chef paying particular attention on attaining favourable labour rate variances.

9.6   The kitchen of Sydney's Deluxe Hotel makes large meat pies for sale in one of the hotel's restaurants and also to a local meat pie retailer. It makes the pastry and also the meat sauce that goes into the pies. The budgeted direct cost of a pie is $2.80, made up as follows:

0.5 kg of meat	$1.50
100 grams of pastry	$0.10
6 minutes of labour	$1.20
Per unit budgeted standard direct cost	$2.80

During June, 2,600 pies were made at the following cost:

1,400 kg of meat used at a cost of:	$3,990
270 kg of pastry used at a cost of:	$300
280 direct labour hours worked at a cost of:	$4,060

Required • • •
(a) Calculate the meat price and efficiency variances. Indicate whether each variance is favourable or unfavourable.
(b) Calculate the pastry price and efficiency variances. Indicate whether each variance is favourable or unfavourable.
(c) Calculate the direct labour price and efficiency variances. Indicate whether each variance is favourable or unfavourable.
(d) Do you see any potential shortcomings arising if significant importance is attached to achieving favourable meat price variances?

9.7   *(This question draws partially on material covered in the previous chapter)*
Val Dizzy Air is a hotel complex located in a well-known ski resort in Queenstown, New Zealand. The town's population doubles during the skiing months of June through to October, and hotel activity also doubles during these months.

A new chief administration officer was hired one year ago as part of an initiative designed to increase the hotel's profitability. Among the new ideas introduced was responsibility accounting. This was formally announced in a memorandum accompanying quarterly cost reports supplied to department heads. Previously, cost data were presented to department heads infrequently. Excerpts from the announcement and the first cost report received by the supervisor of laundry services are presented below.

The new administrator constructed the annual budget for 20X3 and then divided it by four to facilitate the provision of quarterly feedback to the operating managers. The administrator considered establishing a budget according to an average of the prior three years' costs, hoping that installation of the system would reduce costs to this level. However, because of rapidly increasing prices, 20X2 costs, less 3%, were finally chosen for the 20X3 budget. Activity levels were set at the volume achieved in 20X2, which was approximately equal to the volume in each of the previous two years.

Val Dizzy Air Hotel

MEMORANDUM

To: Supervisor, Laundry Department

From: Hotel Chief Administration Officer

Date: 15 October 20X3

As I indicated to you in our last department heads' meeting, I am introducing a quarterly performance reporting system. Please find your performance report for July, August and September attached.

Under this new system, all heads of department will receive quarterly reports, which will identify the costs of operating your department, your departmental budget and variations between your actual performance and budgeted performance. Highlighting variances in this manner will enable you to quickly identify aspects of your operation requiring immediate attention. As you know, I based this year's budget for costs by taking last year's performance less 3%. I believe this to be an appropriate basis for our budget setting as it is consistent with our hotel's philosophy of seeking continuous improvement. I trust we would all agree that there is always scope for improvement.

You will note from the report that your department's costs are significantly above budget (all items over budget are indicated by way of brackets in the variance column). I would be grateful if you could prepare a report for me outlining why these variations have occurred and also what remedial actions you plan to implement.

Val Dizzy Air Hotel
Laundry Department quarterly performance report
3 months to 30 September 20X3

	Actual	Budget	Variance	% Variance
Room occupancy days	9,600	8,000	(1,600)	(20%)
Kilograms of laundry processed	100,000	80,000	(20,000)	(25%)
	$	$	$	
Cleaning products	944	800	(144)	(18%)
Laundry equipment electricity	605	500	(105)	(21%)
Labour	9,200	8,000	(1,200)	(15%)
Salaried supervision	2,995	3,000	5	0.2%
Laundry equipment depreciation	425	425	–	–
Facility maintenance	1,650	1,500	(150)	(10%)
Allocation of central administration overheads	896	800	(96)	(12%)
	16,715	15,025	1,690	

Required • • •
(a) Describe two ways that the budget-setting exercise could be improved at the Val Dizzy Air Hotel. Your answer can refer to technical as well as behavioural aspects of budget-setting.
(b) Explain whether the report effectively communicates the level of efficiency of the laundry department.
(c) Redesign the quarterly performance report so that it provides a more meaningful and fair appraisal of the performance of the supervisor of the Laundry Department.

9.8   Explain what is meant by 'benchmarking' and how it can be used to improve performance.

Cost information and pricing

After studying this chapter, you should have developed an appreciation of:

1 Factors affecting pricing policy

2 Cost-based approaches to F&B pricing

3 Cost-based approaches to setting room rates

4 The importance of variable cost in the context of short-term price setting.

Introduction

Pricing is an important and challenging aspect of hospitality decision making. The choice on restaurant menus highlights the number of meals that have to be priced, and a price differential frequently exists between lunchtime and dinner menus. With respect to accommodation, many hotels offer a range of rooms with different configurations. These different rooms have to be priced in busy as well as quiet seasons. These pricing decisions are made more challenging by the fact that it is rare to find two restaurant meals that represent exactly the same dining experience, and no two hotel stays constitute exactly the same accommodation experience. As a result, a hotel cannot conduct direct price comparisons to the same degree as companies operating in the retail sector. Supermarkets, for example, have a large volume of goods to price, however they can conduct direct price comparisons with competing outlets that offer identical products.

The distinct nature of the various goods and services sold in the hospitality industry constitutes a further factor that complicates pricing. Compare the variable cost to revenue ratio for a room night sold with the variable cost to revenue ratio for a bottle of wine sold through a restaurant. The cost of selling one more room night (i.e. variable cost) is basically the cost of cleaning the room. The cost of selling one more bottle of wine in a restaurant is basically the cost of purchasing the bottle of wine. Cleaning a room might cost $10 and rooms may have a rack rate of $120, while the bottle of wine might cost $20 and command a restaurant price of $40. Note the large difference in the apparent percentage profit margin associated with these two sales. This apparent difference is misleading, however. In the cost data provided we have excluded reference to fixed costs. The ratio of fixed costs to variable costs is typically much higher for accommodation activities than F&B activities. It is frequently difficult to trace fixed costs to individual sales, however. As a result, a high price mark-up over variable cost does not necessarily signify a high mark-up over all costs.

This distinction between F&B and room pricing is particularly apparent when we consider the range of price discretion apparent in the two areas. Exhibit 10.1 demonstrates how there is greater price discretion in the case of rooms. This greater price discretion arises because it is presumed that the hotel would, at a minimum, want to cover its variable cost. As variable cost represents a greater proportion of the selling price for the bottle of wine, an F&B manager is relatively constrained in terms of being able to discount the wine's selling price. Because of the significantly different cost structures in F&B and the rooms division, pricing issues arising in these two areas of hotel management are considered separately in this chapter.

If a hotel or restaurant has many local competitors, its volume of sales will be heavily affected by the prices it sets. A hotel that charges high room rates relative to its local competition will achieve lower occupancy levels than if it were to drop its room rates. This signifies that room managers are bound to be confronted by the need to manage the trade-off between a quest for achieving high room rates and maintaining high levels of occupancy. A parallel can also be noted with restaurant pricing. High pricing can be expected to result in reduced numbers of covers served.

When setting prices, managers obviously need to consider what prices are being charged by competitors. In addition, pricing needs to consider factors such as image sought and whether management believes that setting a low price for a particular

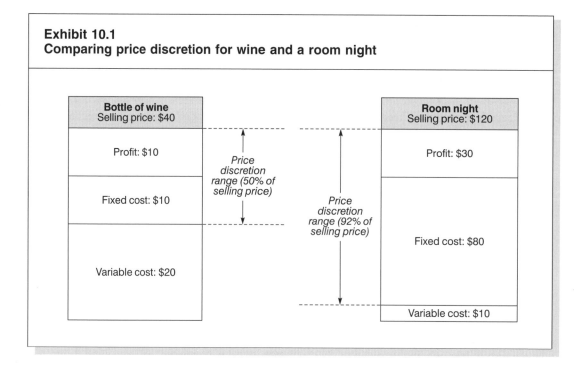

Exhibit 10.1
Comparing price discretion for wine and a room night

| Bottle of wine
Selling price: $40 |
| Profit: $10 |
| Fixed cost: $10 |
| Variable cost: $20 |

Price discretion range (50% of selling price)

Price discretion range (92% of selling price)

| Room night
Selling price: $120 |
| Profit: $30 |
| Fixed cost: $80 |
| Variable cost: $10 |

service will result in more customers and greater sales of other services offered (i.e. using one service as a loss leader). These types of pricing considerations fall within the marketing domain of decision making. As marketing as well as costing issues impact on price setting, it is important to recognize at the outset of this chapter that we are dealing with a complex decision-making area. Any student of hospitality management who is seeking a simple 'off the shelf' costing formula for supporting price decision making is bound to become frustrated. The complexity of the issues at hand preclude the application of any single 'off the shelf' analytical procedure.

It might be stating the obvious to say that prices charged must cover costs incurred. Stating the obvious is important, however, as it highlights that we need to draw on the accounting information system in order to ascertain product and service costs as part of price decision making. In addition to a need to justify different prices charged for comparable services provided (e.g. different menu items provided by a restaurant, different sized rooms, etc.), it is a fundamental reality of commerce that prices must cover costs. Having said that, it should be noted that the hotel industry is characterized by a high proportion of fixed costs. Such costs are typically difficult to allocate across products and services. This factor probably signifies that compared to industries with lower fixed-cost structures, the hospitality industry attaches less importance to cost analysis for pricing decisions. While it might be helpful to bear this factor in mind, we should nevertheless conduct as complete a cost analysis as is reasonably possible in order to maximize our ability to make well-informed pricing decisions.

The remainder of this chapter provides an overview of techniques that can be considered when attempting to draw on cost information for pricing decisions. The chapter is structured as follows. Initially, we will review two factors affecting price decision making. The following section outlines traditional costing perspectives on F&B pricing, room rate setting and also contribution pricing.

Factors affecting pricing

In this section, the manner in which price elasticity and product or service perishability affect pricing policies is described.

Price elasticity

A highly price elastic service is one where a change in price results in a relatively high change in demand for the service. A service with low price elasticity, on the other hand, is one where a change in price results in a relatively low change in the demand for the service. Higher degrees of price elasticity provide a potential for more imaginative approaches to pricing strategy. For example, if a particular hotel has found that room sales are highly price sensitive, decreasing room rates during the off-season might represent an effective strategy to increase occupancy levels and total revenue. If, however, it has been found that room rates are relatively price inelastic, dropping the room rate might not be an appropriate strategy as it will not result in a significant increase in occupancy (if a hotel operates in a remote town with no competitors, relatively low price elasticity is likely to result).

A product or service is viewed as being price elastic if a percentage change in price results in a greater percentage change in demand. For example, imagine that a hotel has found that at a room rate of $120 it maintains an average sales level of 500 room nights per week. In addition, it has also found that that if it increases its room rate by 10% to $132, a 15% reduction in demand will result, i.e. sales will drop to 425 room nights per week. As the percentage change in demand is greater than the percentage change in price the rooms can be described as price elastic. Price elasticity is generally measured using the following formula:

$$\text{Price elasticity} = \frac{\%\ \text{change in quantity demanded}}{\%\ \text{change in price}}$$

If this formula yields a value greater than 1, the demand is price elastic. If it yields a value less than 1, the demand is inelastic.

Most introductory micro-economic texts provide a more detailed discussion of the nature of price elasticity. For the purposes of this text, it is important that hospitality management accounting students are aware of the concept of price elasticity, as it represents an important contextual consideration when determining a pricing strategy for a particular product or service.

Perishability of the product or service

Pricing strategies should take into account the degree to which a product or service is perishable. To illustrate the issue of perishability, let us compare a bottle of wine and a fresh cream cake that are available for purchase from a café that adjoins a hotel's foyer. While these two items are sold through the same cash register, a manager would be justified in implementing very different pricing strategies for the two products. Let us assume that the unit variable cost of making the cakes is $1.20, and that immediately following production, the cakes are priced at $4 each. Let us also assume that if a cake is not sold by the end of the day following its production, it will have to be discarded as waste. On the day following the cake's production, if the cake is not sold by the time the café closes, its revenue-earning potential will be lost forever. Accordingly, a manager might be justified in dropping the retail price of the cakes to $0.5 one hour before the café is due to close. Based on his experience, this results in most cakes selling and the manager justifies his action by saying:

> If I didn't drop the price, none of the cakes would sell in the final hour of their life. Better to make a loss of $0.70 per cake ($1.20 variable cost − $0.5 revenue) than the $1.20 I've effectively lost when they're tossed in the bin. What would you prefer, $0.5 or $0 in the till for the cake?

The bottle of wine does not suffer from the same perishability as the cream cake. The closing of the café on a particular day does not signify that the future revenue potential of the bottle of wine is lost. Accordingly, the rationale for dropping the price of cream cakes to a point that is below their variable cost does not apply to the bottle of wine. This issue of perishability is particularly pertinent in the hospitality industry. Much of what is produced by a restaurant's kitchen is perishable. In addition, rooms and conference facilities can be viewed in a similar light. If, on a particular night, a room is not sold, the revenue-earning potential of that particular room night has been lost forever. As the likelihood of this loss occurring increases as the time for the unsold room night approaches, so the incentive for dropping the price of the room increases. In a manner paralleling the cream cake example, it is better to gain some revenue rather than earn no room revenue for the room.

The room example differs in one key regard to the cream cake example, however. The room sale generates subsequent costs, i.e. the room will have to be cleaned. Therefore, unlike the cake example where earning some revenue was viewed as better than earning no revenue, in the room-pricing situation the room rate should not be set below the variable cost of servicing the room. This difference arises as the sale of the cake does not generate subsequent costs.

This discussion of pricing perishable products and services needs to be placed in the context of marketing issues. Care must be taken when discounting items as they approach their time of expiry. Heavy price discounting can result in damaging a hotel's image. It can also result in customers, who are aware of the practice, deferring their purchase until after the discounted price is offered.

Traditionally applied pricing methods

In this section we initially consider food and beverage pricing issues. This is followed by a description of techniques relating to setting room rates. The section concludes with a discussion of contribution pricing, which concerns the significant nature of variable cost in short-term pricing situations.

Food and beverage pricing

Cost-plus pricing is extensively applied in food and beverage management. The approach involves identifying costs traceable to the food or beverage item to be priced and marking up the cost by a multiple in order to determine a selling price. Compared to pricing meals on a restaurant menu, pricing beverages on a cost mark-up basis is relatively straightforward. This is because beverages served frequently contain only one purchased ingredient, sometimes they contain two ingredients, but seldom more than three ingredients. The situation is very different, however, when costing meal items on a restaurant menu. Meals can comprise many ingredients and determining the cost and quantity of each ingredient used can be challenging. This is because some ingredients have a kitchen labour component, and some are subject to seasonal and daily cost fluctuations. For this reason, when determining the cost of a meal, it is common practice to restrict the costing exercise to the main ingredients used.

Cost-plus pricing of a particular menu item will be illustrated through the following worked example. Imagine that an analysis has been conducted to determine the cost of the ingredients in a fish dinner at Marseille's Poisson restaurant. This analysis has resulted in the preparation of the schedule presented as Exhibit 10.2.

It will be assumed that the Poisson restaurant has a pricing strategy of marking up its ingredient costs by a multiple of 8. From Exhibit 10.2 it is apparent that the ingredients in the fish salad have been estimated to cost €2.80. The price to be charged can be calculated as follows:

Cost of meal ingredients × 'Cost-plus' multiple = Price

i.e. €2.80 × 8 = €22.40

Because of marketing considerations such as customer attitudes to different price bands, prices charged by competitors for similar meals, etc., management is likely to round the 'raw price' of €22.40 to a price that is consistent with its marketing strategy on pricing. For instance, the restaurant may have a strategy of setting its prices at 5 cents below the nearest round Euro. This would mean that the raw price calculated might be rounded down to €21.95 or rounded up to €22.95.

A variation on this pricing example might involve including only the main ingredient in the costing analysis. Such an approach might be justified on several grounds. First, it would make the costing analysis easier. Second, the main

---

Exhibit 10.2
Poisson restaurant – cost of ingredients used in fish salad

Ingredient	€ cost
Fish	2.00
Potato salad	0.18
Green salad (lettuce, tomato, etc.)	0.28
Rice	0.14
Bread roll and butter	0.20
Total	2.80

ingredient accounts for the bulk of the total cost of all ingredients. Third, it may well be that the main ingredient's cost is more volatile than the other ingredients, with the result that changes in restaurant prices need to reflect changes in the cost of the main ingredient. If price is to be determined based on the main ingredient alone, clearly the 'cost-plus' multiple will have to be greater in order for the restaurant to earn the same level of gross profit for the meal. Returning to the example illustrated in Exhibit 10.2, if the Poisson restaurant uses cost-plus pricing based on the main ingredient alone, it might use a multiple of 11. Applying this multiple to the cost of fish served provides the following raw price calculation:

Cost of main ingredient × cost plus multiple = Price

i.e. €2.00 × 11 = €22.00

The issue of applying a multiple to cost in order to determine a desired price raises an issue that frequently troubles students of accounting. A percentage mark-up on cost is not the same as a gross profit margin percentage. The former concerns a percentage of cost while the latter concerns a percentage of selling price. This distinction can be illustrated through a simple example. Imagine a restaurant buys its house wine for $16 per bottle and prices it on the menu at $20. The cost mark-up stated as a percentage is 25% ($4 ÷ $16 × 100). However, gross profit margin as a percentage is 20% ($4 ÷ $20 × 100). From this example it can be seen that if a service is being sold at a 24% gross profit margin, it is earning less profit than a service with a 20% cost mark-up.

Setting room rates

A variety of cost-based approaches can be used to inform the setting of room rates. Three of these approaches are outlined here. First, a rule of thumb approach known as the 'rule of a thousand' can be utilized. Second, where a hotel has several differently sized rooms, room pricing can be based on room size. Third, hotel management can determine the level of profit sought as a function of investment, and attempt to work back to the price that has to be charged in order to provide the required profit level.

Rule of a thousand approach to room rates • • •

The rule of a thousand approach to setting room rates is outlined through a worked example in Box 10.1.

This method should be regarded as a rather vague rule of thumb approach, as it fails to address key issues such as seasonality of demand and the time at which investment was made in competing hotels. If a hotel that was built prior to a period of high inflation in building costs applied the rule of a thousand when setting room rates, it is unlikely that a competing hotel built following the high-inflation period could survive by also applying the same pricing strategy. If the second hotel were to apply the rule of a thousand, it would have higher rates and would lose much custom to its competitor.

Box 10.1
Rule of a thousand approach to setting room rates

One broad sweep indicator of room pricing that has been referred to for many years in the industry is the 'rule of a thousand'. This involves setting room prices at the rate of $1 for every $1,000 capital invested in a room. For example, assume that the total cost of building a 100-room hotel is $15,000,000, and that 20% of the infrastructure investment relates to non-accommodation hotel activities such as F&B. By spreading the $12,000,000 invested in accommodation (80% of $15,000,000) across the 100 rooms we can determine the investment in each room to be $120,000 ($12,000,000 ÷ 100). Application of the $1 charged for every $1,000 invested formula would result in room rates being set at $120 ($120,000 ÷ 1,000).

Relative room size approach to setting room rates • • •

The relative room size approach to pricing is explained via a worked example in Box 10.2.

Required rate of return approach to setting room rates • • •

This approach involves determining what room rate must be charged to generate an annual revenue that is sufficient to cover all costs and taxes and, in addition, provide a sufficient level of profit to meet the owners' targeted return on investment. In the United States this approach is widely referred to as the 'Hubbart formula'. It is also sometimes referred to as the 'bottom-up' approach to setting room rates as, once the owners' required rate of return has been determined (i.e. the hotel's net profit which is on the last line of the profit and loss statement), the technique involves progressing up the elements referred to in the profit and loss statement, culminating in the term referred to on the first line of the statement, i.e. sales revenue. The technique will be illustrated through the following worked example.

Imagine that the ComfortAssured is a 180-room Winnipeg hotel with assets of $10 million and liabilities of $7 million. The hotel's owners are seeking a 14% annual return on their investment. The hotel is subject to 40% tax and pays 9% interest on a loan of $6.75 million. Other fixed costs, which include administration, depreciation and energy, total $2 million per annum. The food and beverage department generates $400,000 in profit prior to the deduction of fixed costs. The hotel projects an average occupancy of 65% and is open 365 days a year, i.e. 42,705 room nights are sold per annum (180 × 0.65 × 365). The rooms department has estimated variable housekeeping costs of $15 per room sold.

The calculations required to determine the average room rate required to provide the owners with their target ROI are shown in Exhibit 10.3. As already noted, the key to understanding this schedule stems from an appreciation that it represents an upward movement through the hotel's profit and loss statement. This approach stems from the fact that in this schedule we are not seeking to calculate profit (which is the last line in a conventional profit and loss statement), instead we are determining the level of revenue (i.e. the first line in a conventional profit and loss statement) that is sufficient to provide a target profit level.

Box 10.2
Relative room size approach to pricing

Imagine London's Britannica Hotel has 20 rooms that are 125 square metres and 40 rooms that are 100 square metres. Both types of room run at a 70% occupancy level. The rooms manager is seeking a revenue of £1,474,200 for the 360 days that the hotel will be open next year. Based on room size, at what rate should the rooms be priced?

Note that the 20 large rooms are 25% larger than the 40 small rooms, therefore, based on room size they will a command a rate that is 25% higher than that charged on the small rooms. The key to determining this problem is to determine how many square metres will be sold on the average night, and then to determine at what rate each square metre must be charged in order to provide the desired level of revenue.

Total square metres that will be sold on the average night:

Number of rooms		Square metres		Occupancy		Total square metres sold
20	×	125	×	0.7	=	1,750
40	×	100	×	0.7	=	2,800
						4,550

Average revenue required per night is the target annual revenue divided by the number of days the hotel is open in the year:

£1,474,200 ÷ 360 = £4,095

Rate to charge each square metre is the average revenue required per night divided by the total square metres sold:

£4,095 ÷ 4,550 = £0.9

As each square metre needs to be charged at £0.9 per night, the 20 large rooms should have an average rate of £112.50 (125 × £0.9), and the 40 smaller rooms should have an average rate of £90 (100 × £0.9).

We can check to see whether this solution is correct by calculating whether it provides the £1,474,200 target annual revenue.

Total square metres that will be sold on the average night:

Number of rooms		Occupancy		£ Rate		Annual operating days		Total £ revenue
20	×	0.7	×	112.50	×	360	=	567,000
40	×	0.7	×	90	×	360	=	907,200
								£1,474,200

Exhibit 10.3
Using required rate of return to set room rates

Description of amount required	Calculation	$ Amount
Net profit required to meet owners' target ROI	Owners equity × 14%: ($10,000,000 –$7,000,000) × 0.14	420,000
Required pre-tax profit	Required profit ÷ (1 – tax rate):[a] $420,000 ÷ (1 – 0.4)	700,000
Required profit before tax and interest	Add interest: $700,000 + (0.09 × $6,750,000) = $700,000 + $607,500 = $1,307,500	1,307,500
Required profit before deduction of all fixed costs	Add fixed costs: $1,307,500 + $2,000,000 = $3,307,500	3,307,500
Profit required from rooms	Deduct profits provided by other departments: $3,307,500 – $400,000	2,907,500
Total revenue required from rooms	Add variable housekeeping costs (rooms sold × $15): (42,705 × $15) + $2,907,500 = $640,575 + $2,907,500 = $3,548,075	3,548,075
Required average room rate	Total revenue required from rooms ÷ number of rooms sold per annum: $3,548,075 ÷ 42,705	**83.08**

[a]See Chapter 7 for a discussion of calculating a pre-tax amount.

The $83.08 computed in Exhibit 10.3 for the ComfortAssured Hotel can be used as a target average room rate, as it is sufficient to provide the owners' their target ROI. If the hotel has a mixture of double and single rooms and management would like to charge a $15 premium for the double rooms, we can determine what price should be charged for each type of room. Imagine that 60 of the ComfortAssured's 180 rooms are doubles and that both room types have an average occupancy of 65%. This signifies that the hotel will sell an average of 39 double rooms per day (0.65×60), and 78 single rooms per day (0.65×120). The price to be charged for each room type can be determined by solving the following equation in which p represents the price to be charged for the single rooms and $p + 15$ is the price to be charged in the double rooms.

Note that average required daily revenue from rooms =

$9,720.75 (i.e. $3,548,075 ÷ 365).

$78p + 39 (p + 15) = 9{,}720.75$

$78p + 39p + 585 = 9{,}720.75$

$117p = 9{,}135.75$

$p = 78.08$

Therefore singles should be priced at an average of $78.08 and doubles should be priced at an average of $93.08 ($78.08 + $15).

Other room rate issues • • •

While the cost-based approaches outlined above can be seen to be helpful as a basis for setting room rates over the long term, in a short-term situation that sees a hotel experiencing low levels of occupancy, aggressive approaches to pricing may be justified. In such a situation, the hotel manager may want to know what is the lowest price that may be charged for a room. The description of contribution pricing presented in the next section will be helpful to the manager seeking the lowest room rates that are consistent with a sound commercial rationale.

Before considering contribution pricing, however, we should consider a final room rate setting concept relating to the maximization of total room revenue across different market segments and also across busy and quiet seasons. To explore this idea further, let us return to the revpar (revenue per available room) concept which was introduced in Chapter 5. Revpar concerns finding an optimal balance between maximizing occupancy levels and average room rates charged. Obviously, higher occupancy levels can be achieved by reducing average room rates, and also vice versa. This factor underlines the relative incompleteness of the occupancy level measure and the average room rate measure as performance indicators. As is shown through the worked example in Box 10.3, bringing the two measures together through the calculation of revpar results in a more complete measure of performance.

Box 10.3
Revpar: a comprehensive room sales performance measure

Which of the following outcomes represents the better marketing achievement for a Chicago 200 room hotel, a Tuesday night with an occupancy of 65% and an average room rate of $90, or a Wednesday night with an occupancy of 70% and an average room rate of $83 (assume Tuesdays and Wednesdays experience similar levels of demand for rooms)? The fact that both occupancy and the average room rate measures provide only a partial picture of performance can be dealt with by multiplying them together to calculate revpar which provides a more complete picture of performance. Revpar indicates the average revenue earned by all rooms in the hotel, regardless of whether or not they are sold.

Occupancy night	Occupancy level		Average room rate		Revpar (revenue per available room)
Tuesday	0.65	×	$90	=	$58.50
Wednesday	0.70	×	$83	=	$58.10

It is evident that of the two results, an occupancy level of 65% with an average room rate of $90 is preferable as it provides a $0.4 higher revpar. This signifies that the hotel earns $80 more revenue (200 rooms × $0.4) for the Tuesday night compared to the Wednesday night. Alternatively, this issue could be considered by comparing the total revenue provided under the two scenarios. The Tuesday night provides a total rooms revenue of $11,700 (130 rooms × $90). The Wednesday night provides $11,620 revenue (140 rooms × $83).

As a performance measure, revpar is preferred to total revenue as it facilitates benchmarking comparisons across hotels with different numbers of rooms. It should, however, be recognized that maximizing revpar does not necessarily signify profit maximization. In a situation of major room rate discounting, the higher revpar associated with an increase in occupancy could result in a lower level of overall profit if the increased total revenue does not outweigh the additional housekeeping and energy costs associated with the hotel's increased level of activity. Although increased costs for the rooms department result from increased levels of occupancy, there will also be increased F&B profit made from additional F&B sales resulting from the higher occupancy level. In addition, greater future profitability may result from favourable word of mouth promotion provided by the additional guests. All these factors need to be borne in mind when using a performance measurement system that attaches high importance to maximizing revpar. When a hotel uses market segment demand data as part of an attempt to maximize revpar over the long term, it is generally described as practising yield management. This approach to pricing is commented upon in Case 10.1.

Case 10.1

Financial Decision Making in Action –
The Sales and Marketing Manager and yield management

The application of pricing strategies designed to maximize revpar is often referred to as 'yield management'. Yield management involves sales and marketing management developing pricing plans that recognize factors such as whether a reservation pertains to a quiet or busy season, weekday or weekend and also the nature of a customer's market segment (e.g. tour group booking vs a single transient guest).

The distinguishing feature of yield management relates to its focus on maximizing revpar rather than simply attempting to maximize occupancy levels. To illustrate yield management decision making, consider the case of a reservation office deliberating whether to make an advanced sale of rooms to a tour operator. The hotel has 200 rooms and charges $80 per room for advanced bookings except for those placed by tour operators who are granted a 25% discount. A tour operator wants to book 30 rooms for three nights in two months' time. The hotel has already sold 170 of its rooms for the three-day period in question, and the sales department projects that if the sale is not made to the tour operator, 80% of the remaining rooms will be sold to full rate paying guests. The reservations office can determine whether the sale should be made to the tour operator by comparing projected revenue with and without the tour operator booking.

Revenue per night if sale is made to tour operator

170 rooms sold at $80	13,600
30 rooms sold at $60	1,800
	$15,400

Revenue per night if sale is not made to tour operator

194 rooms sold at $80	$15,520

As total revenue is greater if the sale is not made to the tour operator, the reservations office should not reserve rooms for the tour operator.

This represents a fairly simplified example. It does, however, highlight that as yield management involves an attempt to match pricing to demand factors, its effectiveness is heavily reliant on the maintenance of a well-developed demand forecasting system. This is a key issue for a hotel's sales and marketing departments. It should be noted, however, that today yield management is generally highly computerized. Yield management computer software can track data such as: occupancy levels by market segment, the incidence of cancelled reservations, proportion of 'no shows', as well as revenue lost through high-price customers being displaced by low-price customers.

Contribution pricing

Contribution pricing is a particular type of cost-plus pricing where a mark-up is attached to a service or product's variable cost. While contribution pricing can be applied in the rooms, restaurant, and bar areas, it will be explored here in the context of conference and banqueting operations. Applying contribution pricing in this area is particularly appropriate due to the fact that it is relatively easy to identify the variable costs associated with hosting conferences and banquets (i.e. the cost of additional refreshments and covers served). In addition, contribution management can provide a useful perspective on conference and banquet price decision making during periods of excess capacity (i.e. during a period of low demand for conferences).

Contribution pricing allows the conference manager to determine the lowest price that can be charged while ensuring a positive contribution towards profit results from hosting the conference. Such an aggressive pricing policy might be particularly pertinent during a period of excess capacity if any of the following applies:

(a) Competitors are very aggressively pricing their conference facilities
(b) Hosting a conference results in the hotel increasing hotel profits in other areas, e.g. the rooms and F&B departments
(c) Hosting a particular conference carries the potential of stimulating further conference sales in the future.

From the example in Box 10.4, it is apparent that the unit of analysis affects the way that we look at variable cost (i.e. in this example we have conducted the analysis at the level of the whole conference as well as the individual attendee level). While this aggressive approach to pricing can be justified in the short term (in order to utilize capacity that would otherwise be idle) or on the basis of one or more of the three factors outlined above, it should be noted that it should not be viewed as a long-term pricing strategy. Over the long term, fixed as well as variable costs have to be covered if a profit is to result. Despite this, a justification could be made for running conferences at a price that results in a loss to the conference department, if increased conference activity has a positive impact on the hotel's overall profitability due to increased F&B and room sales.

Box 10.4
Applying contribution pricing

Imagine a European conference organizer has approached a Munich hotel in connection with a proposed conference to be attended by approximately 200 delegates (the organizer estimates an attendance of not less than 150 and not more than 250 delegates). If a price quotation is being sought where the organizer has confirmed an attendance of exactly 200 attendees, the variable cost can be calculated at the level of the total conference as follows:

Variable cost for hosting conference with 200 attendees

	€
Morning refreshments (€1 per person × 200 attendees)	200
Lunch (€5 per person × 200 attendees)	1,000
Afternoon tea (€1 per person × 200 attendees)	200
Cost of 2 additional casual staff	300
Total variable cost for conference	**1,700**

If, however, the conference organizer is seeking a quotation on a 'per attendee' basis, the variable cost analysis would have to be modified, as the cost of additional casual staff does not vary according to the number of attendees (it is assumed that the two additional casual staff would be required regardless of whether there are 150 or 250 attendees). The cost of two casual staff therefore represents an incremental cost of the conference, but a fixed cost in terms of the number of attendees.

Variable cost per attendee attending proposed conference

	€
Morning refreshments (€1 per person × 200 attendees)	1
Lunch (€5 per person × 200 attendees)	5
Afternoon tea (€1 per person × 200 attendees)	1
Total variable cost per attendee	**7**

In variable costing, it is generally claimed that so long as a price is charged that exceeds variable cost, a positive contribution towards profit results. In this case, the variable cost analysis conducted at the 'per attendee' level has resulted in the exclusion of casual labour. As the two additional casual staff represent an incremental cost of holding the conference, if pricing is based on the above 'per attendee' analysis, an additional mark-up would have to be included to cover the incremental cost of casual staff.

Summary

Due to the subject matter of this book, the pricing approaches outlined in this chapter have a financial orientation. As noted in the introduction, the provision of accurate financial information is imperative in a price-sensitive industry such as the hospitality industry. This price sensitivity has doubtlessly resulted in some managers, uninformed by an appropriate financial analysis, setting prices below cost. The significance of cost information for pricing becomes particularly apparent when we recognize that setting prices below variable cost means that the more we sell, the more we lose. We should nevertheless remind ourselves that provision of costing information is only part of the management information required for well-informed pricing setting. Marketing factors, which can include issues such as competitor pricing, image sought, the possibility of loss-leader pricing etc., also need to be considered when formulating a pricing strategy.

In the chapter we have reviewed how factors such as perishability affect pricing policy. We have also seen how 'cost-plus' pricing approaches can be used in the context of F&B. Due to the high fixed cost structure associated with the provision of accommodation, room pricing is slightly more complicated. Several approaches to setting room rates, including basing prices on room size and a required rate of return, were reviewed. In addition, the importance of yield management was described in the context of a hotel's sales and marketing function.

Having read the chapter you should now know:

- The meaning of price elasticity and the significance of product and service perishability when approaching pricing decisions
- How a 'cost-plus' approach can be used in F&B pricing
- How to apply the 'rule of a thousand' when setting room rates
- How to apply the 'relative room size' approach to setting room rates
- How to apply the required rate of return approach to setting room rates
- What is meant by yield management
- The importance of maintaining a positive contribution margin (i.e. covering variable cost) when discounting prices.

References

Atkinson, H., Berry, A. and Jarvis, R. (1995) *Business Accounting for Hospitality and Tourism & Leisure*, International Thomson Publishing, London, Chapter 14.

Coltman, M. M. and Jagels, M. G. (2001) *Hospitality Management Accounting*, 7th edition, John Wiley, Chichester, Chapter 6.

Hansen, D.R. and Mowen, M. M. (2000) *Management Accounting*, 5th edition, South-Western, Cincinnati, OH, Chapter 17.

Harris, P. (1999) *Profit Planning*, Butterworth-Heinemann, Oxford, Chapter 6.

Kotas, R. (1999) *Management Accounting for Hospitality and Tourism*, 3rd edition, International Thomson Publishing, London, Chapter 8.

Owen, G. (1994) *Accounting for Hospitality, Tourism & Leisure*, Pitman Publishing, London, Chapter 12.

Schmidgall, R. F. (1997) *Hospitality Industry Managerial Accounting*, 4th edition, Educational Institute – American Hotel & Motel Association, East Lansing, MI, Chapter 8.

Problems

✓ indicates that a solution appears at the back of the text

✓ 10.1 Aberdeen's Thrifty hotel has forty rooms and has historically achieved an average occupancy of 55%. The hotel's assets have a book value of £450,000 and the owners believe the assets should generate a 15% return after tax. Assume tax is charged at the rate of 50%.

The hotel has several fixed costs which include 9% interest charged on a £250,000 bank loan, £40,000 of equipment and fittings depreciation and other fixed costs of £65,000 per year.

The hotel's manager believes that the 55% occupancy level will again be achieved next year, and estimates that this level of activity will result in £85,000 of operating expenses.

Required ▪ ▪ ▪
Assuming the hotel is open 365 days per year, calculate the room rate that should be charged in order to provide the owners with their target profit level.

✓ 10.2 The following information relates to a family-owned Adelaide restaurant:

Manager's salary:	$55,000 p.a.
Interest:	Loan of $100,000 is outstanding; 8% annual interest rate
Depreciation:	Equipment and furniture with book value of $120,000 is being depreciated at 25% of book value
Licence:	$5,000 p.a.
Insurance:	$6,000 p.a.
Maintenance:	$4,000 p.a.
Other salaries:	$28,000 p.a.
Variable costs:	75% of revenue
Before-tax operating profit target:	50% of owners' investment of $120,000

Required ▪ ▪ ▪
(a) What sales revenue does the restaurant have to achieve in order to make its before-tax operating profit target?
(b) The restaurant is closed for three weeks each year. In the remainder of the year (assume 49 weeks) it opens every day except Mondays. The restaurant has 50 seats, and averages a seat turnover of two times per day in the week and three times per day on Saturdays and Sundays. What must the average cover price be in order to achieve the target profit level?

✓ 10.3 The rooms manager of a new 90-room hotel in Texas has approached you seeking advice on what room rates should be charged. The hotel, which will be open for 365 days of the year, has the following three types of room:

Number of rooms	Type	Size
30	Economy	60 sq. metres
30	Double	80 sq. metres
30	Deluxe	110 sq. metres

The hotel's balance sheet indicates that $18,000,000 has been invested in the building and 30% of the building is dedicated to non-accommodation activities such as F&B.

Required • • •

(a) According to the 'rule of a thousand' approach ($1 charge for each $1 invested), what should be the average room rate charged?

(b) Assume the rooms manager projects that each type of room will achieve a 70% occupancy level. If the hotel is seeking to achieve a total revenue of $3,066,000 from rooms next year and wishes to set room rates based on size, what rate should the hotel charge for each of its rooms?

10.4   The manager responsible for pricing merchandise in a souvenir shop located in the foyer of a hotel is discussing pricing strategy with a shop assistant. The two have agreed on a policy of aggressively pricing a specific set of items. When discussing pricing, the shop assistant is used to talking of marking up cost by a specific percentage. The manager, however, is more familiar with referring to 'gross profit margin', a term which tends to be used at management meetings in the hotel. The assistant has indicated that based on her experience in other merchandising situations, the minimum acceptable cost mark-up is 25%. Following discussions at the most recent monthly management meeting, the manager feels that a gross profit margin of 20% is acceptable for loss-leader items. The manager realizes, however, that he is using a different terminology from that used by the assistant. As a result of this he has decided to phone the accounting department to clarify the difference between '% cost mark-up' and '% gross profit margin'.

Required • • •

Through the use of a hypothetical example, demonstrate whether a 25% cost mark-up results in more profit than a 20% gross profit margin.

10.5   Hamilton's Carvery restaurant has had a Sunday seat turnover of 5 while charging $40 per cover for its lunch to dinner 'all you can eat roast' special. The chef is considering increasing the price of the special meal to $45 and estimates that this will reduce the Sunday seat turnover to 4.5.

Required • • •

For the price change proposed, determine whether the 'all you can eat' Sunday special is price elastic or inelastic.

10.6   Bristol's Severn Bridge restaurant uses cost-plus pricing as an aid to determining what prices to charge for its menu items. Identified below are the findings of a recent analysis of the cost of the ingredients used in a traditional roast beef dinner. The restaurant has a policy of marking up the cost of its ingredients by a multiple of 8.

Ingredient	£ Cost
Beef	1.68
Potatoes	0.24
Carrots	0.16
Peas	0.14
Sprouts	0.20
Yorkshire pudding	0.10
Total	2.52

Required • • •

(a) What price should the restaurant charge for the roast beef dinner if it wishes to achieve a mark-up multiple of 8?

(b) The restaurant is considering taking a simpler approach to its mark-up calculations of menu items. Under this simplified approach, only the main ingredient of each meal will be costed and price will be determined by using a revised cost mark-up multiple. If the restaurant wishes to earn the same level of profitability from its roast beef dinner what mark-up multiple should it attach to the cost of the main ingredient?

10.7   Quebec's BonVivant hotel has 200 rooms. It sets its room rates according to a policy of charging $120 per night to business clients and $90 per night for group bookings. It has found that most guests stay for three nights. A manager is attempting to determine whether a four-week advance reservation should be made for a group of 40 seeking accommodation on the nights of 20, 21 and 22 June. Eighty rooms for these three nights have already been booked by business clients and past purchasing patterns suggest that, subject to availability, 90% of the remaining 120 rooms will also be sold to business clients.

Required • • •

Determine whether it is in the hotel's interest to accept the group booking for the party of 40.

CHAPTER 11

Working capital management

After studying this chapter, you should have developed an appreciation of:

1 The manner in which cash budgeting represents an important tool in cash management

2 The reasons profit is not the same as cash

3 Factors that need to be considered when extending credit to a customer

4 The role of an accounts receivable ageing schedule in credit management

5 How the economic order quantity (EOQ) can inform purchasing decisions

6 When to take advantage of a supplier's offer of a discount for early payment

7 The risk/return tradeoff apparent in short- vs long-term financing of current assets.

Introduction

Working capital was defined in Chapter 5 as current assets minus current liabilities. In this chapter we explore financial management issues relating to the main elements comprising current assets and current liabilities, i.e. cash, accounts receivable, inventory and accounts payable.

Initially, we will highlight the distinction between cash flow and profit. A clear understanding of this distinction is important. The immediate cause of bankruptcy is not a business's failure to make profit. Bankruptcy occurs when a firm does not have enough cash to honour liabilities that are due for payment. We will highlight this distinction between cash flow and profit by working through the mechanics of preparing a **cash budget**. The cash budget is particularly important as it predicts the timing of cash surpluses and deficits. Knowing when there will be a cash surplus allows investment plans to be formulated. Knowing the timing of a projected cash deficit allows short-term borrowing arrangements to be made in advance of the cash shortfall occurring. Failure to predict the timing of cash shortfalls can result in costly borrowing arrangements, or, much worse, bankruptcy.

In connection with **accounts receivable management**, we will consider factors that should be taken into account when deciding whether to extent credit to a customer. In addition, the nature and use of an ageing of accounts receivable schedule will be introduced. Following this, the economic order quantity (EOQ), which is a tool that can shed light on the optimal purchase order size for **inventory**, will be described.

In connection with **accounts payable management**, a technique enabling you to determine whether to accept a supplier's offer of a discount for early payment will be introduced. This technique is not only useful in accounts payable management, it also represents a fundamentally important analytical tool for any manager considering offering corporate customers a discount for early payment.

Finally, issues surrounding different approaches to financing a hotel's investment in current assets will be explored. We will see that a risk/return trade-off underlies the question of how much short-term, relative to long-term, borrowing should be undertaken. If a hotel uses a relatively high degree of short-term financing, it will be reducing its costs (i.e. increasing its return) but decreasing its net working capital (i.e. increasing its risk), and vice versa.

Cash management

It is important to understand that net cash flow is not the same as profit earned in a period. It is an alarming reality that many business managers have a negligible appreciation of this fundamental aspect of accounting. As a result, business failures can frequently be attributed to managers' failure to recognize a looming liquidity crisis (liquidity refers to the ability to honour short-term financial obligations when they are due). Part of the problem stems from management's tendency to give insufficient attention to cash management, due to an overly blinkered focus on profit. This management tendency is understandable when we recognize the widespread use of profit as a key business performance indicator.

By requiring regular and careful preparation of cash budgets, we can counter this tendency for 'profit myopia'. This is because cash budgets:

1 Identify periods in which a cash deficit is anticipated. Failure to predict such periods is not only potentially costly, it can represent commercial suicide. If a hotel unexpectedly runs out of cash and no lender can be found at short notice, it will have to either liquidate some assets, quickly arrange some long-term finance, or default on liabilities due. An attempt to hastily pursue either of the first two options is likely to result in a costly outcome. By predicting cash deficit periods, however, early negotiations can be conducted with a lending institution (e.g. a bank), and a crisis avoided by establishing a short-term borrowing facility. By taking these steps in a timely manner, not only will a hotel greatly enhance its chances of negotiating favourable loan terms, in extreme cases financial collapse will be averted.

2 Identify periods in which a cash surplus is anticipated. By predicting cash surpluses, plans concerning the optimal investment of the surplus can be developed.

The need for cash budgeting is especially apparent in the hotel industry due to the degree of seasonality experienced in many properties (see discussion in Chapter 1). As careful cash budgeting is a key element of effective cash management, in this section we closely review a cash budget's preparation. By working through the example, your understanding of how cash differs from profit will be consolidated. Although it is an important management tool, you should not be intimidated by the idea of a cash budget. In many ways it is very similar to your bank statement, i.e. it identifies an opening cash balance, lists cash inflows and outflows, and shows the closing cash balance. To minimize any sense of intimidation, prior to working through the example, you should take a quick sneak preview of the cash budget presented in Exhibit 11.5.

For the cash budgeting example, imagine the BackWoods Escape, a hotel located in Banff, Canada. The hotel offers accommodation, dining, bar and also seminar facilities. Sue George, BackWoods' General Manager, wishes to refocus the marketing of the hotel's seminar facilities by pursuing the small corporate convention and retreat market. Consistent with this, plans have been finalized to refurbish the hotel's two seminar rooms and equip them with state of the art presentation technology.

Following two meetings with the hotel accountant, the projected profit and loss statements presented in Exhibit 11.1 have been developed for January, February and March next year. In compiling this budgeted statement, it has been assumed that the hotel's seminar facilities will be refurbished during December this year and that the first conventions will be sold in January next year. No convention, restaurant or bar sales will be made in December while the refurbishment work is underway. Consistent with the higher prices that will be charged upon completion of the refurbishment, the projections indicate higher profit margins than those earned in the past by the hotel. Sue George is particularly encouraged by the projected profit and would like to draw up plans to invest cash earned during this period. It is in connection with this that she has asked you to prepare a cash budget for the January–March period.

In addition to the budgeted profit and loss statements, the information detailed in Exhibit 11.2 has been gathered to facilitate your preparation of BackWoods' cash budget.

The profit and loss statements presented in Exhibit 11.1, together with the projected cash receipts and payments details in Exhibit 11.2, provide you with

Exhibit 11.1
BackWoods Retreat budgeted profit and loss statements for January, February and March

Revenue	January $	$	February $	$	March $	$
Conventions	34,000		36,000		40,000	
Restaurant & Bar	16,000		17,000		20,000	
		50,000		53,000		60,000
Expenses						
Food & drink	8,000		9,000		10,000	
Wages & salaries	7,000		7,400		7,800	
Supplies	1,000		1,100		1,200	
Electricity	400		400		400	
Insurance	500		500		500	
Advertising	2,000		2,000		2,000	
Depreciation	3,000		3,000		3,000	
		21,900		23,400		24,900
Profit		28,100		29,600		35,100

sufficient information to prepare BackWoods' cash budget for next January, February and March.

The easiest way to compile a cash budget involves breaking the exercise into the following three steps:

1 Prepare a schedule of projected receipts by month.
2 Prepare a schedule of projected cash disbursements (payments) by month.
3 Prepare the monthly cash budget by consolidating the monthly receipts and payments schedules and also the estimated cash balance at the beginning of the budget period.

We will now work through each of these steps, in turn, for the BackWoods Retreat.

BackWoods' schedule of projected cash receipts

Preparing the schedule of cash receipts can be tricky when there is a significant variation in the period of credit taken by customers. In the BackWoods Retreat case, we have convention receipts occurring in three instalments (5% in the month prior to the sale, 40% in the month of the sale, and 55% in the month following the sale). In addition, we have 40% of restaurant & bar receipts coinciding with the month of sale (i.e. cash sales) and 60% of receipts occurring one month after the sale.

The best way to deal with this slightly awkward pattern of collections is to develop a table with months as columns and types of receipt as rows. The types of receipt are classified according to the period of credit taken (e.g. month prior to sale, month of sale, one month's credit, etc.). BackWoods' schedule of projected cash

---

Exhibit 11.2
Information relating to BackWoods projection of cash flows

(i) Receipts: It is anticipated that favourable credit terms will have to be extended to the corporate clients targeted when marketing the hotel's new convention facilities. It is projected that 5% of convention revenue will be received in the month prior to the convention as a deposit, 40% of convention revenue will be received at the time the seminar is held, and the remaining 55% will be received in the month following the convention. $42,000 in convention sales are predicted for April. In the past, 40% of restaurant and bar sales have been for cash and 60% have been charged and collected in the month following the sale. This cash to credit ratio for restaurant and bar sales is expected to continue.

(ii) Food and drink purchases: Food and drink stocks are replenished frequently. This signifies that food and drink purchases in a month are approximately equal to food and drink expenses for the month. One month's credit is taken for all food and drink purchases.

(iii) Wages, salaries and supplies payments: Wages, salaries and supplies are paid in the month they are incurred as an expense.

(iv) Electricity payments: Electricity is paid quarterly. The cost per quarter has been estimated at $1,200 and the first annual payment is made in March.

(v) Insurance payments: The annual insurance premium of $6,000 is paid in February.

(vi) Advertising payments: In order to promote the hotel's new seminar facilities, a major advertising campaign costing $5,000 per month will be undertaken during the first four months of the year. In May, following the initial period of intensive promotion, advertising will revert to the hotel's traditional level of $500 per month. This signifies that $24,000 will be spent on advertising over the course of the year ([4 × $5,000] + [8 × $500]). The hotel's accountant felt that for profit and loss statement purposes, it is reasonable to pro rata this $24,000 equally across the year at the rate of $2,000 per month. He defended this approach on the grounds that sales for the whole year would benefit from the additional market exposure achieved during the initial intensive advertising campaign. All advertising is paid for in the month the service is provided.

(vii) Fixed asset payments: Following an appraisal period in which tests will be conducted to ensure that the new presentation equipment is meeting the vendor's specifications, a final installment payment of $150,000 for the seminar room equipment will be made in February. The expense associated with this refurbishment has been included in the depreciation figure in BackWoods' budgeted profit and loss statement for January–March.

(viii) Opening bank balance: It is projected that BackWoods will be holding a bank balance of $6,000 at the beginning of January.

---

receipts is presented in Exhibit 11.3. Most people find it easier to prepare this schedule by moving along the rows (i.e. consider each type of receipt in turn), rather than moving down the columns. The total monthly receipts is found by adding the convention monthly receipts to the restaurant and bar monthly receipts. The total presented as the final column is not strictly needed, however, it does provide a useful check that the sum of the rows equals the sum of the columns.

BackWoods' schedule of projected cash disbursements

Consistent with the projected cash receipts schedule, the schedule of cash disbursements can be compiled by placing months in columns and cash flow type in rows. BackWoods' schedule of projected disbursements is presented in Exhibit

Exhibit 11.3
Schedule of projected cash receipts for BackWoods Retreat

	Jan.	Feb.	March	Total
Convention sales	**$34,000**	**$36,000**	**$40,000**	
Deposit (5% of next month's sales)	$1,800	$2,000	$2,100[a]	$5,900
40% received in month of sale	13,600	14,400	16,000	44,000
55% received in month following sale	0	18,700	19,800	38,500
Total convention receipts	$15,400	$35,100	$37,900	$88,400
Restaurant & bar sales	**$16,000**	**$17,000**	**$20,000**	
40% cash sales	$6,400	$6,800	$8,000	$21,200
60% received in month following sale	0	9,600	10,200	19,800
Total restaurant & bar receipts	6,400	16,400	18,200	41,000
Total all receipts	**$21,800**	**$51,500**	**$56,100**	**$129,400**

[a]Point (*i*) in Exhibit 11.2 indicates that $42,000 is predicted for April's convention sales.

Exhibit 11.4
Schedule of projected cash disbursements for BackWoods Retreat

	$	$	$	$
Disbursements	**January**	**February**	**March**	**Total**
Food and drink (paid in month following purchase)	0	8,000	9,000	17,000
Wages and salaries (paid in month expense is incurred)	7,000	7,400	7,800	22,200
Supplies (paid in month expense is incurred)	1,000	1,100	1,200	3,300
Electricity (paid quarterly)			1,200	1,200
Insurance (paid annually)		6,000		6,000
Advertising (paid in month advertising is conducted)	5,000	5,000	5,000	15,000
Final instalment payment for presentation equipment		150,000		150,000
Total disbursements	**13,000**	**177,500**	**24,200**	**214,700**

11.4. The key to accurately projecting cash receipts and also cash disbursements lies in using well-laid-out schedules such as those presented in Exhibits 11.3 and 11.4. If your schedule is well-designed, compiling the data required becomes a relatively straightforward exercise. Now work carefully through Exhibit 11.4 to ensure you can see how each disbursement item has been determined. Again, you will find it easiest to approach the table on a 'row by row', rather than 'column by column' basis. The disbursement items are presented in Exhibit 11.4 in the same sequence as in Exhibit 11.2.

BackWoods' cash budget

Once the projected cash receipts and cash disbursements schedules have been prepared, preparation of the cash budget becomes a relatively straightforward exercise. In the cash budget we determine each month's net cash flow by subtracting the month's total disbursements from the month's total receipts. We then add the opening cash balance to determine the projected cash balance at each month-end. This is the approach that has been taken in preparing BackWood's cash budget presented in Exhibit 11.5.

Cash versus profit

It is very important to note that while BackWoods is profitable throughout the quarter (see Exhibit 11.1), it is projected that over the same period its cash balance will decline. Having seen the budgeted monthly profit and loss statements, BackWoods' General Manager had anticipated a growing cash balance for the quarter. It is surprising how often in business you will encounter the misconception that cash equates to profit. This example, however, should give you a strong sense of why **cash flow is not the same as profit**. If you have any continuing uncertainty over this issue, you should review Box 11.1 which provides an overview of some of the main reasons why profit is not the same as cash.

Appreciating that profit is not the same as cash is important for two reasons:

1 It shows why we need to prepare budgeted cash flow statements in addition to budgeted profit and loss statements.
2 It highlights the potential of profitable firms becoming bankrupt. Many new profitable ventures expand very quickly. This period of expansion can be a very dangerous stage in the life of an organization, as expansion signifies an outflow of funds on assets such as accounts receivable, inventory, and fixed assets. The cash flow associated with this expansion can result in a liquidity crisis, i.e. the

---

Exhibit 11.5
A cash budget for BackWoods Retreat

	$ January	$ February	$ March	$ Total
Total cash receipts[a]	21,800	51,500	56,100	129,400
less Total cash disbursements[b]	13,000	177,500	24,200	214,700
Net cash flow	8,800	(126,000)	31,900	(85,300)
add Opening cash balance[c]	6,000	14,800	(111,200)	6,000
Ending cash balance (negative balance in brackets)	14,800	(111,200)	(79,300)	(79,300)

[a]From Exhibit 11.3.
[b]From Exhibit 11.4.
[c]January's opening balance provided in Exhibit 11.2 (point *viii*).

Box 11.1
Why is profit not the same as cash?

Revenue versus receipts	We recognize revenue at the time a service is provided, not when cash is received. When a sale is made on account, an account receivable is created and the receipt will lag behind revenue. For BackWoods, as 55% of convention sales and 60% of restaurant and bar sales are on credit, receipts will tend to lag behind revenue.
Purchases versus payments	To facilitate trade, many suppliers extend credit. BackWoods' supplier of food and drink items extend one-month credit. This signifies that payments lag behind purchases.
Wages and salaries	Employees are paid following the completion of work or a working period. While most waged employees are paid weekly, the payment nevertheless lags behind the time when work is performed, which is the time wage expense is recognized. This is more marked for salaried employees, especially in those countries where monthly salary payments are common.
Electricity	In many countries, electricity accounts are settled on a quarterly basis. This signifies at least a three-month discrepancy between some of the electricity expense incurred and payment for electricity.
Insurance	Insurance and rent are paid in advance of charging the associated expense to the profit and loss statement. In the case of insurance, payment is made a year in advance of a portion of the expense.
Fixed asset accounting (i.e depreciation)	One of the most significant reasons causing a discrepancy between cash and profit arises in connection with depreciation accounting. There are two reasons for this: 1 Fixed assets can be very expensive items. 2 The time lag can be considerable. If a fixed asset is being depreciated over 10 years, a portion of the asset's expense lags 10 years behind the actual payment for the asset.
Long-term financing	When a company arranges a loan or increases its share capital there is an immediate large positive impact on cash flow. The only profit and loss statement impact concerns the loan's annual interest expense, however.

expanding firm can run out of cash. Just look at the highly profitable BackWoods Retreat example. The hotel's investment in assets resulted in it having a negative cash balance in February. If BackWoods management did not take care to produce a cash budget and arrange a loan to cover its projected cash deficit period, its inability to pay creditors could put it out of business. This clearly shows how profitable firms can go bankrupt. **If you ensure maintenance of sufficient cash, you will ensure maintenance of a business.**

Accounts receivable management

One of the closest to cash assets is accounts receivable. This is because in the normal course of business an account receivable will become cash in the short term. There are two costs associated with extending credit to customers:

1 The cost of the selling company not being able to deposit the monetary value of a completed sale in its bank, i.e. as a result of not collecting cash at the time of a sale, the vendor will forgo some bank account interest (or if the vendor has a bank overdraft, it will incur additional interest expense).
2 The cost associated with lost revenue due to some accounts receivable proving to be uncollectible.

These costs might cause you to question why companies extend credit. The answer is because credit facilitates trade. Considerable sales would be lost if credit was not extended. It is hard to contemplate a 5-star hotel not allowing customers to use a credit card to settle their accounts. This shows how much we are conditioned to expect the granting of credit whenever we purchase a service from a hotel. In addition to credit card sales, many large hotels have corporate clients that purchase on account.

The cost associated with extending trade credit signifies that hotels have to perform a credit balancing act, i.e. they have to ensure the credit period extended is neither too much nor too little. In addition, a hotel has to ensure that credit is only granted to creditworthy customers. The widely acknowledged five C's of credit management provides a useful checklist of factors to consider when deciding whether to grant credit to a particular customer. The five C's comprise character, capacity, capital, conditions and collateral, and are described in Box 11.2.

Box 11.2
The five C's of credit management

The following issues should be appraised when considering whether to extend trade credit to a customer:

1 *Character*: does the customer have a predisposition towards timely payment of accounts?

2 *Capacity*: does the customer have the capacity to run a successful business?

3 *Capital*: does the customer have sufficient working and long-term capital to honour the account when it is due for payment?

4 *Conditions*: are there any particular economic conditions that might affect the potential customer's ability to pay? In addition, there might be particular circumstances such as low occupancy in the off-season that might cause a hotel to consider extending credit to less creditworthy customers.

5 *Collateral*: does the customer have assets that could be liquidated relatively easily in the event of a liquidity crisis that threatened timely reimbursement of the account due?

When appraising a hotel's accounts receivable strategy and performance, it can be useful to determine the average number of days' credit it extends to customers. We saw in Chapter 5 that we can gauge the accounts receivable turnover and average number of days' credit advanced by a company if we can determine its level of credit sales and average accounts receivable balance. For example, imagine that London's HighTowers hotel made £2,835,000 in credit sales during the most recent calendar year and that its year-end accounts receivable balance was £270,000. By dividing credit sales by the accounts receivable balance, we can determine HighTowers' accounts receivable turnover as follows:

$$\frac{\text{Credit sales}}{\text{Accounts receivable balance}} \quad \text{i.e.} \quad \frac{£2,835,000}{£\,270,000} = 10.5$$

By dividing 365 days (i.e. the days in a year) by the accounts receivable turnover, we can determine the average number of days that credit is extended as follows:

$$\frac{\text{Days in a year}}{\text{Accounts receivable turnover}} \quad \text{i.e.} \quad \frac{365}{10.5} = 34.8 \text{ days}$$

For those working within a company, a more detailed analysis of the accounts receivable balance can be conducted by preparing an 'Ageing of Accounts Receivable' schedule. An example of such a schedule is presented in Exhibit 11.6. This provides a breakdown of HighTowers' total accounts receivable balance according to the number of days that each amount owing is overdue. When reviewing the schedule, assume that we are currently standing at the end of December and that HighTowers has a policy of extending 30-day credit terms. This signifies that credit arising from sales made during December can be described as current, i.e. it is not yet overdue.

With the exception of the 31–60 days' overdue accounts, the schedule reveals a fairly typical time distribution of the accounts receivable balance. To have 20% of the accounts receivable balance falling within the 31–60 days overdue category is cause for some concern, however. Immediate management action addressing this issue may be warranted. It may be that one large account is in dispute, or one or more debtors are experiencing liquidity problems. If further detail is sought, an accounts receivable ageing schedule that separately analyses the age of each individual

Exhibit 11.6
Ageing of accounts receivable schedule

	Current	0–30	Days overdue 31–60	61–90	Over 90	
Sale period	December	November	October	September	August	Total
Accounts receivable	£4,900	£490	£1,400	£140	£70	£7,000
Percentage of total	70%	7%	20%	2%	1%	100%

Box 11.3
Accounts receivable collection techniques

The following account collection methods are listed in the order with which they are generally used in connection with a particular account:

1 *Letters*: once an account has been overdue for a number of days, a polite reminder can be mailed. Following a designated period, if payment is not forthcoming, a second more strongly worded letter can be sent.

2 *Telephone calls*: in addition to letters, one or more telephone calls to the accounts payable officer concerned can be made. This technique can be particularly effective if the credit manager possesses good negotiating skills and has extensive business contacts.

3 *Site visits*: visiting the debtor can be an effective counter to the 'cheque is in the mail' syndrome, as payment can be made on the spot. It is only feasible, however, when the debtor is located in the vicinity of the company seeking reimbursement.

4 *Collection agency*: there are an increasing number of factoring companies that specialize in credit management and debt collection. As this can represent an expensive way to collect accounts receivable, it should only be used if none of the techniques referred to above have been successful.

5 *Legal action*: this can be regarded as the most radical step in a collection strategy. It is expensive and can trigger the debtor company's bankruptcy. Even if successful, legal action might sour relations with the debtor firm and signify the end of a trading relationship.

---

debtor's account can be prepared. Most computerized accounting systems have the capacity to provide accounts receivable aging schedules in such a format.

Once problem accounts have been identified, a series of steps designed to collect outstanding debts can be initiated. These steps are summarized in Box 11.3. If an account is particularly large, several initial steps can inform what collection strategy would be most appropriate. These include:

1 Determine why the customer has withheld payment.
2 Determine the payment history of the customer.
3 Determine whether the customer is a large client that might take their business elsewhere if a significant dispute over credit develops.
4 Determine whether we have personnel who might be able to expedite payment through their contacts in the debtor firm.

Inventory management

Paralleling the balancing act that has to be performed when determining the credit period to be extended to customers, care has to be taken in inventory management to ensure that neither too little nor too much inventory is held. A hotel that holds low inventory balances runs the risk of experiencing stock-outs. This can result in the immediate loss of sales and, perhaps more significantly, it can also significantly damage customer goodwill (e.g. a restaurant customer becoming disgruntled when several menu items are unavailable). If too much inventory is held, the hotel will experience high inventory carrying costs that include:

1 The opportunity cost of money tied up in inventory, i.e. money invested in inventory can be viewed as money that could be earning interest if it was invested in a bank account.
2 The cost of pilferage.
3 Cost of deterioration of perishable items.
4 Cost of inventory insurance.
5 Handling costs, i.e. if large amounts of inventory are held, additional costs may result from problems associated with storing, locating and moving inventory.
6 The cost of maintaining and financing storage space.

Box 11.4   Using the EOQ model to determine optimal order size

The EOQ model assumes:

• rate of demand for inventory item in question is relatively predictable
• administrative order costs do not vary with size of order processed.

The EOQ can be calculated by applying the following formula:

$$EOQ = \sqrt{(2 \times U \times O \div C)}$$

where:

U = Usage per period of time (same period of time as used for carrying cost).

O = Cost of ordering and receiving an order.

C = Carrying cost per unit of inventory per period of time (same period of time as used for usage).

Example
Imagine that New York's Elite Restaurant offers an extensive menu of fine wines. The average case of wine costs Elite $360. Past experience indicates 750 cases of wine are sold per year by the restaurant. Following discussions with Elite's purchasing and store managers, Elite's accountant has estimated that the cost of ordering and receiving a shipment of wine is $30. As the restaurant holds any excess working capital as marketable securities that earn 5% per annum, the accountant estimates the cost of holding a case of wine for a year to be $18 (i.e. $360 \times 5\%$).
   The EOQ for Elite's wine inventory can be calculated as follows:

$$\sqrt{(2 \times 750 \times \$30 \div \$18)} = \sqrt{(2,500)} = 50 \text{ cases per order.}$$

By applying the EOQ, we have determined that if Elite orders its wine in shipment sizes of 50 cases, the sum of its annual carrying and ordering costs will be minimized.

Hospitality, Leisure & Tourism Series

The correct amount of inventory to be held is largely a matter of judgement. One way to inform such a judgement is to monitor inventory turnover. As noted in Chapter 5, this can be computed by dividing the cost of sales by the average inventory balance. If a hotel is part of a chain, it can be a useful exercise to benchmark inventory turnover rates in order to identify those members of the chain holding relatively high or low levels of inventory.

A second aspect of inventory management that lends itself to analysis is the question of how much inventory should be ordered when making a purchase order. The economic order quantity (EOQ) model is a technique enabling us to estimate the optimal order size for purchase orders. While theoretically correct, the model does require fairly restrictive assumptions. Despite this, the model can be applied in many hotel situations and it does highlight how purchasing officers should attempt to balance the trade-off between minimizing inventory holding costs and the costs of processing orders and shipments. The model is outlined in Box 11.4.

Accounts payable management

Accounts payable management can be seen as the flip side of accounts receivable management. For an account receivable, bank interest that could be earned is lost due to money that relates to a sale being held by a customer. For an account payable, we can gain bank interest from holding money that relates to a purchase already made. Care should be taken not to abuse credit terms extended by suppliers, however. Good supplier relations can be a key source of competitive advantage. Characteristics of a good supplier include a willingness to:

1 meet rush orders
2 tailor shipments to specific requests
3 maintain high quality in goods and services supplied
4 provide flexible credit terms.

One particular issue that can arise in connection with accounts payable management is a discount offered by a supplier for early payment of an account. This type of trade discount is typically stated using abbreviated terms such as '1/10 *net* 30'. This means that the purchaser can deduct a 1% discount off the invoiced amount if payment is made 10 days after the start of the credit period (typically the invoice date), and if the discount is not taken, the invoiced amount is due for payment 30 days after the start of the credit period. A method enabling you to appraise whether the discount should be taken is described in Case 11.1.

Case 11.1

Financial decision making in action –
The Financial Controller determining whether to take a trade discount

In most organizations, accounts payable management falls within the financial controller's jurisdiction. An issue that needs to be managed in accounts payable management is the question of whether to take the early payment discount offered by some suppliers. This issue can be analysed by viewing an early payment as an advance of funds that earns a return. We can determine the effective annual rate of return on this advance relatively easily in the following way.

Imagine British Airways has received a £1,000 invoice and credit terms of 2/10 net 45 from one of its contract food suppliers. This means BA can either pay £980 in 10 days' time, or £1,000 in 45 days' time. By advancing £980 35 days earlier than necessary, BA will get a return of £20 (i.e. the £20 saved on the invoice payment). To find what this represents in terms of an annual rate of return, we have to gross up the £20 return on the £980 advance to translate it from a 35-day period to 365 days, i.e.:

$$\frac{£20}{£980} \times \frac{365}{35} = 0.213 \text{ (or 21.3\%)}$$

This calculation used the actual monetary amounts involved. Alternatively, the following generic formula can be used:

$$\frac{\% \text{ discount offered}}{100 - \% \text{ discount offered}} \times \frac{\text{Days in a year}}{\text{Days difference in final due date and discount date}}$$

This generic formula can be applied to the above example as follows:

$$\frac{2}{98} \times \frac{365}{(45 - 10)} = 0.213 \text{ (or 21.3\%)}$$

For this example, the financial controller would conclude that if BA has enough cash to enable early payment, and if it is earning less than 21.3% per annum interest on any cash balances held, then it should take the discount and gain the benefit of an effective 21.3% annual rate of return. If BA does not have sufficient cash and must borrow to take the discount, then as long as the cost of borrowing is less than 21.3%, it is in its interest to borrow £980 and take advantage of the trade discount offered.

Working capital management

As noted in the chapter's introduction, net working capital is defined as current assets – current liabilities. So far we have considered management issues arising in connection with the main elements of working capital, i.e. cash, accounts receivable, inventory and accounts payable. We now turn to consider a more holistic dimension of working capital management. Working capital management can be a particularly important dimension of financial management in hotels, as high seasonality translates into high working capital volatility. During the busy season, a hotel will have a relatively high level of current assets. This is because:

- Higher levels of cash will be needed to support the above-average levels of daily purchase payments
- Higher accounts receivable will result from the above-average levels of sales
- Higher inventory levels will be needed to support the above-average levels of activity.

Figure 11.1 depicts investment in fixed and current assets for a resort hotel that experiences a busy mid-summer and mid-winter season. Note how the hotel's fixed

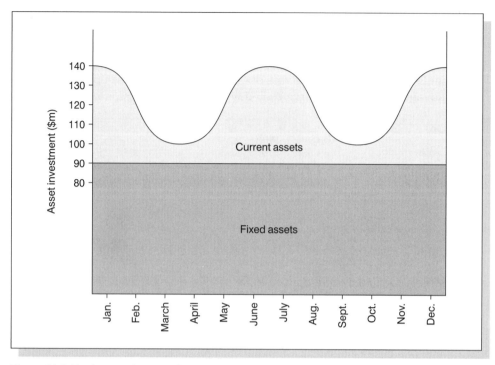

Figure 11.1 The impact of seasonality on asset investment

assets remain constant throughout the year. Its current assets, however, exhibit considerable volatility, rising to highs during busy seasons and lows during quiet seasons. It is this volatility in current assets that results in the volatility of the hotel's total asset base.

A key working capital management issue that arises in connection with Figure 11.1 concerns the mix of current liabilities and long-term capital that should be used to finance a hotel's fluctuating asset base. It is widely acknowledged in the finance literature that long-term assets (i.e. fixed assets) should be financed through long-term capital. Therefore, for the hotel depicted in Figure 11.1, the minimum amount of long-term financing that should be raised is $90 m. It is also apparent from Figure 11.1 that the permanent amount of funds required during the year is $100 m (total assets never drop below $100 m), and a case could be made for financing all of this permanent portion of total assets with long-term capital.

The issue of what proportion of the floating current asset base should be financed through current liabilities reduces to a profit versus risk trade-off decision. This is because, as is explained in Box 11.5, a relatively high ratio of current liabilities to long-term capital signifies a high profit/high risk strategy, and a relatively low ratio of current liabilities to long-term capital signifies a low profit/low risk strategy. While all managers like to see increased profit levels, it is obvious that care must be taken not to jeopardize an organization's solvency by becoming too dependent on current liability financing.

When considering this short- versus long-term financing issue, if an aggressive financing approach is taken, it should be noted that not all incremental investments in current assets have to be financed by short-term loans. This is because part of the

---

Box 11.5
The profit/risk trade-off in current liability financing

The profit aspect: Current liabilities are cheaper to finance than long-term capital. Accounts payable and wages accrued generally have no cost associated with them. In addition, except for times when there is a widespread expectation that interest rates will decline in the future, it is normal for short-term lending rates to be below long-term lending rates.

The risk aspect: If a hotel increases its current liabilities relative to long-term capital its net working capital will decline. Net working capital is a key indicator of a firm's ability to pay its debts over the short term. A decrease in net working capital signifies increased risk due to the lower short-term asset coverage of short-term liabilities.

Effects of high current liability financing: Synthesizing the profit and risk aspects of current liability financing, we can conclude that a relatively high short- to long-term financing ratio has a positive impact on profit and risk.

Effects of low current liability financing: It follows that a relatively low short- to long-term financing ratio has a negative impact on profit and risk.

---

extra current asset investment occurring during busy seasons will be financed spontaneously by higher current liabilities that also arise during busy seasons. The greater business activity levels that stimulate higher current assets will also result in higher accounts payable and average wage accruals due to increased levels of purchasing and casual staff employment.

Summary

In this chapter we have looked at management issues associated with the main accounts that comprise working capital, i.e. cash, accounts receivable, inventory and accounts payable. A particularly important aspect of the chapter concerned an illustration of how cash flow is not the same as profit.

Having read the chapter you should now know:

- How cash budgeting represents an important aspect of cash management
- How cash differs from profit
- What issues need to be considered when deciding whether to extend credit to a new customer
- How an accounts receivable ageing schedule can aid the identification of customer accounts warranting particular attention
- How application of the EOQ model can aid the reduction of costs associated with inventory management
- How to analyse whether to accept a supplier's offer of a discount for early payment of an account payable
- How a risk/return trade-off exists when deciding what proportion of short- versus long-term capital should be used to finance current asset investments.

Hospitality, Leisure & Tourism Series

References

Atkinson, H., Berry, A. and Jarvis, R. (1995) *Business Accounting for Hospitality and Tourism & Leisure*, International Thomson Publishing, London, Chapter 17.

Coltman, M. M. and Jagels, M.G. (2001) *Hospitality Management Accounting*, 7th edition, John Wiley, Chichester, Chapter 11.

Gitman, L. J., Juchau, R., Flanagan, J., Pearson, K. and Clemens, M. (1998) *Principles of Managerial Finance*, 2nd edition, Addison-Wesley Longman Australia Pty Ltd, Sydney, Chapters 16–19.

Hansen, D. R. and Mowen, M. M. (2000) *Management Accounting*, 5th edition, South-Western, Cincinnati, OH, Chapter 19.

Kotas, R. (1999) *Management Accounting for Hospitality and Tourism*, 3rd edition, International Thomson Publishing, London, Chapter 18.

Kotas, R. and Conlan, M. (1997) *Hospitality Accounting*, 5th edition, International Thomson Publishing, London, Chapter 23.

Owen, G. (1994) *Accounting for Hospitality, Tourism & Leisure*, Pitman Publishing, London, Chapter 17.

Problems

✓ indicates that a solution appears at the back of the text

✓ **11.1** The marketing department of Singapore's CrownJewel Hotel has projected the following sales in the last half of the current financial year.

CrownJewel projected sales (in $000)

	July	August	September	October	November	December
Rooms	630	660	600	540	500	600
Restaurant & Bar	90	100	80	70	60	80

Most of CrownJewel's room sales are made to corporate clients. Past experience indicates that 10% of room sales are for cash, 50% is collected in the month following the sale, 35% is collected two months following the sale and 5% of sales are to a large company that takes three months to settle accounts.

In the past, 30% of restaurant and bar sales have been for cash and 70% have been charged and collected in the month following the sale.

Required • • •
Prepare a schedule showing CrownJewel's projected cash receipts in October, November and December.

✓ **11.2** In connection with the CrownJewel sales estimates provided in Problem 11.1, experience has shown that room variable costs are 20% of room revenue. Sixty per cent of these variable costs are paid for in the month the expense is incurred and the remainder is paid for in the following month.

Restaurant and bar variable costs comprise wages, food and drink. Wages are 10% of restaurant and bar revenue and are paid for in the month incurred. The cost of food and drink is 15% of restaurant and bar revenue. Due to the CrownJewel's inventory stocking policy, 40% of food and drink is purchased one month before it is sold. The remainder is purchased in the month of sale. All food and drink is purchased from the same company which extends one-month trade credit.

The hotel has fixed costs of $15,000 per month which are paid for in the month incurred. In addition, the hotel estimates it will make a quarterly electricity payment of $3,000 in November and its annual insurance premium of $7,500 is due for payment in December.

Required • • •
Prepare a schedule showing CrownJewel's projected cash disbursements for October, November and December.

✓ 11.3 Draw on your solutions provided to Problems 11.1 and 11.2 to prepare CrownJewel's cash budget for October, November and December. It has been estimated that the hotel will have a positive cash balance of $12,000 on 30 September.

11.4 The ShireLodge provides a residential convention service in England's Yorkshire Dales. The lodge's general manager is concerned about cash flow in the next few months particularly as insurance will soon be due for payment.

The following revenue and expense estimates have been developed for the first four months of 20X2:

	January £	February £	March £	April £
Convention sales revenue	10,000	12,000	13,000	14,000
Fixed costs:				
Salaries	4,000	4,000	4,000	4,000
Ground maintenance	500	500	500	500
Insurance	420	420	420	420

It has been estimated that sales in December 20X1 will be £8,000. Previous cash collections indicate that 10% of all sales are collected in the month prior to the sale as a deposit. Fifty per cent of all sales are collected in the month of the sale, and 40% of sales are collected in the month following the sale.

Variable costs are 15% of revenue. Ninety per cent of variable costs are paid in the month of the sale to which they relate, and the remainder are paid in the month prior to the sale (purchase of some food and other items in preparation for conventions). Salary and ground maintenance fixed costs are paid for as they are incurred. Insurance is paid for twice a year, in January and July. It is estimated that on 1 January 20X2 the lodge will have £4,200 in its bank account.

Required • • •
Prepare a cash budget showing receipts, disbursements and opening and closing cash balances for each of the first three months of 20X2.

11.5   A review of the accounts receivable records of Auckland's CreatureComforts Hotel reveals the following year-end information.

CreatureComforts Hotel
Analysis of age of accounts receivable as at 31/12/X1

Month of sale	Accounts receivable $	%
July	2,594	1
August	13,448	5
September	2,782	1
October	7,890	3
November	26,300	10
December	210,000	80
Total year-end balance	263,014	100

The credit manager believes that the report accurately shows the proportion of the year-end accounts receivable balance that can be traced to months in which credit sales were made. Forty per cent of the hotel's $6,000,000 annual sales are on credit. The hotel extends 30-day credit terms.

Required ▪ ▪ ▪
(a) Using the year-end account balance, evaluate the effectiveness of the hotel's accounts receivable collection system.
(b) If the hotel's peak season runs from November through to January, how does this additional information affect your answer to part (a)?
(c) Prepare an ageing of accounts receivable schedule in order to obtain additional insight into the status of the hotel's accounts receivable balance. What further observations can be made from the ageing schedule?

11.6   The laundry department of the Edinburgh hotel, TartanDays, orders concentrated laundry detergent in 10-kilogram boxes. Each box costs £32. It costs £20 to place, process and receive a laundry detergent order and TartanDays has estimated that it would cost £2 to hold a box of detergent in inventory for a year. The hotel uses 25 boxes of detergent per month.

Required ▪ ▪ ▪
What is the TartanDays' EOQ for laundry detergent?

11.7   Toronto's Roma Pizzeria sells a variety of pizzas. The largest inventory item held by Roma is cheese. The owner has approached you for advice in connection with the size of orders that should be placed when ordering cheese. You have ascertained the following:

• Cheese is ordered in blocks at $20 per block.
• Roma currently places an order with its cheese supplier every two weeks and the average order size is 500 blocks. Roma has a policy of timing its cheese reordering so that its inventory of cheese has declined to 40 blocks when the new shipment arrives.

- Money not invested in inventory could be invested in a bank account to earn Roma 5% per annum.
- The cheese is shipped in refrigerated transport and the cost of ordering, shipping and receiving a shipment is $30.

Required • • •
(a) What is the Roma's EOQ for cheese? Assume 52 weeks in a year.
(b) What is the sum of Roma's current cheese carrying and ordering costs? Assume 52 weeks in a year.
(c) What would Roma save in total carrying and ordering costs if it changed its order size to the most economic order quantity (EOQ)?

11.8 Johannesburg's 'MouthWatering' Restaurant has approached you for assistance in determining whether it should take the 1/10 net 30 trade discount terms offered by its main food supplier. The restaurant currently has invested excess liquidity in marketable securities earning an 8% average annual rate of return.

Required • • •
Conduct an analysis to demonstrate whether the MouthWatering Restaurant should take the trade discount offered.

11.9 Feast'N'Run provides a contract catering service to several university and college campuses. One of its main suppliers has offered trade discount terms of 1/10 net 40. In the past, Feast'N'Run has taken an average of 50 days' credit when settling its trade accounts. The chief accountant feels that this policy has not damaged relations with any of its suppliers and proposes to continue with it, except when making an early payment to secure a discount. Feast'N'Run finances its investment in working capital by short-term borrowing that carries an annual interest rate of 9.5%.

Required • • •
Conduct an analysis to demonstrate whether Feast'N'Run should take the trade discount offered.

11.10 Le SlopeVerticale is a French skiing hotel complex offering accommodation, restaurant, bar, ski shop and equipment hire facilities. The complex has estimated it will have the following assets for the forthcoming year:

Month	Current assets €	Fixed assets €	Total assets €
January	60,000	1,000,000	1,060,000
February	60,000	1,000,000	1,060,000
March	60,000	1,000,000	1,060,000
April	40,000	1,000,000	1,040,000
May	6,000	1,000,000	1,006,000
June	2,000	1,000,000	1,002,000
July	2,000	1,000,000	1,002,000
August	2,000	1,000,000	1,002,000
September	2,000	1,000,000	1,002,000
October	6,000	1,000,000	1,006,000
November	40,000	1,000,000	1,040,000
December	60,000	1,000,000	1,060,000

With respect to the cost of financing these assets, no interest is paid on the balance of trade accounts payable or accrued wages, which fluctuate through the year. At any time, the aggregate of these two accounts is generally 60% of current assets. The remainder of SlopeVerticale's investment in assets is financed by:

- Long-term financing costing an average of 10% per annum
- A floating short-term bank loan carrying an interest rate of 6% per annum (used to cover any financing shortfall).

Required • • •

(a) If SlopeVerticale's long-term financing is €1,000,000:
   1 Based on the asset projections provided, determine the floating short-term bank loan required in each month of the year.
   2 Determine SlopeVerticale's total financing cost for the year.
(b) If SlopeVerticale's long-term financing is €1,020,000:
   1 Determine the floating short-term bank loan required in each month of the year.
   2 Determine SlopeVerticale's total financing cost for the year.
(c) What are the profit/risk trade-offs associated with the different financing options identified in parts (a) and (b)?

Investment
decision making

Learning objectives

After studying this chapter, you should have
developed an appreciation of:

1 How the accounting rate of return, payback, net
present value and internal rate of return
investment appraisal techniques can be applied

2 The relative merits of these investment appraisal
techniques

3 What is meant by the 'time value of money'

4 How the present value of a cash flow occurring in
the future can be determined using discounting
tables.

Introduction

This topic focuses on analytical methods that can be used to assess the merit of long-term investment proposals. The process of rationing funds to long-term investment proposals is often referred to as 'capital budgeting'. In the context of financial management, the term 'capital' is used when referring to long-term funds (we talk of a company 'raising capital' when it issues more equity finance or borrows long-term debt). In the earlier chapter concerned with budgeting, it was noted that the 'budget' relates to plans for the forthcoming year. It follows that 'capital budgeting' relates to longer-term budgeting, i.e. decision making concerned with investing in fixed assets such as laundry or kitchen equipment, or the decision to refurbish rooms. As a large proportion of a hotel's assets are fixed assets, it is evident that **capital budgeting is an important decision-making area for hotel managers**.

The chapter is structured around the following four investment appraisal techniques:

- Accounting rate of return
- Payback
- Net present value
- Internal rate of return.

Accounting rate of return

A worked example that highlights the calculation of the accounting rate of return is presented in Box 12.1.

At first glance the ARR might appear conceptually appealing. It has major shortcomings, however. These shortcomings include:

1 The ARR fails to consider the period of the investment. Suppose a hotel is deciding whether to take this 40% ARR investment option with a 3-year life, or a second $8,000 investment option that has a 10-year life and an ARR of 38%. Both returns appear very high. Consequently, we are left to question, would you like to make an investment that provides a very high return for 3 years, or an investment that provides a very high return for 10 years? Let us assume that the hotel in question generally makes an average return of 12% on its assets. By investing in the 10-year asset that provides a 38% ARR, it will be able to increase its average return on assets for 7 years longer than if it invests in the 3-year asset that provides a 40% ARR. In this case, it appears that the 10-year 38% ARR investment option is preferable to the 3-year 40% ARR option.

2 The ARR is based on accounting profits. These figures involve some apportioning of cash flows to different accounting periods (e.g. depreciation). As a result, profits are not 'real' in a tangible sense. They represent nothing more than the accountant's 'account' of performance. Cash flows, however, are real, and it is the commercial reality of the timing of money entering and exiting the organization, and not the accountant's account, that we need to incorporate into the decision model.

Box 12.1
Finding an investment proposal's accounting rate of return

The accounting rate of return (ARR) can be found by applying the following formula:

$$ARR = \frac{\text{Average annual profit generated by the investment}}{\text{Average investment}}$$

Usually, ARR is stated as a percentage, therefore multiply the above formula by 100.

Imagine Auckland's KiwiStay Hotel is appraising a 1 January 20X0 investment of $8,000 in a drinks vending machine that will increase accounting profits by $1,000 in 20X0, $2,000 in 20X1 and $3,000 in 20X2. At the end of 20X2, it is estimated the vending machine will be sold for $2,000.

Calculating the average annual profit generated by the investment is relatively straightforward. We find it is $2,000 by taking the average of the profit generated in years 20X0, 20X1 and 20X2 ([$1,000 + $2,000 + $3,000] ÷ 3).

The average investment is a slightly more challenging concept to grasp, however. Try thinking of it as 'The average amount of money invested in the asset during its life'. At the beginning of 20X0, it is evident that $8,000 is invested in the asset (i.e. the initial investment). At the end of the life of the asset, it is evident that $2,000 is effectively invested, as this is the amount that could be liquidated if the asset is sold. As the asset is worth $8,000 at the beginning of its life and $2,000 at the end of its life, its average value over the duration of its life is $5,000. This is the midpoint between $8,000 and $2,000, and can be computed as follows: ([$8,000 + $2,000] ÷ 2).

As the average annual profit is $2,000 and the average investment in the asset is $5,000, the ARR can be computed as follows:

$$ARR = \frac{\$2,000}{\$5,000} \times 100 = 40\%$$

Payback

Surveys of capital budgeting practice highlight the popularity of the payback investment appraisal technique (e.g. Lamminmaki *et al.*, 1996). Payback's popularity may result from it being an intuitively appealing approach that is relatively simple to understand. In addition, payback can be used as an initial screening mechanism prior to the use of more sophisticated investment appraisal techniques. Application of the payback approach to appraising an investment proposal is outlined in Box 12.2.

Like accounting rate of return, the payback technique has several shortcomings. Two major shortcomings of the payback approach are:

1 It fails to consider any cash flows occurring after the payback period. The second of the two examples presented in Box 12.2 has the faster payback, but the first example generates the most lifetime cash inflows. In the first payback example,

---

Box 12.2
Finding an investment proposal's payback

Payback can be calculated as follows:

Payback = The time taken to recoup the cash invested in an asset

Payback example 1
Imagine an initial investment of $20,000 will increase operating cash inflows by $5,000 in each of the 8 years of an asset's life.

Payback = 4 years

(It takes 4 years to get the $20,000 back)

Payback example 2
A 1 January 20X0 investment of $10,000 will increase operating cash inflows by $3,000 in 20X0, $4,000 in 20X1 and $6,000 in 20X2.

Payback = 2.5 years

(After two years, $7,000 of the $10,000 investment will have been recouped. As the operating cash inflow in the third year is $6,000, it is assumed that the final $3,000 needed will have been recouped half-way through 20X2)

---

note that if the projected operating cash inflows had been $100,000 in each of the last four years of the investment's life, the payback would still be 4 years.

2 It fails to recognize the time value of money, i.e. $1 today does not have the same value as $1 in a year's time. Payback treats cash flows occurring in different time periods as if they have the same value.

Net present value (NPV)

NPV is based on the concept that $1 in one time period is not worth the same as $1 in another time period ($1 today is worth more than $1 in a year's time). If $1 could be invested in a bank account to earn 10%, then we would be indifferent between having $1 now or $1.1 in a year's time. Therefore, if we expect an interest rate of 10% for the foreseeable future, $1 today has the same value as $1.1 in one year's time.

The view that $1 today does not have the same value as $1 in a year's time is not recognized in the accounting rate of return nor in the payback method. Note that in the examples above, no attempt was made to adjust the value of future profits (in the ARR example), or future cash flows (in the payback example) in order to bring them into line with cash flows occurring at the beginning of the project's life.

The NPV investment appraisal technique involves finding today's value of future cash flows associated with an investment proposal. When today's value of a project's inflows are greater than today's value of the project's outflows, the project is described as having a positive 'net present value'. A positive net present value signifies that a project is acceptable; a negative net present value (i.e. the present value of a project's outflows are greater than the present value of its inflows) signifies that a project should be rejected.

Today's value of a future cash flow can be found by multiplying the future cash flow by the appropriate factor appearing in Table 12.1 or Table 12.2. These tables are widely referred to as 'discounting tables'. Table 12.1 presents the present value factors to be used when finding the present value of a single cash flow. Table 12.2 presents the present value factors to be used when finding the present value of a series of equal cash flows (a series of equal cash flows is referred to as an 'annuity'). Box 12.3 presents two small examples that illustrate how the tables can be used to find the present value of a future cash flow.

Box 12.3
Using discounting tables to find the present value of future cash flows

Discounting example 1

Assuming an interest rate of 10%, what is today's value of a $300 cash inflow occurring in 4 years' time?

Answer: First, note that we are dealing with a single cash flow, therefore we turn to Table 12.1 (present value factors for a single cash flow). In this table, move along the columns until you come to the column headed 10%. Then move down the rows in this column until you come to the 4-year row. The factor you will find is 0.683. This signifies that if we multiply $300 by 0.683, we will have found today's value (or the present value) of a $300 cash flow occurring in 4 years' time.

In the calculation presented below, the term 'PV' is an abbreviation of 'present value' and is used to highlight the fact that the factor used has been drawn from the 'present value of a single cash flow' table. The first number following the 'PV' term refers to the relevant interest rate and the second number following the term refers to the relevant number of years. We find the present value of $300 in four years' time to be $204.90.

Present value = $300 (PV10%, 4 years) = $300 × 0.683 = $204.90

Discounting example 2

Assuming an interest rate of 12%, what is today's value of receiving an annual payment of $400 in each of the next 5 years? Assume the first payment is in 1 year's time.

Answer: First, note that in this second example we are dealing with a series of equal cash flows, therefore we turn to Table 12.2 (present values factors for an annuity). This table has been compiled on the basis that the first cash flow of the stream of equal cash flows will occur one year from today. In the same manner to that used in the first discounting example, move along the columns until you come to the column headed 12%. Then move down the rows in this column until you come to the 5-year row. The factor you will find is 3.605. In the calculation presented below, the term 'PVA' is an abbreviation of 'present value of an annuity' and is used to highlight the fact that the factor used has been drawn from the 'present value factors for an annuity' table.

Present value = $400 (PVA12%, 5 years) = $400 × 3.605 = $1,442

Year	1%	2%	3%	4%	5%	6%	7%	8%	9%	10%	11%	12%	13%	14%	15%	16%	17%	18%	19%	20%
1	0.990	0.980	0.971	0.962	0.952	0.943	0.935	0.926	0.917	0.909	0.901	0.893	0.885	0.877	0.870	0.862	0.855	0.847	0.840	0.833
2	0.980	0.961	0.943	0.925	0.907	0.890	0.873	0.857	0.842	0.826	0.812	0.797	0.783	0.769	0.756	0.743	0.731	0.718	0.706	0.694
3	0.971	0.942	0.915	0.889	0.864	0.840	0.816	0.794	0.772	0.751	0.731	0.712	0.693	0.675	0.658	0.641	0.624	0.609	0.593	0.579
4	0.961	0.924	0.888	0.855	0.823	0.792	0.763	0.735	0.708	0.683	0.659	0.636	0.613	0.592	0.572	0.552	0.534	0.516	0.499	0.482
5	0.951	0.906	0.863	0.822	0.784	0.747	0.713	0.681	0.650	0.621	0.593	0.567	0.543	0.519	0.497	0.476	0.456	0.437	0.419	0.402
6	0.942	0.888	0.837	0.790	0.746	0.705	0.666	0.630	0.596	0.564	0.535	0.507	0.480	0.456	0.432	0.410	0.390	0.370	0.352	0.335
7	0.933	0.871	0.813	0.760	0.711	0.665	0.623	0.583	0.547	0.513	0.482	0.452	0.425	0.400	0.376	0.354	0.333	0.314	0.296	0.279
8	0.923	0.853	0.789	0.731	0.677	0.627	0.582	0.540	0.502	0.467	0.434	0.404	0.376	0.351	0.327	0.305	0.285	0.266	0.249	0.233
9	0.914	0.837	0.766	0.703	0.645	0.592	0.544	0.500	0.460	0.424	0.391	0.361	0.333	0.308	0.284	0.263	0.243	0.225	0.209	0.194
10	0.905	0.820	0.744	0.676	0.614	0.558	0.508	0.463	0.422	0.386	0.352	0.322	0.295	0.270	0.247	0.227	0.208	0.191	0.176	0.162
11	0.896	0.804	0.722	0.650	0.585	0.527	0.475	0.429	0.388	0.350	0.317	0.287	0.261	0.237	0.215	0.195	0.178	0.162	0.148	0.135
12	0.887	0.789	0.701	0.625	0.557	0.497	0.444	0.397	0.356	0.319	0.286	0.257	0.231	0.208	0.187	0.168	0.152	0.137	0.124	0.112
13	0.879	0.773	0.681	0.601	0.530	0.469	0.415	0.368	0.326	0.290	0.258	0.229	0.204	0.182	0.163	0.145	0.130	0.116	0.104	0.093
14	0.870	0.758	0.661	0.577	0.505	0.442	0.388	0.340	0.299	0.263	0.232	0.205	0.181	0.160	0.141	0.125	0.111	0.099	0.088	0.078
15	0.861	0.743	0.642	0.555	0.481	0.417	0.362	0.315	0.275	0.239	0.209	0.183	0.160	0.140	0.123	0.108	0.095	0.084	0.074	0.065
16	0.853	0.728	0.623	0.534	0.458	0.394	0.339	0.292	0.252	0.218	0.188	0.163	0.141	0.123	0.107	0.093	0.081	0.071	0.062	0.054
17	0.844	0.714	0.605	0.513	0.436	0.371	0.317	0.270	0.231	0.198	0.170	0.146	0.125	0.108	0.093	0.080	0.069	0.060	0.052	0.045
18	0.836	0.700	0.587	0.494	0.416	0.350	0.296	0.250	0.212	0.180	0.153	0.130	0.111	0.095	0.081	0.069	0.059	0.051	0.044	0.038
19	0.828	0.686	0.570	0.475	0.396	0.331	0.277	0.232	0.194	0.164	0.138	0.116	0.098	0.083	0.070	0.060	0.051	0.043	0.037	0.031
20	0.820	0.673	0.554	0.456	0.377	0.312	0.258	0.215	0.178	0.149	0.124	0.104	0.087	0.073	0.061	0.051	0.043	0.037	0.031	0.026

Table 12.1 Present value factors for a single cash flow (PV)

Year	1%	2%	3%	4%	5%	6%	7%	8%	9%	10%	11%	12%	13%	14%	15%	16%	17%	18%	19%	20%
1	0.990	0.980	0.971	0.962	0.952	0.943	0.935	0.926	0.917	0.909	0.901	0.893	0.885	0.877	0.870	0.862	0.855	0.847	0.840	0.833
2	1.970	1.942	1.913	1.886	1.859	1.833	1.808	1.783	1.759	1.736	1.713	1.690	1.668	1.647	1.626	1.605	1.585	1.566	1.547	1.528
3	2.941	2.884	2.829	2.775	2.723	2.673	2.624	2.577	2.531	2.487	2.444	2.402	2.361	2.322	2.283	2.246	2.210	2.174	2.140	2.106
4	3.902	3.808	3.717	3.630	3.546	3.465	3.387	3.312	3.240	3.170	3.102	3.037	2.974	2.914	2.855	2.798	2.743	2.690	2.639	2.589
5	4.853	4.713	4.580	4.452	4.329	4.212	4.100	3.993	3.890	3.791	3.696	3.605	3.517	3.433	3.352	3.274	3.199	3.127	3.058	2.991
6	5.795	5.601	5.417	5.242	5.076	4.917	4.767	4.623	4.486	4.355	4.231	4.111	3.998	3.889	3.784	3.685	3.589	3.498	3.410	3.326
7	6.728	6.472	6.230	6.002	5.786	5.582	5.389	5.206	5.033	4.868	4.712	4.564	4.423	4.288	4.160	4.039	3.922	3.812	3.706	3.605
8	7.652	7.326	7.020	6.733	6.463	6.210	5.971	5.747	5.535	5.335	5.146	4.968	4.799	4.639	4.487	4.344	4.207	4.078	3.954	3.837
9	8.566	8.162	7.786	7.435	7.108	6.802	6.515	6.247	5.995	5.759	5.537	5.328	5.132	4.946	4.772	4.607	4.451	4.303	4.163	4.031
10	9.471	8.983	8.530	8.111	7.722	7.360	7.024	6.710	6.418	6.145	5.889	5.650	5.426	5.216	5.019	4.833	4.659	4.494	4.339	4.192
11	10.368	9.787	9.253	8.760	8.306	7.887	7.499	7.139	6.805	6.495	6.207	5.938	5.687	5.453	5.234	5.029	4.836	4.656	4.487	4.327
12	11.255	10.575	9.954	9.385	8.863	8.384	7.943	7.536	7.161	6.814	6.492	6.194	5.918	5.660	5.421	5.197	4.988	4.793	4.611	4.439
13	12.134	11.348	10.635	9.986	9.394	8.853	8.358	7.904	7.487	7.103	6.750	6.424	6.122	5.842	5.583	5.342	5.118	4.910	4.715	4.533
14	13.004	12.106	11.296	10.563	9.899	9.295	8.746	8.244	7.786	7.367	6.982	6.628	6.303	6.002	5.724	5.468	5.229	5.008	4.802	4.611
15	13.865	12.849	11.938	11.118	10.380	9.712	9.108	8.560	8.061	7.606	7.191	6.811	6.462	6.142	5.847	5.575	5.324	5.092	4.876	4.675
16	14.718	13.578	12.561	11.652	10.838	10.106	9.447	8.851	8.313	7.824	7.379	6.974	6.604	6.265	5.954	5.669	5.405	5.162	4.938	4.730
17	15.562	14.292	13.166	12.166	11.274	10.477	9.763	9.122	8.544	8.022	7.549	7.120	6.729	6.373	6.047	5.749	5.475	5.222	4.990	4.775
18	16.398	14.992	13.754	12.659	11.690	10.828	10.059	9.372	8.756	8.201	7.702	7.250	6.840	6.467	6.128	5.818	5.534	5.273	5.033	4.812
19	17.226	15.679	14.324	13.134	12.085	11.158	10.336	9.604	8.950	8.365	7.839	7.366	6.938	6.550	6.198	5.877	5.585	5.316	5.070	4.843
20	18.046	16.352	14.878	13.590	12.462	11.470	10.594	9.818	9.129	8.514	7.963	7.469	7.025	6.623	6.259	5.929	5.628	5.353	5.101	4.870

Table 12.2 Present value factors for an annuity (PVA)

Box 12.4
Finding an investment proposal's net present value

A project's NPV is determined by deducting its initial investment from the present value of the cash inflows that the project will generate.

NPV example 1: A proposed investment of $20,000 will increase net cash inflows by $5,000 in each of the following 8 years. The company considering the investment has determined that it requires a 12% return for this proposal to be acceptable.

> NPV = −$20,000 + $5,000 (PVA 12%, 8 years)
>
> = −$20,000 + $5,000 (4.968)
>
> = −$20,000 + $24,840 = $4,840

NPV is positive, therefore proposal is acceptable

NPV example 2: A 1 January 20X0 investment of $10,000 will increase cash inflows by $3,000 in 20X0, $4,000 in 20X1 and $6,000 in 20X2. The company considering the investment requires a 12% return on investments.

> NPV = −$10,000 + $3,000 (PV 12%, 1 year) + $4,000 (PV 12%, 2 years) + $6,000
> (PV 12%, 3 years)
>
> = −$10,000 + $3,000 (0.893) + $4,000 (0.797) + $6,000 (0.712)
>
> = −10,000 + 2,679 + 3,188 + 4,272 = $139

NPV is positive, therefore proposal is acceptable

Having seen how the discounting tables can be used, we can now turn to calculating the NPV of an investment proposal. To do so, we need to isolate all incremental cash flows resulting from a decision to invest (including changed taxation cash flows), then bring these cash flows to present value. Remember, if a proposed investment has a positive NPV, it is acceptable. If it has a negative NPV, it should be rejected. If we are choosing between two mutually exclusive projects, select the one with the higher NPV. Two examples that illustrate the determination of an investment proposal's NPV are provided in Box 12.4.

The discount rate to be used when calculating NPV

It is widely suggested that the discount rate that should be used when calculating a project's net present value is the risk-adjusted cost of capital. Much finance research and discussion has focused on this issue. Stated simply, the cost of capital is the average cost (stated as a percentage) of the capital funds raised by a company. Its calculation is illustrated in Box 12.5.

Box 12.5
Calculating the cost of capital

The cost of capital can be defined as a firm's average cost of long-term financing. It is widely used by companies as the discount rate to be used when calculating NPV.

Imagine the UK-based Trafalgar Hotel group has raised £1,000,000 in capital. £400,000 comprises long-term debt with an annual interest of 8%. £600,000 has been raised in equity. Equity holders expect an annual return of 12% on their investment.

From the table below it can be seen that calculating Trafalgar's cost of capital involves using weights that reflect the relative size of each of Trafalgar's long-term sources of finance (i.e. equity is 60% of capital, debt is 40% of capital). Multiplying the cost of each source of finance by its weighting, and summing the products we find the Trafalgar group's weighted average cost of capital to be 10.4%.

	Cost	Relative size of capital source (weighting)	Cost × weighting
Equity (£0.6 m)	12%	0.6	7.2%
Debt (£0.4 m)	8%	0.4	3.2%
Cost of capital			10.4%

The 10.4% cost of capital computed for the Trafalgar group in Box 12.5 would be an appropriate discount rate to use when appraising one of the company's average risk investment proposals. If appraising a higher risk investment, a risk premium reflecting the higher risk should be added to the cost of capital. This is because investors are risk averse and they would want to be compensated via a higher return if the hotel group were to assume a more risky profile. Likewise, if a below-average risk investment is under consideration, net present value should be calculated using a rate below the 10.4% cost of capital. Readers seeking more information on the cost of capital will find extensive discussion devoted to the topic in most introductory corporate finance texts.

Concluding comments on NPV

In the interest of simplification, we have treated future cash flows as if they occur at the end of the year rather than during the year. This approach is widely taken and signifies that if the investment proposal under consideration fits the typical cash flow pattern of a large initial outlay followed by incremental net inflows, the net present value of the project will be slightly understated.

In theory, NPV is the preferred investment appraisal technique. If a company commits itself to a project with an NPV of $5 m, and the share market is working efficiently, the company's value should increase by $5 m. This is because today's value of all the company's future cash flows has been increased by $5 m.

Internal rate of return

Like the NPV, the internal rate of return (IRR) investment appraisal technique is also based on discounting cash flows that occur in the future. Calculation of the IRR is illustrated through a worked example in Box 12.6.

This example represents a relatively easy IRR computation, as the cash inflows are in the form of an annuity. Where the inflows are not an annuity, a trial and error approach has to be adopted. This involves trying different discount rates until one is found that results in an NPV of zero. If you have an advanced pocket calculator, it might be able to compute the IRR, otherwise it can be a lengthy exercise!

The IRR approach to investment appraisal has the following shortcomings:

1 In some cases, where a project's cash flows include future cash outflows, two different discount rates can result in an NPV of zero (i.e. two IRRs for one project).
2 In a single project, accept or reject situation, NPV and IRR will give the same indication (i.e. if IRR > required rate of return, NPV will be > 0). When ranking

---

Box 12.6
Finding an investment proposal's internal rate of return

Internal Rate of Return (IRR) = the discount rate that causes the present value of the project's inflows to equal the present value of the project's outflows, i.e. the discount rate that causes the project's NPV to equal zero.

If a proposed project's IRR is greater than the company's risk-adjusted cost of capital, the project is acceptable.

An IRR example
Imagine a proposed investment of $20,000 will increase cash inflows by $5,000 in each of the following 8 years. The company considering the investment has determined that it requires a 12% return for this proposal to be acceptable.

The method taken to find the IRR of a proposed investment that generates future equal annual inflows (an annuity) involves setting the 'NPV equation' equal to zero. We then determine what discount rate yields the zero NPV.

IRR calculation:

0 = −$20,000 + $5,000 (PVA IRR, 8 years),

$20,000 ÷ $5,000 = (PVA IRR, 8 years),

4 = (PVA IRR, 8 years)

In the PVA table, looking along the 8-year row, we find 4 corresponds to between 18% and 19%.

IRR = is between 18% and 19%

Project is acceptable as IRR > 12%

projects, however, NPV and IRR can give conflicting signals, i.e. the highest NPV project will not necessarily be the highest IRR project. If this situation arises, preference should be given to the NPV indication as it is the theoretically preferred technique.

Despite IRR's shortcomings (which are not as great as those apparent for ARR and payback), it is widely used in practice. This may be because managers can conceive of a proposed investment's projected rate of return more easily than its projected net present value.

Integrating the four investment appraisal techniques

In capital budgeting decision making, most large companies use more than one of the four investment appraisal techniques described in the previous section. Lamminmaki *et al.* (1996) report on the degree to which large companies use a combination of the techniques, with payback and NPV proving to be the most popular.

Case 12.1 is designed to underline the fact that most organizations use more than one investment appraisal technique. In addition, it highlights that investment appraisal techniques can be used when considering a cost-saving investment.

Case 12.1

Financial Decision Making in Action – The Chief Engineer and investment appraisal

Imagine the Bermuda Beach Hotel's chief engineer is deliberating whether to upgrade the hotel's old air-conditioning system. Investment in the new system would be $250,000 and it has been estimated that it will save the hotel $75,000 in electricity and maintenance expenses in each of the next five years. The investment would be depreciated at the rate of $50,000 per annum and have no salvage value at the end of its five-year life. The hotel has a 10% cost of capital and operates in a tax haven (i.e. no tax applies).

If the chief engineer knows that the hotel's finance department uses a breadth of investment appraisal techniques, he could review the financial viability of the proposed investment by computing its ARR, payback, NPV and IRR in the following manner:

Accounting rate of return (Annual profit generated ÷ Average investment × 100)

ARR = ($75,000 −$50,000) ÷ $125,000 × 100 = 20%

Payback (time taken to recoup the cash invested in an asset)

Payback = $250,000 ÷ $75,000 = 3.33 (i.e. 3 years and 4 months).

Net present value

NPV = −$250,000 + $75,000 (PVA 10%, 5 years)

= −$250,000 + $75,000 (3.791)

= −$250,000 + $284,325 = $34,325.

Hospitality, Leisure & Tourism Series

Internal rate of return

$0 = -\$250{,}000 + \$75{,}000$ (PVA IRR, 5 years),

$\$250{,}000 \div \$75{,}000 = $ (PVA IRR, 5 years),

$3.33 = $ (PVA IRR, 5 years),

In the PVA table, in the 5-year row, we find 3.33 corresponds to between 15% and 16%.

IRR = is between 15% and 16%

From the above analysis, the chief engineer would have established that the air-conditioning upgrade is financially justifiable as its projected NPV is positive and its IRR is greater than the cost of capital. Capital budgeting is not always conducted in a completely rational way, however.

It may be that the Bermuda Beach Hotel has a risk-averse general manager who is unwilling to authorize any capital expenditure that does not meet a predicted payback of less than three years. It may also be that the proposal is rejected as its submission coincides with a year of several other worthy investment projects. While the proposal may be financially justifiable, the chief engineer will soon realize that it cannot be approved if the hotel has insufficient capital funds available.

Summary

In this chapter we have looked at the main financial techniques that can be used to appraise investment proposals. You should now know:

- How to compute a proposed investment's accounting rate of return, payback period, net present value and internal rate of return
- The relative merits of these four investment appraisal techniques
- What is meant by the 'time value of money'
- How present values can be determined using discounting tables.

References

Atkinson, H., Berry, A. and Jarvis, R. (1995) *Business Accounting for Hospitality and Tourism & Leisure*, International Thomson Publishing, London, Chapter 19.

Carnegie, G., Jones, S., Norris, G., Wigg, R. and Williams, B. (1999) *Accounting: Financial and Organisational Decision Making*, Irwin/McGraw-Hill, New York, Chapter 24.

Coltman, M. M. and Jagels, M. G. (2001) *Hospitality Management Accounting*, 7th edition, John Wiley, Chichester, Chapter 12.

Eyster, Jr, J. J. and Geller, A. N. (1981) 'The Capital-Investment Decision: Techniques Used in the Hospitality Industry', *The Cornell Hotel and Restaurant Administration Quarterly*, May, 69–73.

Harris, P. (1999) *Profit Planning*, Butterworth-Heinemann, Oxford, Chapter 12.

Kotas, R. (1999) *Management Accounting for Hospitality and Tourism*, 3rd edition, International Thomson Publishing, London, Chapter 19.

Lamminmaki, D., Guilding, C. and Pike, R. (1996) 'A Comparison of British and New Zealand Capital Budgeting Practices', *Pacific Accounting Review*, 1–29.

Owen, G. (1994) *Accounting for Hospitality, Tourism & Leisure*, 1st edition, Pitman Publishing, London, Chapter 16.

Schmidgall, R. F. (1997) *Hospitality Industry Managerial Accounting*, 4th edition, Educational Institute – American Hotel & Motel Association, East Lansing, MI, Chapter 13.

Problems

✓ indicates that a solution appears at the back of the text

✓ 12.1 Michael Johnson has been given the opportunity of investing in a financial security that will pay him $600 in five years' time. Assuming similar risk investments earn an annual return of 8%, what value should Michael put on this investment opportunity today?

✓ 12.2 (a) What is the value today of a stream of cash flows paying $500 at the end of each of the next 8 years? Assume an interest rate of 10%.

(b) What is the value today of a stream of annual cash flows paying $500 at the beginning of each of the next 8 years (i.e. the first cash flow will occur today)? Assume an interest rate of 10%. (Helpful hint: remember that the PVA table is compiled on the basis that the first cash flow occurs in one year's time.)

✓ 12.3 Given the following two sets of cash flows, determine whether A or B has the higher present value. Assume an interest rate of 12%. (Helpful hint: remember that the PVA table is compiled on the basis that the first cash flow occurs in one year's time.)

Year[a]	Cash stream A $	Cash stream B $
1	3,000	3,500
2	3,000	3,500
3		3,500
4	3,000	3,500
5	3,000	
6	3,000	
7	3,000	3,500
8	3,000	3,500

[a] Assume that year 1 refers to a cash flow occurring in 1 year's time, year 2 refers to a cash flow occurring in 2 years' time, etc.

12.4 As part of its annual capital budgeting cycle, the Welsh Westmede hotel is deciding whether investment proposal A or investment proposal B is more financially justifiable. Investment proposal A requires an initial outlay of £36,000. It is estimated that £3,000 of this initial investment will be salvaged at the end of the investment's five-year life. Investment B also requires an initial investment of £36,000. It is estimated that this asset will be salvaged for £7,000 in five years' time.

The schedule below presents the timing of estimated increases to Westmede's operating cash flows and also operating profit that would result if either investment were to be made.

	Investment A		Investment B	
	Net cash operating inflows	Increased operating profit[a]	Net cash operating inflows	Increased operating profit[a]
Year	£	£	£	£
1	14,000	6,400	5,000	0
2	12,000	4,900	7,000	800
3	10,000	3,400	15,000	8,400
4	8,000	1,900	18,000	10,400
5	8,000	2,400	13,000	5,400

[a] Annual depreciation charges associated with the new investment will cause operating profits to be less than operating cash flows.

Required

(a) Calculate the accounting rate of return for the two investment proposals.
(b) Calculate the payback for the two investment proposals.
(c) Calculate the net present value for the two investment proposals assuming that the company has a required rate of return of 12%. Assume that no tax implication will arise as a result of salvaging either of the proposed investments at the end of their useful lives.
(d) Which is the preferred investment opportunity?

12.5 Edmonton's Green Park Hotel is considering purchasing some new laundry equipment for $200,000. Currently the hotel is outsourcing its laundry activities. The hotel's financial controller has estimated that if the laundry equipment is purchased, annual cash flows of $50,000 will be saved in each of the next five years, at which time the laundry equipment will have a zero salvage value. The hotel has a 10% cost of capital.

Required

(a) What is the laundry equipment's approximate internal rate of return?
(b) In light of your answer to part (a), would you recommend that the hotel invests in the laundry equipment?

12.6 (a) Imagine you are trying to find the IRR of an investment project that has increasing estimated future cash inflows in each of the next eight years. You have tried a discount rate of 12% and have discovered that this results in a positive NPV for the investment project. Explain whether the project's IRR is more or less than 12%.
(b) Your hotel is considering two options with respect to a major overhaul of an existing restaurant. The restaurant will either be themed as an Italian restaurant, which will require the installation of a wood-fired pizza oven, or as a British pub which will require the installation of extensive bar facilities. It has been estimated that the Italian restaurant option will provide an IRR of 16% and an NPV of $420,000. It has also been projected that the British pub option will provide an IRR of 17% and an NPV of $350,000. From a financial perspective, explain which of the two options is preferable.

12.7   Viking Hotels, a large international hotel chain, is structured according to seven geographically based divisions worldwide. Shortly after he joined the company, the Chief Executive of the European division informed General Managers in Viking's European hotels that he wanted an improved profit performance. This head of the European division believes in a decentralized policy and likes to give Hotel General Managers considerable autonomy in running their hotels as they see fit.

Eighteen months after the European Division's Chief Executive took up his position, the performance of the group's Birmingham and Manchester hotels caught his eye. Both hotels had managed to increase their return on capital employed, following some expansion in the Birmingham hotel's assets and some contraction in the Manchester hotel's assets. The schedule below summarizes the performance of the two hotels.

| | Birmingham hotel | | Manchester hotel | |
	20X2	20X1	20X2	20X1
Net operating profit	£144,000	£60,000	£228,000	£288,000
Capital employed	£2,400,000	£1,500,000	£1,200,000	£1,600,000
Return on capital employed	6%	4%	19%	18%

In addition to providing a financial summary of their hotel's performance, each Hotel General Manager is expected to provide the division's Chief Executive with a written commentary that provides background to the financial performance. The following represents extracts taken from the commentaries provided by the General Managers in the Birmingham and Manchester hotels.

The Birmingham hotel General Manager commented:

> We've managed to expand operations this year following the completion of the hotel's east wing extension. This expansion is already proving to be highly successful with operating profit more than doubling and return on capital employed increasing from 4% to 6%. I, together with the hotel's senior management, am confident that continued expansion is possible and that next year we will again be able to increase return on capital employed by a further percentage point to 7%.

The General Manager of the Manchester Hotel commented:

> 20X2 has been a year of rationalization. We've managed to sell off some of the hotel's grounds where we used to operate a restaurant, bar and night club. This has had a positive impact on our return on capital employed. Further increases in return on capital employed may be possible as we may be able to phase out other below average rate of return activities.

Required . . .
In light of Viking's cost of capital, which is 12%, explain whether the actions of the two hotels give cause for any concern. (Helpful hint: consider the return on capital employed of the assets acquired at the Birmingham hotel and also the return on capital employed of the assets sold at the Manchester hotel.)

12.8   Len, the head of general stores in a large Australian hotel complex, has been asked to defend his 'gut feel' that an upgrade in the currently used stores computerized information system is warranted. He has visited a company operating the recently developed 'Super store' software and has returned very favourably impressed. He now needs to prepare an investment proposal in a manner that will find favour with the finance group that closely scrutinizes all capital expenditure proposals.

Len has determined that the upgrade will cost the hotel $40,000 in new computer hardware. An annual software operating licence fee would also have to be paid. Len recommends that the licence agreement be entered into for 5 years as the software company is providing an introductory special of 'sign up for 5 years and pay a fee of only $5,000 per annum – a saving of 10% off the standard fee charge'. Due to computer technology advancement, it is widely believed that the hardware will be worthless after five years. For this reason, the company's policy will be to view the investment as having a life of five years.

Len believes that the new system will enable him to reduce clerical time associated with inputting data on the old computer system by 25 hours per week. This clerical work has been performed by a casual employee who cost the hotel $15,000 in wages last year. He also believes that the greater accuracy resulting from the improved record keeping that would be achieved will reduce the investment in average stock held by $10,000.

Required • • •
(a) Ignoring tax, determine the payback of this investment.
(b) Assuming a 40% tax rate and that computer hardware capital expenditure is written off straight line over a five-year period for tax purposes, use NPV to determine whether the proposed computer upgrade is justified. The hotel has a 10% cost of capital.

12.9   The General Manager of Eating Extravagance Ltd has approached you seeking advice on two competing investment opportunities that he has under consideration. Each investment requires an initial investment of $40,000 and will result in the following annual cash flows over a six-year period.

Year	Alternative 1 $	Alternative 2 $
1	2,000	16,000
2	8,000	13,000
3	10,000	11,000
4	12,000	8,000
5	16,000	6,000
6	24,000	4,000

Required • • •
(a) Calculate the payback for each of the investment alternatives. Based on the payback method, state which is the preferred investment.
(b) Calculate the net present value of each of the alternatives, assuming the general manager uses a discount rate of 10% in all NPV calculations.
(c) Based on your calculations, comment on which, if either, of the investment alternatives should be taken.

12.10 The Stellar Views' Chapel Case Study

Introduction • • •

This is a case that draws on a real investment opportunity that was under consideration in a large Australian hotel. The numbers stated in the case have been modified and also the name of the hotel changed in order to provide anonymity to the hotel concerned. The case is presented partly as an illustration of the difficult nature of estimating future cash flows when a hotel is considering an investment in a new activity that is significantly different from its existing activities. Textbooks that provide an overview of capital budgeting too frequently give extensive consideration to the different appraisal techniques that can be used, but give little attention to the problem of generating a proposed investment's cash flow estimates.

Case description • • •

The Stellar Views Hotel is located in a popular tourist region of Australia. The hotel comprises two adjoining buildings located near a beach. The main building is 25 storeys high, and the second is 6 storeys high. The smaller of the two buildings has a large flat roof with easy pedestrian access available from the large building. A small tennis facility comprising two courts has occupied this roof for the last ten years and the courts are now in need of a major overhaul. The tennis facility has been provided as a free service to hotel guests.

Stellar Views' management is considering dismantling the tennis facility and replacing it with a small 100-seat wedding chapel. The management believes there is considerable potential demand for this service, especially in light of the photo opportunities that the chapel's position would offer. In addition to catering to the local market, the chapel would be targeted towards the many Japanese visitors that come to the region to get married. Part of the rationale for the strong anticipated demand relates to a change in the type of wedding/reception/accommodation mix currently sought in the market for weddings. In earlier years it was typical for different venues to be used for the wedding service, wedding reception and also the accommodation booked before and after the wedding. Following consultation with a Japanese tourist operator, Stellar Views' management has determined that couples are increasingly seeking a facility that can enable the wedding service, reception and accommodation to be provided at a single site. Convenience and cost issues are the main factors that lie behind this change. A single venue signifies that couples can benefit from packaged prices and also save on additional costs such as limousine hire and church decorators.

The hotel's management has commissioned a consulting group to develop estimates of the initial costs of building the chapel and also the demand for wedding ceremonies. It has been estimated that the chapel will cost $1,000,000 to build. The schedule overleaf presents the consulting company's demand estimates. The demand estimates are based on a ceremony fee of $550. This ceremony price also covers the provision of floral arrangements, pew bows, topiary trees and a red carpeted aisle.

The hotel has also projected that each ceremony will have a variable cost of $100 and that annual fixed costs associated with maintaining the chapel and surrounding gardens will be $10,000. Further, it has been estimated that 90% of the Japanese inbound market ceremonies will result in a reception held at the hotel and extra guests staying at the hotel. It has been estimated that each Japanese reception held at the hotel will generate a contribution of $2,000. For the 90% of Japanese

Projected demand for ceremonies[a]

	Jan. & Feb.	March & April	May & June	July & August	Sept. & Oct.	Nov. & Dec.	Total
Local market							
Friday	0	0	2	0	4	1	7
Saturday	6	16	14	7	40	10	93
Sunday	0	2	4	0	8	1	15
Sub-total	6	18	20	7	52	12	115
Japanese inbound market							
Monday	0	1	2	0	2	0	5
Tuesday	0	3	10	0	8	3	24
Wednesday	0	3	10	0	8	3	24
Thursday	0	3	9	0	8	3	23
Friday	0	1	1	0	2	0	4
Sub-total	0	11	32	0	28	9	80
Total ceremonies held	6	29	52	7	80	21	195

a The projected demand for ceremonies is based on a proposed ceremony fee of $550.

ceremonies that will result in extra guests staying at the hotel, it has been estimated that each ceremony will result in an additional $1,000 of accommodation profit earned by the hotel.

With respect to the wedding ceremonies booked by locals, it is estimated that 20% will result in a reception at the hotel and these receptions will contribute $5,000 per reception. Further, it is estimated that the average local market ceremony will result in 15 extra room sales which will generate an additional contribution of $100 per room. The hotel's financial controller has determined that the viability of this chapel investment will be assessed using a 14% discount rate.

Required • • •

(a) Prepare an NPV analysis of the proposed chapel investment for Stellar Views' management. Assume that the hotel's management feels that the projected demand schedule presented above will apply for the first five years following the chapel's construction. In addition, it feels the contributions earned from receptions and accommodation associated with ceremonies will be constant in the chapel's first five years. When calculating NPV, the management has a policy of not looking at cash flow estimates beyond a five-year period.

(b) Describe whether you see the proposed chapel investment as risky. With respect to the discount rate that should be used when calculating the chapel's NPV, do you feel Stellar Views should use its cost of capital?

(c) What sources of information do you feel the hotel might use with respect to developing its initial estimate of the cost of building the chapel?

Solutions to problems

Chapter 1 Hospitality decision makers' use of financial management

Problem 1.1

(a) Functional interdependency exists when the performance of one functional area is affected by the performance of a separate functional area. For example, in a hotel complex that is dominated by a casino, the success of the rooms and food and beverage departments will be affected by the success of the casino operations in attracting clients to the complex.

(b) Functional interdependency is an important issue for the designers of a hotel's system of accountability because care should be taken to hold a manager accountable for only those aspects of the hotel's performance that he or she can influence. For example, the heads of rooms and food and beverage departments should not be held accountable for a decrease in their room sales if it is caused by reduced casino activity.

Problem 1.2

(a) The four main dimensions of sales volatility in the hotel industry are:
1 Economic cycle-induced sales volatility,
2 Seasonal sales volatility,
3 Weekly sales volatility,
4 Intra-day sales volatility.

(b) The implications that these dimensions of sales volatility carry for hotel accounting systems are as follows:

1 ***Economic cycle-induced volatility***: Hotel sales' high susceptibility to general economic conditions highlights the importance of hotels carefully forecasting economic cycles as part of the annual budgeting process.

2 ***Seasonal sales volatility***: Three accounting implications arise:

- Seasonal sales volatility can be so severe to warrant temporary closure for some resort properties. This possibility of having to make a closure decision signifies that cost and revenue data should be recorded in a manner that will enable a well-informed financial analysis of the pros and cons of closing.
- Seasonal sales volatility can also pose particular cash management issues. During the middle and tail-end of the busy seasons, surplus cash balances are likely to result, while in the off-season and the build-up to the busy season, deficit cash balances are likely to result. Careful cash budgeting will therefore need to be conducted.
- Seasonal sales volatility will also affect price discounting decisions. To ensure such decisions are well informed, careful forecasting as part of the annual budgetary process will have to be conducted.

3 ***Weekly sales volatility***: Accurate forecasting of weekly sales volatility will inform management's decision making with respect to the amount and timing of room rate discounting, staffing needs as well as restaurant purchasing needs.

4 ***Intra-day sales volatility***: Intra-day demand volatility has led to widely used pricing strategies such as 'early bird specials' in restaurants and 'happy hours' in bars. Records concerning demand at different times of the day will have to be maintained in order to inform such hotel pricing issues.

Problem 1.3

(a) High product perishability signifies that an item cannot be held in inventory for sale at a later time. Food items have a limited life inventory because of their rapid physical deterioration. Room nights and conference facilities cannot be placed in inventory because they relate to a particular time period that expires.

(b) The absolute perishability of rooms, conference and banquet facilities and the relative perishability of food underlines the importance of accurate hotel demand forecasting as part of the budgeting process. Generally, the most important aspect of forecasting is room occupancy, as room sales drive sales levels of other hotel services. Accurate restaurant forecasting provides the basis for maintaining a full menu of options while also minimizing the cost of food wastage.

Chapter 2 Analysing transactions and preparing year-end financial statements

Problem 2.1

(a) Simply defined, assets are things that are owned by a business. Typical hotel assets include: cash, accounts receivable, prepayments, inventory, cars, china, silver, glass, linen, uniforms, equipment, land and buildings.

(b) Simply defined, liabilities comprise financial obligations of the organization. Typical liabilities include: wages & salaries payable, accounts payable and bank loans.

(c) Simply defined, owners' equity represents the residual claim that owners have on the assets of an organization subsequent to the acquittal of all liabilities. Owners' equity increases when owners introduce more funds to the organization and when the organization makes a profit.

Problem 2.2

The balance sheet equation relates to the fact that assets minus liabilities equals owners' equity. The equation can also be stated as assets equal liabilities plus owners' equity.

Underlying the first equation is the notion that the value of the owners' equity in a business equals the surplus assets that would remain following acquittal of all liabilities. Sense can also be made of the second equation as a business raises money and then invests the money in various assets.

Problem 2.3

A business balance sheet summarizes the assets, liabilities and owners' equity pertaining to the business. It can thus be seen to be one representation of the wealth of the organization. It relates to a particular moment in time.

In the profit and loss statement sales revenue and expenses (i.e. resources consumed) for a period of time are summarized. The deduction of total expenses from total revenue provides profit (or loss if expenses are greater than revenue).

Chapter 3 Double entry accounting

Problem 3.1

No, it is inappropriate and misleading to suggest a debit to an account represents a good or a bad thing. It is true that a debit to the cash or bank account may be seen as beneficial as it signifies that an inflow of money has occurred. However, a debit to an expense account signifies an increase in the expense account and not many businesses would regard an increase in an expense as beneficial. We can conclude that we can only say that a debit to an account is a good thing if we know what type of account we are talking about.

Problem 3.2

No, in double entry accounting we cannot say that a debit represents a plus and a credit represents a minus. Debiting an asset account will usually represent a plus as asset accounts generally have a debit balance (the bank account can be an exception, however, if it is overdrawn). Liability accounts (e.g. accounts payable), however, generally have a credit balance, therefore a debit entry will have the effect of reducing the account's credit balance.

Problem 3.3

'Fixed assets' is the term given to all physical assets that will be held by the owning company for more than a year. They are acquired for use in operations rather than for resale to customers. 'Current assets' include cash and other assets that through the business's operating cycle will be converted into cash, sold or consumed within one year of the balance sheet date. The main current assets are: cash, prepayments (discussed in Chapter 4) accounts receivable and inventory.

Chapter 4 Adjusting and closing entries

Problem 4.1

'Adjusting entries' is the term used to describe the set of bookkeeping entries that need to be made in order to update some accounts prior to the preparation of the accounting year-end profit and loss statement and balance sheet. This 'tidying up' of accounts, which is really what the adjusting entries represent, has to be completed prior to closing entries. In many cases, the need for adjusting entries arises because the timing of cash flows (either receipts or disbursements) does not coincide with the period in which it is appropriate to recognize the revenue or expense. This distinction between the timing of a cash flow and the timing of the recognition of a revenue or an expense item stems from the accrual concept of accounting which holds that:

* Revenue is recognized when it is earned and certain, rather than simply when cash is received.
* An expense is recognized in the period when the benefit derived from the associated expenditure arises.

Closing entries involve rolling all the accounts that feed into the profit and loss statement (plus the drawings account) back to zero at the end of the accounting year. For this reason, these accounts are sometimes referred to as temporary accounts. Accounts that feed directly into the balance sheet are sometimes referred to as permanent accounts as they are not rolled back to zero at the end of the accounting year. The revenue, expense and drawings accounts have to be wound back to zero at the end of the accounting year, otherwise they would carry amounts that relate to the business since its inception, rather than the current accounting year.

Problem 4.2

(a)

Telephone expense		Telephone payable	
500			500

(b)

Rent expense		Rent accrued	
2,400			2,400

(c)

Depreciation expense		Accumulated depreciation	
1,000			1,000

(d)

Salary & wage expense		Salaries & wages accrued	
70,000			70,000

(e)

Unearned revenue		Revenue	
1,200			1,200

(f)

Rental revenue		Unearned revenue	
400			400

Problem 4.3

(a)

1.

Cash		Accounts receivable	
(92,000)		OB 141,500	(92,000)

2.

Accounts receivable		Revenue	
141,500	92,000		OB 1,320,000
(101,000)			(101,000)

(b) The first entry is to record the write down of the accounts receivable for the 180 days' due balance:

Allowance for doubtful accounts		Accounts receivable	
(4,500)	OB 2,400	141,500	92,000
		101,000	(4,500)

Following the review of the accounts receivable ledger, it has been determined that the allowance for doubtful accounts should have a credit balance of $2,080 (($84,000 × 0.0075) + ($44,000 × 0.0125) + ($18,000 × 0.05)).

An inspection of the balance on the 'allowance for doubtful accounts' account reveals that following the above debit entry of $4,500, it has a debit balance of $2,100. In order to achieve the requisite closing credit balance of $2,080, an adjusting credit entry of $4,180 has to be made to the 'allowance for doubtful accounts'. This adjusting entry signifies that the allowance for doubtful accounts entries made throughout the year were insufficient to reflect the doubtful account reality at the year-end. It is presumed that through the year, when the monthly entry has been made to allow for doubtful accounts, the 'bad debts expense' account has been debited. Accordingly, we need to increase the bad debts expense account at the year-end, i.e. make an adjusting debit entry of $4,180 to the 'bad debts expense' account.

Allowance for doubtful accounts		Bad debts expense	
4,500	2,400	OB 12,400	
	(4,180)	(4,180)	

Chapter 5 Financial statement analysis

Problem 5.1

(a) **Dupont (ROI)**

$$\frac{EBIT}{TA} = \frac{EBIT}{Revenue} \times \frac{Revenue}{TA}$$

HoJo:

$$\frac{50 \div 250}{0.2} = \frac{50 \div 500}{0.1} \times \quad \frac{500 \div 250,}{2}$$

EasyRest

$$\frac{15 \div 75}{0.2} = \frac{15 \div 300}{0.05} \times \quad \frac{300 \div 75,}{4}$$

(b) Both companies' F&B activities have achieved a 20% return on total assets. However, their methods of achieving this return have been quite different. HoJo has earned a 10% profit margin and a 200% turnover of sales to total assets, whereas EasyRest has had a much higher sales turnover (4 or 400%) with a smaller profit margin (5%).

The companies appear to have different pricing policies. HoJo's mark-up on cost of sales is 150% (300/200), whereas EastRest only marks up cost of sales by 36% (80/220).

Problem 5.2

(a) Cost of sales $= 0.6 \times £28,750,000 = £17,250,000$

$$\text{Average inventory} = \frac{£400,000 + £800,000 + £900,000 + £200,000}{4}$$

$$= £575,000$$

$$\text{Inventory turnover} = \frac{£17,250,000}{£575,000} = 30$$

$$\text{Average age of inventory} = \frac{365}{30} = 12.17 \text{ days}$$

(b) Enwad appears to have less liquid inventory than the average firm in the industry. Enwad's inventory is converted into a sale after 12 days while the average firm in the industry is taking approximately 9 days ($365 \div 40$).

Problem 5.3

(a) Year ending 20X1 working capital:
($10,800 + 27,000 + 7,500 + 10,400 + 1,500) − ($8,400 + 3,600 + 4,500 + 700 + 10,700) = $57,200 − $27,900 = $29,300
Year ending 20X2 working capital:
($14,300 + 26,000 + 7,500 + 12,000 + 1,600) − ($12,200 + 5,600 + 3,400 + 400 + 9,500) = $61,400 − $31,100 = $30,300

(b) Year ending 20X1 current asset ratio: $57,200 ÷ $27,900 = 2.05
Year ending 20X2 current asset ratio: $61,400 ÷ $31,100 = 1.97

(c) Year ending 20X1 acid test ratio: ($57,200 − 10,400 − 1,500) ÷ $27,900 = 1.62
Year ending 20X2 acid test ratio: ($61,400 − 12,000 − 1,600) ÷ $31,100 = 1.54

(d) The working capital shows a marginal increase, however both the current asset ratio and the acid test ratio have decreased marginally. It appears the increase in the working capital has largely been accounted for by an increase in the size of the business (all things being equal, as a business doubles in size, so its working capital needs to double in order to maintain the same level of liquidity). Overall, we can conclude that there has been a marginal decrease in the restaurant's level of liquidity.

(e) Accounts receivable turnover = Credit sales ÷ average accounts receivable
Credit sales = $500,000 × 0.55 = $275,000
Average accounts receivable = ($27,000 + $26,000) ÷ 2 = $26,500
Accounts receivable turnover = $275,000 ÷ $26,500 = 10.38

(f) Accounts receivable collection period = 365 ÷ A.R. turnover:
365 ÷ 10.38 = 35.16 days

(g) Inventory turnover = Cost of sales ÷ average inventory
   Cost of sales = $150,000
   Average inventory = ($10,400 + $12,000) ÷ 2 = $11,200
   Inventory turnover = $150,000 ÷ $11,200 = 13.39
(h) Inventory collection period = 365 ÷ inventory turnover:
   365 ÷ 13.39 = 27.25 days

Chapter 6 Cost management issues

Problem 6.1

The range of cost classifications arises due to the wide diversity of management decision-making and control situations that can arise. In the text of the chapter it was noted that the cost classifications that can arise include the following:

(a) Outlay versus opportunity costs
(b) Direct versus indirect costs
(c) Variable versus fixed costs
(d) Controllable versus non-controllable costs
(e) Incremental versus sunk costs.

   An opportunity cost can be a significant issue if management is considering taking an action that will result in a lost opportunity. The issue of direct versus indirect costs is an issue when attempting to determine the profitability of revenue-generating departments, as calculation of each departments' net profit would necessitate the allocation of indirect costs. Many issues arise that necessitate a distinction between fixed and variable costs; one significant issue addressed in this chapter concerns the aggressive pricing strategy of setting prices over the short term at a level designed to cover variable costs. In responsibility accounting it is important that managers are only held accountable for costs that they can control. Finally, sunk costs are irrelevant in decision making; the decision maker need only focus on costs that will be affected by whatever decision is at hand.

Problem 6.2

(a) Variable costs:

	£
Food and drink	7.0
Conference materials	6.0
Fixed costs (£360 ÷ 80)	4.5
	17.5

(b) Variable costs:

	£
Food and drink	7
Conference materials	6
Fixed costs (£360 ÷ 120)	3
	16

(c) The cost per attendee declines with more attendees because the fixed cost is spread across more attendees.
(d) If 120 people attend, the cost per attendee is £16.
If profit is to be 20% of revenue, then cost must be 80% of revenue.
As cost = £16 per person when 120 people attend, revenue per person must be
£16 ÷ 0.8 = £20.
(e) The lowest price that does not result in the conference adversely affecting this year's profit is the variable cost, i.e. £13 (£7 + £6).

Problem 6.3

(a) *Determination of variable cost function:*
When 20,000 kg of laundry was processed (highest level of activity),
cost = $22,000.
When 18,000 kg of laundry was processed (lowest level of activity),
cost = $20,400.
It therefore costs an extra $1,600 ($22,000 − $20,400), to process an extra 2,000 kg of laundry (20,000 − 18,000).
Therefore, the variable cost per kg is $1,600/2,000 = $0.80 per kg.
Determination of fixed cost function:
Calculation based on July's performance:
HighFlyer's laundry costs for July are $22,000, and their variable laundry costs are $16,000 ($0.80 × 20,000 kg). Fixed housekeeping costs must therefore be $6,000 ($22,000 − $16,000).
(b) Total laundry costs if 25,000 kg of laundry are processed: (25,000 × $0.80) + $6,000 = $26,000

Chapter 7 Cost–volume–profit analysis

Problem 7.1

(a) The contribution margin format enables us to quickly answer questions such as 'What will happen to profit if our hotel's revenue increases by $100,000?' If variable costs are 20% of revenue, then the contribution margin ratio is 80%. This signifies that a $100,000 increase in revenue will result in an $80,000 increase in profit (0.8 × $100,000).
　　The contribution margin format can also be seen as helpful to management's understanding of cost structure as it places revenue alongside those costs that are affected by the level of revenue achieved.
(b) Cost–volume–profit analysis can be helpful if a manager is considering questions such as:

1 'How many units will we need to sell in order to break even?'
2 'How much will we need to sell in order to achieve our target profit level?'
3 'What will happen to profit if we manage to increase sales volume by 10%?'
4 'By what volume of sales are we currently surpassing our breakeven point?'
5 'If fixed costs increase by $20,000, how much more would we have to sell in order to maintain our current level of profit?'

Problem 7.2

(a)
The Hulsey Restaurant
Profit and loss statement for the year ending 31 December 20X1
(Contribution margin layout)

	$	Percentage
Sales revenue	500,000	100.0
Variable costs		
Variable cost of sales	100,000	20.0
Variable operating expenses	16,000	3.2
Contribution margin	384,000	76.8
Fixed costs		
Salaries and wages	144,000	28.8
Marketing	10,000	2.0
Rent	48,000	9.6
Maintenance	5,000	1.0
Other	10,000	2.0
	217,000	43.4
Net Profit	167,000	33.4

(b) Breakeven point = Fixed costs ÷ Contribution per cover = $217,000 ÷ (25 − [5 + 0.8]) = $217,000 ÷ $19.2 = 11,302 meals per annum

(c) From the profit and loss statement prepared using the contribution margin layout, it is evident that the contribution margin is 76.8%. An increase in sales of 10% represents a $50,000 sales increase ($500,000 × 0.1). As the contribution margin ratio is 76.8% a 10% increase in sales will result in a $38,400 increase in profit ($50,000 × 0.768).

(d) Profit = Contribution margin − Fixed costs. ($600,000 × 0.768) − $217,000 = 460,800 − 217,000 = $243,800

(e) A 10% increase in revenue would signify that profit would increase by $50,000 ($500,000 × 0.1). Alternately stated, profit would increase by $2.5 for each cover served. As there are 20,000 covers sold, profit would increase by $50,000 ($2.5 × 20,000).

Problem 7.3

(a) Room nights to be sold to break even =
Fixed costs ÷ Contribution per room night
£360,000 ÷ (£68 − £8) = 6,000 room nights.

Room nights available per annum = 365 × 60 = 21,900
∴ Percentage occupancy necessary to break even =
6,000 ÷ 21,900 × 100 = 27.4%

(b) Room nights to be sold to achieve a before-tax profit of £60,000 =
(Fixed costs + target profit) ÷ Contribution per room night =
(£360,000 + £60,000) ÷ (£68 − £8) = 7,000 room nights.

(c) Room nights to be sold to achieve an after-tax profit of £72,000 =
[Fixed costs + (After-tax target profit ÷ '1 – tax rate')]
÷ Contribution per room night =
[£360,000 + (£72,000 ÷ 0.6)] ÷ (£68 – £8) =
(360,000 + 120,000) ÷ 60 = 8,000 room nights

Chapter 8 Budgeting and responsibility accounting

Problem 8.1

Responsibility accounting involves sub-dividing an organization into units of accountability. It is fundamental to control as it involves holding managers accountable for the performance of their respective units. Budgeting is closely associated with responsibility accounting because it involves allocating resources to an organization's sub-units. In addition, the budget highlights benchmarks that are used when appraising a unit manager's performance. As the budgeting system sets targets for all of an organization's sub-units, it is difficult to conceive of any meaningful budgeting occurring in the absence of a responsibility accounting system.

Problem 8.2

There is no single 'easy' answer to this question. Issues that might be addressed in a well-reasoned answer include:

- So long as Bromwich provided the requisition to Joe in reasonable time (i.e. sufficient purchasing lead time), it would be inappropriate to hold the head of banqueting and conferences responsible for the part not arriving. Despite this issue, it would appear that the head of banqueting and conferences was responsible for the refund decision and therefore justification could be given for charging at least a portion of the lost revenue to her department. One could also argue that given the importance of the part, Maxine should have followed up with Joe more times.
- The following rationale could be developed for charging all of the lost revenue to the purchasing department:

  1 In the whole organization, the purchasing manager is the one who is most closely associated with the role of ensuring timely delivery.
  2 Joe could be criticized for not getting another staff member or Maxine to follow up on the order while he was away on holiday.
  3 Joe could have requested that a copy of the consignment be faxed when told that the delivery was underway.
  4 Joe should have informed Maxine earlier of the potential problem with the delivery.
  5 By requiring Joe's department to carry the loss, he may take greater care when ordering one-off special parts in the future.

- It could also be argued to be inappropriate to attach blame to Joe (it was really the supplier's fault), as it appears he may well have made reasonable efforts to ensure timely delivery.

- Joe and Maxine could attempt to recoup some of the loss from the supplier. At the very least, this would inform the supplier of the cost of their mistake.
- This case appears to be a situation highlighting how it can be very inappropriate to use the responsibility accounting system as an apportioning blame system rather than a 'determining who should have the opportunity to explain' system.

Problem 8.3

(1) The first thing to note is that the responsibility accounting system appears to be perceived as an 'apportioning blame' system. This is highly undesirable as it is likely to give rise to ill-feeling that is more damaging than helpful. A properly used responsibility system emphasizes information rather than blame. If managers feel they are beaten around the head when unfavourable variances occur, they are likely to view the system as a tool of bureaucracy and start conjuring up ways to undermine the system. When the numbers are used in a manner that emphasizes the informational role of the responsibility system, managers are more likely to be open to discussion with colleagues in a quest for gaining improved performance. Scheduling an inter-departmental management meeting following the receipt of monthly performance reports may be one way of focusing on the information aspect of the responsibility accounting system.

(2) The accountant could agree that in the future 'pastry cutters' wages will be charged to Maintenance at the rate of $9 per hour and that a correction will be made for last month's entry. The $4.50 premium could be charged to a 'Loss from unused capacity' account which is charged back to the F&B department because it was the F&B director who elected to retain these staff. The Maintenance manager should be told that it is up to him to get $9 of work per hour out of the staff placed under his direction. The fact that these are non-preferred personnel could be recognized in a note to the monthly report.

(3) Theoretically, the accountant could argue that the $4.50 (or even the whole $13.50) represents investment in an asset as:

   (a) It is an investment today that will yield a benefit in the future (i.e. retention of preferred kitchen staff)

   (b) It is an investment today that will result in a saving in the future (i.e. no need to expend resources recruiting and training new skilled kitchen staff).

Due to conservatism, accountants would not tend to take this view, however. The distinction is nevertheless important. An 'expense' tends to be viewed in a negative light, while an 'investment' tends to be viewed in a positive light.

Chapter 9 Flexible budgeting and variance analysis

Problem 9.1

(a) As the lodge has made 15% more room sales than was budgeted for ([12,420 − 10,800] ÷ 10,800 × 100), we can produce a flexible budget by increasing the revenue and variable cost figures stated in the static budget by 15%. A simple way to achieve this is to multiply them by a factor of 1.15.

The Curbside Motor Lodge
Flexible budget performance report
for the quarter ended 30 September 20X1

	Actual	Budget	Flexible budget	Flexible budget variances
Room nights sold	12,420	10,800	12,420	
	£	£	£	£
Revenue (sales)	1,179,900	1,080,000	1,242,000	62,100 (U)
Variable Costs:				
Labour	84,456	75,600	86,940	2,484 (F)
Room amenities	5,216	5,400	6,210	994 (F)
Contribution Margin	1,090,228	999,000	1,148,850	58,622 (U)
Fixed Costs	241,000	235,000	235,000	6,000 (U)
Operating Profit	849,228	764,000	913,850	64,622 (U)

(b) A shortcoming of isolating variances between actual performance and the static budget is that much of a variance may be attributable to the fact that it is practically impossible to correctly estimate the volume of sales that will occur in a forthcoming accounting period. Variances occurring as a result of an organization being busier or quieter than expected are not really reflective of the performance of many managers. If we were to take static budget variances to the extreme, we can see that very favourable variable cost variances can be achieved if we have no one staying at our hotel! To remove the effect of actual volume of sales being different from the budgeted volume of sales, we can produce a flexible budget. In a flexible budget, the static budget figures are restated as if the actual volume of sales achieved had been known at the time the budget was set.

The flexible budget performance report provides very different management insights to those provided by the static budget variances computed by Curbside's conventional performance report. The extent of these differences is highlighted by the following table.

Curbside: Comparison of static budget and flexible budget variances

	Static budget variances	Flexible budget variances
Revenue (sales)	(F)	(U)
Variable Costs:		
Labour	(U)	(F)
Room amenities	(F)	(F)
Contribution Margin	(F)	(U)
Fixed Costs	(U)	(U)
Operating Profit	(F)	(U)

- The unfavourable flexible budget variance for revenue signifies that rooms must have been sold below the rate budgeted for. This fact was not evident from the static budget variance.
- The favourable flexible budget variance for labour signifies that labour worked efficiently or the labour rate was below the rate budgeted for. This fact was not evident from the static budget variance.
- The size of the unfavourable revenue flexible budget variance is sufficient to have turned the favourable static budget contribution margin variance into an unfavourable flexible budget variance. This impact is also apparent at the operating profit level.

Problem 9.2

(a)   **Curbside: Room cleaning labour rate and efficiency variances for quarter ending 30/9/X1**

Actual labour hours × Actual rate	Actual labour hours × Budgeted rate	Budgeted labour hours × Budgeted rate
5,630.4	5,630.4	6,210
×	×	×
£15	£14.00	£14.00
£84,456	£78,825.6	£86,940

←——————————→ ←——————————→

£5,630.4 Unfavourable labour rate variance   £8,114.4 Favourable labour efficiency variance

←——————————————————————→

£2,484 Labour favourable flexible budget variance

(b) **Curbside: Room amenities price and efficiency variances
for quarter ending 30/9/X1**

Actual packs × **Actual price** 13,040 × £0.40 £5,216	**Actual packs** × **Budgeted price** 13,040 × £0.50 £6,520	**Budgeted packs** × **Budgeted price** 12,420 × £0.50 £6,210

←————————————————→ ←————————————————→

£1,304 Amenities favourable   £310 Amenities unfavourable
price variance   efficiency (or usage) variance

←————————————————————————————————→

£994 Amenities favourable flexible budget variance

(c) **Curbside: Selling price and sales volume variances
for quarter ending 30/9/X1**

Actual volume of sales × **Actual selling price** 12,420 room nights × £95* £1,179,900	**Actual volume of sales** × **Budgeted selling price** 12,420 room nights × £100** £1,242,000	**Budgeted volume of sales** × **Budgeted selling price** 10,800 room nights × £100 £1,080,000

←————————————————→ ←————————————————→

£62,100 Unfavourable selling   £162,000 Favourable sales
price variance   volume variance

←————————————————————————————————→

£99,900 Favourable revenue variance

* £1,179,900 ÷ 12,420 = £95
** £1,080,000 ÷ 10,800 = £100

Problem 9.3

(a)

Tiff's Restaurant
Flexible budget performance report
for the month ended 30 June

	Actual €	Flexible budget €	Flexible budget variance €	Flexible budget variance %[a]
Breakfasts (actual served: 110)				
Revenue (sales)	759	770	11 (U)	1.4%
Variable Costs	242	275	33 (F)	12.0%
Breakfast contribution margin	517	495	22 (F)	4.4%
Lunches (actual served: 100)				
Revenue (sales)	1,700	1,400	300 (F)	21.4%
Variable Costs	540	500	40 (U)	8.0%
Lunch contribution margin	1,160	900	260 (F)	28.9%
Dinners (actual served: 300)				
Revenue (sales)	6,600	7,500	900 (U)	12.0%
Variable Costs	2,850	3,000	150 (F)	5.0%
Dinners contribution margin	3,750	4,500	750 (U)	16.7%
Total restaurant contribution	5,427	5,895	468 (U)	7.9%
Less: Fixed costs	740	800	60 (F)	7.5%
Net profit	**4,687**	**5,095**	**408 (U)**	**8.0%**

[a] Flexible budget variance as a percentage of the flexible budget.

(b) From the above table's final column, it is evident that there is a large lunch revenue flexible budget variance that is 21.4% of the flexible budget amount. This variance has resulted from the average lunch revenue being €17, i.e. €3 more than the budgeted average lunch revenue. If this higher average revenue stems from higher than anticipated menu prices, the higher prices may have resulted in the below-budget volume of lunch sales achieved (the restaurant has sold 50 lunches less than was budgeted for). Management may need to consider whether the higher prices have resulted in a reduced volume of sales.

A second factor that might be worthy of further investigation is the €900 unfavourable variance that has resulted from dinner average revenue being below budget. Average dinner revenue was budgeted at €25, however actual average dinner revenue is €22. Management might review what has caused the failure to meet budgeted average dinner revenue and whether dinner menu prices need to be increased.

Chapter 10 Cost information and pricing

Problem 10.1

Total costs:

	£
Bank loan (£250,000 @ 9%)	22,500
Depreciation	40,000
Other fixed costs	65,000
Operating expenses	85,000
Total costs	212,500

After-tax profit sought by owners = £450,000 × 0.15 = £67,500.
Before-tax profit needed to provide after-tax profit of £67,500 =
     £135,000 (tax is 50%).
Total revenue needed to provide before tax profit of £135,000 =
Total costs + desired before-tax profit, i.e. £212,500 + £135,000 = £347,500
Room rate = Total revenue ÷ Room nights sold in a year
Room nights sold in a year = 40 × 0.55 × 365 = 8,030
Room rate = £347,500 ÷ 8,030 = £43.27

Problem 10.2

(a) Profit = Revenue − Variable costs − Fixed costs
    Contribution = Revenue − Variable costs

   In this problem Variable costs are 75% of Revenue,
   ∴ Contribution = 25% of Revenue

   We can therefore say:
   Target profit = 0.25 of Revenue − Fixed costs, or:
   50% of $120,000 = 0.25R − ($55,000 + $8,000 + $30,000 + $5,000 +
                         $6,000 + $4,000 + $28,000)

   $60,000 + $136,000 = 0.25R,
   $196,000 ÷ 0.25 = R
   R = $784,000

   Answer: total revenue of $784,000 will provide a 50% before-tax return on the owners' investment of $120,000.

(b) Total number of weekdays restaurant is open = 49 × 4 = 196.
    Total number of weekday covers sold = 196 × 50 × 2 = 19,600.

   Total number of Saturdays and Sundays restaurant is open = 49 × 2 = 98.
   Total number of weekend covers sold per annum = 98 × 50 × 3 = 14,700

   Total number of covers sold per annum = 19,600 + 14,700 = 34,300
   ∴ average selling price per cover to provide target profit =
        $784,000 ÷ 34,300 = $22.86

Problem 10.3

(a) Total investment in rooms = $12,600,000 (70% of $18 m).
Average room investment = $140,000 ($12.6 m ÷ 90).
Average room rate = $140 ($140,000 ÷ 1,000).

(b) Revenue required per day = $3,066,000/365 = $8,400
Let M represent price charged per square metre.
$(21 \times 60\,M) + (21 \times 80\,M) + (21 \times 110\,M) = \$8,400$
$1,260\,M + 1,680\,M + 2,310\,M = \$8,400$
$5,250\,M = \$8,400$
$M = \$1.6$

For the economy rooms the rate should be: $1.6 × 60 = $96.
For the double rooms the rate should be: $1.6 × 80 = $128.
For the deluxe rooms the rate should be: $1.6 × 110 = $176.

Chapter 11 Working capital management

Problem 11.1

Schedule of projected cash receipts
for CrownJewel in ($000)

	October	November	December	Total
Room sales	540	500	600	
10% cash sales.	54	50	60	164
50% received in month following sale	300	270	250	820
35% received 2 months following sale	231	210	189	630
5% received 3 months following sale	31.5	33	30	94.5
Total room receipts	616.5	563	529	1,708.5
Restaurant & bar sales	70	60	80	
30% cash sales	21	18	24	63
70% received in month following sale	56	49	42	147
Total restaurant & bar receipts	77	67	66	210
Total all receipts	**693.5**	**630**	**595**	**1,918.5**

Problem 11.2

Schedule of projected cash disbursements
for CrownJewel Hotel (in $000)

	October	November	December	Total
Room variable costs paid in month incurred (Room revenue $\times 0.2 \times 0.6$).	64.8	60.0	72.0	196.8
Room variable costs paid one month after incurred (Room revenue $\times 0.2 \times 0.4$).	48.0	43.2	40.0	131.2
Restaurant & bar wages (Restaurant revenue $\times 0.1$).	7.0	6.0	8.0	21.0
Food & drink costs paid in month incurred (Rest. & bar revenue $\times 0.15 \times 0.4$)	4.2	3.6	4.8	12.6
Food & drink costs paid following month incurred (R&B revenue $\times 0.15 \times 0.6$)	7.2	6.3	5.4	18.9
Fixed costs	15.0	15.0	15.0	45.0
Electricity and insurance		3.0	7.5	10.5
Total disbursements	146.2	137.1	152.7	436.0

Problem 11.3

Cash budget for CrownJewel

	October $	November $	December $	Total $
Total cash receipts [a]	693.5	630.0	595.0	1,918.5
less Total cash disbursements [b]	146.2	137.1	152.7	436.0
Net cash flow	547.3	492.9	442.3	1,482.5
add Opening cash balance	12,000.0	12,547.3	13,040.2	12,000.0
Ending cash	12,547.3	13,040.2	13,482.5	13,482.5

[a] From solution to Problem 11.1.
[b] From solution to Problem 11.2.

Chapter 12 Investment decision making

Problem 12.1

Present value = $600 (PV8,5 year) = $600 × 0.681 = $408.60

Problem 12.2

(a) Present value = $500 (PVA10,8 years) = $500 × 5.335 = $2,667.50
(b) In this problem, as the PVA table is compiled on the basis that the first cash flow occurs in one year's time, we need to isolate the first cash flow as it is due to occur today. As this cash flow is occurring today, it is already stated in terms of today's $, therefore there is no need to discount it. The present value of this stream of cash flows will be calculated on the following basis:

> Present value = Today's cash flow + The present value of the annuity to be received at the end of the next seven years

Present value = $500 + $500 (PVA10,7 years) =
$500 + ($500 × 4.868) = $500 + $2,434 = $2,934

Problem 12.3

In this problem, each cash stream comprises two annuities (cash stream A comprises a $3,000 annuity occurring at the end of year's 1 and 2 and a cash flow annuity occurring at the end of years 4–8). We will find the present value of each cash stream by treating them as comprising two separate annuities.

Cash stream A

Present value of cash flows occurring in years 1 and 2 =
$3,000 (PVA12,2 years) = $3,000 × 1.690 = $5,070

Finding the present value of the cash flows occurring in years 4–8 is slightly challenging and will be calculated in two stages. First, the annuity table will be used as normal to find the present value of the five annual cash flows. However, as the annuity table has been compiled on the basis that the first cash flow occurs in one year's time, the answer provided will represent the value of the cash flows one year before the first cash flow occurs, i.e. at year 3. Consequently we will then have to discount the amount back over a three-year period using the PV table (we use the PV table as, at this point, we will be dealing with a $ value stated at one point in time).
Present value of cash flows occurring in years 4–8 = $3,000 (PVA12,5 years)
(PV 12,3 years) = $3,000 × 3.605 × 0.712 = $7,700.28

We now add together the present value of the cash flows occurring in years 1 and 2 to the present value of the cash flows occurring in years 4–8 to find the total present value of cash stream A.

Present value cash stream A = $5,070 + $7,700.28 = **$12,770.28**

Cash stream B

There is another method for dealing with an interruption in an annuity. While the present value of cash stream B could be calculated using the same approach as that used for cash stream A we will use the alternative approach in order to illustrate how it can be applied. In this approach we will initially assume that the $3,500 cash flow is present in the years 1–8 (i.e. we will use (PVA12,8 years). From the answer computed through this first step we will then deduct the present value of the two cash flows that are actually missing from the 8 year annuity (years 5 and 6).

PV cash stream B = $3,500 (PVA12,8 years) – $3,500 (PV12,5 years) – $3,500 (PV 12,6 years) =

$3,500 (4.968) – $3,500 (0.567) – $3,500 (0.507) =
$17,388 – 1,984.5 – 1,774.5 = **$13,629**

From the above, it can be seen that the present value of cash stream A ($12,770.28) is $858.72 less than the present value of cash stream B ($13,629).

Index

Hospitality, Leisure and Tourism Series 2002

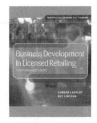

07506 53345
**Business Development
in Licensed Retailing**
(Lashley & Lincoln)

07506 54317
In Search of Hospitality
(ed. - Lashley & Morrison)

07506 5659X
**Financial Management
for Hospitality
Decision Makers**
(Guilding)

07506 52446
Empowerment
(Lashley)

07506 47728
**Franchising Hospitality
Services**
(ed. - Lashley & Morrison)

07506 47965*
Events Management
(Bowden et al.)

07506 45563
Stats To Go
(Buglear)

07506 4480X
**Strategic Questions in
Food and Beverage
Management**
(Wood)

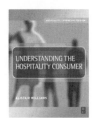

07506 52497
**Understanding the
Hospitality
Consumer**
(Williams)

07506 46160
**Hospitality Retail
Management**
(Lashley)

* Available in UK and Europe only.

**BUTTERWORTH
HEINEMANN**
An imprint of Elsevier Science
www.bh.com